The Ernst & Young Tax Saver's Guide 1997

By the Tax Partners and Professionals of Ernst & Young LLP

Peter W. Bernstein, Editor

John Wiley & Sons, Inc.

New York   Chichester   Brisbane   Toronto   Singapore   Weinheim

In the preparation of this book, every effort has been made to offer current, correct, and clearly expressed information. The information included in this book is based on the Internal Revenue Code amended as of August 31, 1996.

The information in the text is intended to afford general guidelines on matters of interest to taxpayers. The application and impact of tax laws can vary widely from case to case, however, based upon the specific or unique facts involved. Accordingly, this book is not intended to serve as legal, accounting, or tax advice. Moreover, tax rules and regulations often change. Readers are encouraged to consult with professional advisors for advice concerning specific matters before making any decision. The author and publishers disclaim any responsibility for positions taken by taxpayers in their individual cases.

ISBN: 0-471-16334-1 regular edition
ISBN: 0-471-17857-8 special edition

Printed in the United States of America

10 9 8 7 6 5 4 3 2 1

The Ernst & Young Tax Saver's Guide 1997

Editorial Board

Chairman: Harvey B. Wishman

Special thanks to Philip A. Laskawy, Chairman of Ernst & Young LLP; William J. Lipton, Vice Chairman–Tax Services; Herbert J. Lerner, National Director—Tax Policy and Standards; Richard S. Bobrow, National Director—Tax Services; Robert J. Garner, National Director—Personal Financial Counseling; Patrice Ingrassia; and Bari Zahn.

With more than 3,500 tax practitioners, Ernst & Young LLP has one of the largest professional tax practices in the United States. This book draws upon the experience of many of those professionals for its content.

ABOUT THE AUTHOR

Ernst & Young LLP is a member of Ernst & Young International, a leader among professional service organizations in delivering value—ideas, solutions, and results. Ernst & Young has more than 21,000 personnel in 93 locations and is one of the fastest growing major professional services firms in the United States.

Ernst & Young is the largest firm delivering integrated professional services in the United States. It audits more of the 1996 *Fortune* 500 largest U.S. corporations than any other firm, and it is a leader in providing services to the following industries: aerospace and defense; consumer products; energy; financial services; health care; information, communications, and entertainment; insurance; life sciences; manufacturing; real estate and construction; and service firms.

Through its Entrepreneurial Services group, Ernst & Young is the leading firm providing a broad range of services to owner-managed companies, and audits more companies with initial public offerings than any other firm.

ABOUT THE EDITOR

Peter W. Bernstein, executive editor of *U.S. News & World Report,* is the editor of *The Ernst & Young Tax Guide.*

QUICK REFERENCE

Contents

How to Use this Book

The Ernst & Young Tax Saver's Guide 1997 is a year-round tax planner with easy-to-follow, money-saving tax strategies. This book, with its concise explanations of key provisions of federal tax law, can also be used for quick reference to provide guidance on important personal and business transactions. It is not intended to give you line-by-line instructions on how to prepare your federal tax returns. A separate Ernst & Young LLP publication—The Ernst & Young Tax Guide—is available for that purpose.

This book is organized into three sections:

Part I, Tax Strategies for Individuals, contains chapters that tell you what to include as income, what you can deduct, and how you calculate your tax. It also has chapters that relate specifically to your business travel and entertainment expenses; your home; retirement plans, such as IRAs and 401(k)s; charitable contributions; capital gains and losses; and mutual funds. In addition, sprinkled throughout all the chapters are money-saving tips about options and strategies you might consider to cut your tax bill. Part I concludes with a chapter on year-end planning for individuals.

Part II, How to Improve Your Financial Future, should help you with some of the tax considerations guiding your current investments. In addition, options you might consider to ensure yourself a comfortable and secure retirement are presented here. The chapter on estate planning offers tax-saving ideas on gifts, estate, and generation-skipping taxes.

Part III, Tax Strategies for Businesses, discusses many of the fundamental tax questions that confront the owner of any business. There is a special chapter on S corporations. The last chapter contains year-end planning suggestions that can save businesses money.

Among its many benefits, this book offers the following special features:

E&Y FOCUS:

This feature considers topics of current interest, such as leasing a car or deferred compensation plans, and suggests smart money moves that you may want to consider.

TaxSaver

Highlighted throughout every chapter in the book are numerous TaxSavers—specific strategies and recommendations that can help you cut your tax bill.

TaxOrganizer

Do you need to save that receipt for tax purposes? TaxOrganizers point out things you need to do *now* to make it easier to file your taxes later.

TAX*ALERT*

This feature highlights recent changes in the tax law that you should know about. Tax law changes that have been enacted recently are included. If you are aware of a new development in the law before the end of the year, you can often take timely and appropriate action and save yourself some money.

■ *Special chapters on year-end tax planning for individuals and businesses.* The prudent taxpayer must make decisions before December 31 about a number of important tax questions—for example, whether to report income now or defer it to next year and whether to pay a deductible expense this year or in the future.

■ *Important information on the tax aspects of "life-cycle events."* These are the occasions, transactions, and eventualities that most of us will almost certainly have to deal with at some time during our adult lives. A special index to the "life-cycle events" discussed in this book follows this introduction.

■ *Concisely presented rules of the tax law pertaining to individuals, estates, gifts, and business entities.* Included in each section are examples that show you how the rules work and "TaxSavers"—strategies to help you plan better.

The Ernst & Young Tax Saver's Guide contains two more features that will be of year-round use to individuals and businesses alike:

■ *Up-to-date tax tables*—the ones that you will use most often can be found at the end of this book; and

■ *Tax calendar*—a month-by-month reminder of important tax action dates for individuals and businesses.

Index to Life-Cycle Events

This special index can be used to locate the sections of the text that contain important information on the tax aspects of "life-cycle events"— those milestones that most adults will be facing at one time or another during the course of their lives. By reading this information, you'll get off to a good start in understanding and planning for the tax consequences associated with various life-cycle events.

Changes in the Tax Law You Should Know About

On August 20, 1996 the President signed the Small Business Job Protection Act (which includes the minimum wage increase) and the Health Insurance Portability and Accountability Act was signed on August 21, 1996. The small business act contains extensions of some expired tax provisions, S corporation enhancement provisions, and pension simplification items, among other provisions. The health insurance act contains provisions to increase the deduction for health insurance costs of self-employed individuals, a pilot program for medical savings accounts, and also includes incentives for long-term care insurance.

A third bill, the Taxpayer Bill of Rights 2 (T2) was signed into law on July 30, 1996. It contains over three dozen pro-taxpayer provisions designed to help taxpayers in their dealings with the Internal Revenue Service (IRS). One provision establishes a new high-level position of Taxpayer Advocate within the IRS. The new law also affords taxpayers relief from the retroactive application of Treasury regulations in some circumstances. Under T2, the effective date of a regulation is usually the date of publication in the *Federal Register*, with exceptions for such cases as when the regulation is issued within 18 months of the enactment of the statute to which it relates in order to prevent abuse.

Lawmakers have raised the possibility of considering yet another tax bill before the end of the 104th Congress in 1996, specifically, a bill to provide a child tax credit for middle-income families. This bill could be largely financed by "savings" from the recently passed welfare reform legislation. However, time remaining before adjournment of the 104th Congress for the November elections is limited.

The following table highlights some of the 1996 tax law changes:

Item	New Law
Health Insurance Deduction for Self-Employed Individuals and Certain S Corporation Employee-Shareholders	The deduction for premiums paid is gradually phased up from 30% to 80% over a 10-year period, beginning in 1997. **See page 166.**
Medical Savings Accounts (MSAs)	A pilot program—1997–2000—will allow certain taxpayers to make tax-deductible contributions (subject to caps) to tax-deferred MSAs to fund uninsured medical expenses. **See pages 39 and 242.**
	Effective: After 12/31/96.
Spousal Individual Retirement Accounts (IRAs)	The maximum annual deductible IRA contribution is increased from $250 to $2,000 for a non-working spouse. **See page 88.**
	Effective: Taxable years after 12/31/96.
Damage Awards for Personal Injuries	Only compensatory damages for physical injury or illness are nontaxable. Punitive damages are generally taxable. **See page 30.**
	Effective: Amounts received after 8/21/96 unless binding settlement in effect on 9/13/95.
Employer-Provided Educational Assistance (Sec. 127) Income Exclusion	Exclusion is reinstated retroactively from 1/1/95 through 5/31/97 but tuition reimbursements for graduate education courses begun after 6/30/96 will be taxable. **See page 50.**
State Prepaid Tuition Plans: Clarification of Tax Treatment	"Interest" earned on qualified state prepaid tuition programs is tax exempt. **See page 7.**
	Effective: Taxable years ending after July, 1996 (e.g., calendar year 1996 for most individuals).
S Corporation Reform	S corporation eligibility rules are substantially expanded. **See page 254.**
	Effective: Generally after 12/31/96.
Research and Development Credit	The R&D credit, with modifications and an elective incremental credit, is reinstated for the period 7/1/96 through 5/31/97. **See page 249.**
Equipment Expensing Election	The annual equipment expensing election is incrementally increased from $17,500 to $25,000 by 2003. **See page 231.**
	Effective: Generally after 12/31/96.

Item	New Law
Pension Simplification	Pension rules modified, including repeal of combined plan limit and relaxation of nondiscrimination rules. New employer-sponsored plans available to small employers. Various effective dates. **See pages 88–97.**
Adoption Tax Credit	Generally after 1996, taxpayers can receive a nonrefundable income tax credit of $5,000 per child for qualified adoption expenses. The credit phases out at modified adjusted gross income (AGI) above $75,000. **See page 151.**

10 Smart Tax Planning Tips

1. Start your planning early. This allows you time to take advantage of strategies that may take several months to implement.

2. Make your contributions to an IRA or Keogh plan early in the year. The combination of making contributions early in the year and compounding will make your money grow faster than if you wait until the last minute. See page 88.

3. Contribute the maximum to your 401(k) plan and start early in the year. If you wait too long, you may not be able to contribute the full amount because of limitations. See page 162.

4. If you roll over a pension distribution to an IRA account, be sure you do it in a timely fashion. Caution: there is a 20% withholding tax on lump-sum distributions. See page 94.

5. If you plan to work after your normal retirement date, consider how it will affect your Social Security benefits. Also, consider whether you would be better off applying for your benefits by age 62 or waiting until you are 65. See page 113.

6. If you have publicly traded stock that would generate a long-term capital gain if sold, consider using it to make your charitable contributions. (Your contribution deduction will be based on the fair market value of the stock and you won't have to pay tax on the gain.) See page 121.

7. Charitable contributions are subject to certain tax limitations. Some of your contributions to charities may not be deductible until a later year if you exceed the prescribed limits. Futhermore, if you do not meet the substantiation requirements the contribution won't be deductible at all. See page 105.

8. Replace personal debt with mortgage debt to the extent possible. Interest expense on mortgage loans is—subject to some limitations—deductible; personal or consumer interest is not. See page 168.

9. Consider the after-tax yield of an investment when comparing returns on different investments. See page 185.

10. Consider giving gifts to your children. You may be able to shift income to them since children are usually in lower tax brackets and so pay less in taxes. However, if your children are under age 14, their income above certain levels will be subject to the special "kiddie tax" rates. See page 144.

I

Tax Strategies for Individuals

There are lots of tax-saving strategies you can use to lower your tax bill. This book has been organized in a way that will assist you in developing and implementing the most effective tax-saving strategies for you. Step 1, as anyone who has collected information for an annual tax return knows, is to determine what portion of your income is subject to tax and what may not be. Income, of course, is not just the money you get in your paycheck. It includes interest and dividends, rent and royalties, pensions and annuities, alimony and separate maintenance payments, among many other things—all of which are explained in Chapter 1. We've also pointed out permissible ways you can reduce the amount of income you have to report.

The second step (described in Chapter 2) is to figure out which of the expenses you incurred during the year can be deducted from your taxable income. We've included suggestions about how you can maximize your deductions and therefore lower the amount of tax you owe. The chapters on Travel and Entertainment Expenses, Tax Planning and Your Home, IRAs and 401(k) Plans, Charitable Contributions, Capital Gains and Losses, and Mutual Funds explain in greater detail strategies that can help you deal with these important topics.

The third step, the calculation of your tax, is explained in Chapter 9. It involves several calculations—you need to figure out, for example, whether to claim the standard deduction or to itemize, and for some heavy hitters whether or not you are subject to the alternative minimum tax. We've tried to describe the process in as simple and straightforward a way as possible. The results—some of which can help to lower your bottom line—can be richly rewarding.

The last step represents both an end and a new beginning. The sophisticated taxpayer can take steps at the end of the year that can defer taxes until next year. This is the primary focus of Chapter 10. If you can shift the tax from this taxable year to the next taxable year, you have saved the use of those deferred funds for a year. More importantly, Chapter 10 illustrates how a taxpayer can start planning so that less tax will have to be paid in future years.

1

What You Have to Include as Income

INTRODUCTION

The first step in determining how much in taxes you'll have to pay is to figure out your *taxable income*. That is the amount, figured by subtracting from your gross income certain adjustments and allowable deductions, upon which your tax is based. Your gross income includes income from all sources, including:

- Alimony and separate maintenance payments
- Compensation for services, including salary, wages, fees, commissions, and certain employee benefits
- Gains from dealings in property
- Gross income from a business
- Income from an interest in an estate or trust
- Income from paying off a debt for less than you owe
- Certain income from life insurance and endowment contracts
- Interest and dividends
- Pensions and annuities
- Rents and royalties
- Court awards in non-injury or non-sickness cases (e.g., job discrimination)
- Your share of income from a partnership or S corporation, *whether it is distributed or not.*

This chapter discusses what you have to include in calculating your taxable income. Along the way, you'll find many tax-saving suggestions that should help you lower your taxable income—and your tax bill.

WAGES, SALARIES, AND OTHER EARNED INCOME

As a general rule, you must include in your gross income everything you receive as payment for personal services including wages, salaries, commissions, and tips. If you receive property or services as compensation, you generally should include the fair market value of the property or services as wages in the year you receive it.

Unless you anticipate a tax rate increase next year (and we don't expect that there will be one), you will generally find it to your advantage to defer recognizing income, where permissible, to a later year. Usually the date of receipt determines the year income is taxable. So, failure to cash a check or refusal to accept a payment will not defer income.

E&Y FOCUS: Deferred Compensation Plans

Deferred compensation plans are designed by employers for executives who can afford to defer a portion of their earnings. Under such plans you make an election to defer some portion of your income until a stated time; you are taxed on the deferred income only when it is received.

Deferrals can be made from your regular salary or from bonuses. You must make an election to defer income before that income is earned. Furthermore, you and your employer must enter into a written deferral agreement.

Deferred compensation plans serve one or two functions, depending on whether they are short-term or long-term plans:

- Short-term arrangements are generally most effective when used to take advantage of tax-rate changes. For example, suppose that in the current year the top rate on your taxable income is 40%. The next year you expect the top rate to drop to 30%. You might use a deferred compensation plan to shift income from one year to the next so that it will be taxed at a lower rate.
- Long-term arrangements are aimed primarily at providing key employees with bonuses and retirement income in excess of the amounts allowed by law under the employer's qualified pension and profit-sharing plans. Some experts are dubious about the benefits of long-term deferrals, mainly because they believe tax rates will be higher in the future than they are currently. If they're right, the deferred income would be taxed at a higher rate—defeating one of the primary purposes of deferring the income. Some deferred compensation plans include a provision for increasing the amounts to reflect an earnings factor for the period of deferral. Moreover, given the restrictions on qualified plans, nonqualified plans continue to be popular with executives.

Make Sure You Collect Your Deferred Compensation. Many traditional "nonqualified" (i.e., unfunded) deferred compensation plans are based on an unsecured promise from your employer to pay compensation in the future. But how can you be sure your company will pay up?

Various arrangements have been developed to provide the employee with an additional sense of security that the promise will be honored without causing the income to be immediately taxable. One such device is known as a "rabbi trust," so named because the first arrangement approved by the IRS was developed by a synagogue for its rabbi.

Under a rabbi trust arrangement, amounts sufficient to pay the deferred compensation are placed into an irrevocable trust by your employer. Once in the trust, these amounts can be accessed by the employer's creditors only upon the employer's bankruptcy or insolvency; the amounts are not otherwise available for use by the original employer or a successor employer. This means that, unless the employer becomes bankrupt or insolvent, amounts in the rabbi trust will be available to pay the deferred compensation in future years.

"Noncash" Compensation. The following are some of the more common forms of noncash compensation that are subject to tax:
1. *Employer-provided automobile for personal use.* If your employer provided you with a car, your personal use of the car is considered taxable noncash compensation.
2. *Educational assistance.* You generally must include in income any educational expenses your employer paid for you, unless the courses are required by your employer, are job-related, or the expenses are paid for under a special plan meeting IRS requirements.
3. *Bargain purchase of employer's assets.* If you are allowed to purchase property from your employer at a price *below* its fair market value as compensation for your services, you must report as income the difference between the property's fair market value and the amount you paid for it (see the exception following under "Qualified employee discount").
4. *Stock options.* The difference between the stock's fair market value and the option price should generally be reported as additional income when you exercise an option to buy stock from your employer. A special rule, however, applies to certain stock options. This rule usually delays the tax until you sell or exchange your stock. (See pages 25–27 in this chapter.)
5. *Group life insurance premiums for over $50,000 of coverage.* An employer's payments for group term life insurance premiums for coverage over $50,000 are considered to be additional income to you unless the beneficiary of the "over $50,000 life insurance" is an organization to which a contribution would be a charitable contribution.
6. *Club memberships.* If your employer provides you with a membership in a country club or similar social organization, you are subject to tax on the value of the membership.

Tax-Free Fringe Benefits. Certain fringe benefits you receive from your employer are specifically excluded from taxation. These include:
1. *No-additional-cost service.* If you receive services from your employer that are regularly offered for sale to customers and your employer incurs no substantial additional cost in providing them to you, you do not have to include the value of these services as income. *Example:* Stand-by space on flights for airline employees.

2. *Qualified employee discount.* You do not have to report additional income if the discount your employer extended to you is less than the discount your employer would regularly offer to customers. For the purchase of services, the discount must be less than 20% of the price regularly charged to customers. *Example:* Appliance retailers' discounted sales of their merchandise to their employees at the lowest discounted price offered to customers.
3. *Working condition fringe benefits.* You do not have to include in income the value of property or services provided to you by your employer if you would be entitled to a business deduction for such items on your personal return had you paid for these items. *Example:* Business periodical subscriptions.
4. *De minimis fringe benefits.* Fringe benefits items so small in value that it would be unreasonable or administratively impractical for your employer to account for them. *Examples:* Personal use of copying machine, occasional parties for employees.

We've mentioned just a few examples. You should consult with your employer and your tax advisor to find out how to treat a particular item.

401(k) Plans. If your employer has a 401(k) plan or another plan that allows you to postpone income, you can elect to defer a certain amount of your salary on a pre-tax basis. Such amounts are withheld from your salary and are not reported as income until withdrawn from the plan. For further information about 401(k)s and other retirement plans see Chapter 5.

TaxSaver

A key element of tax planning is reducing your income. One way to do that is to take advantage of your employer's 401(k) plan, particularly if the deductible amount you are permitted to contribute to an IRA is limited (see page 20). With a 401(k), you can elect to defer up to a maximum of $9,500 in 1996.

TaxSaver

Although the funds in your 401(k) plan are meant to be set aside for your retirement, you may still have access to them if you need money. Your plan may permit you to borrow from the plan, subject to strict rules. Despite the restrictions, you may be better off borrowing from your retirement fund than getting a loan from your bank. If the loan from the bank is for personal purposes, it could result in nondeductible interest. While a loan from your 401(k) plan does not generate deductible interest, the interest you pay is allocated to your account.

INTEREST AND DIVIDENDS

Interest that you receive on bank accounts, on loans that you have made to others, or from other sources is taxable. However, interest received on obligations of a state or one of its political subdivisions, the District of Columbia, or a possession of the United States or one of its political divisions, is usually tax-exempt for federal purposes.

TAX*ALERT*

The Small Business Job Protection Act of 1996 clarifies that qualified state tuition programs are tax exempt. Thus participants will not be subject to income or gift taxes arising from such contributions made to qualified programs. If disbursed for education, no tax will apply.

Interest is paid by the IRS on a tax refund arising from any type of original tax return if the refund is not issued by the 45th day after the later of the due date for the return (determined without regard to any extensions) or the date the return was filed. Interest you receive from the IRS is taxable. (The interest rates on such payments are set periodically by the IRS.)

U.S. Saving Bonds

U.S. saving bonds are direct obligations of the United States government. Two series of bonds are available: Series EE bonds and Series HH bonds. Both are subject to federal income tax, though in some circumstances (explained below) interest on Series EE bonds may be deferred for many years, and if used for certain educational purposes may even be exempt from tax. Both series of bonds, however, are not subject to state or local income taxes.

Series EE Bonds. These are bonds that are issued at a discount—that is, they're purchased at a fixed amount, and are redeemed at a higher amount depending upon how long the bonds were held. Cash method taxpayers have the option of reporting income on the bonds when the bonds are redeemed or reporting it annually as it accrues. Accrual method taxpayers must report the income as it accrues.

TAX*SAVER*

Series EE bonds can be an interesting tax-sheltered investment in two ways. First, because most individuals are cash-method taxpayers paying taxes on income as it is received, interest income from Series EE bonds is not recognized until it is received (i.e., when the bonds are redeemed). But, there is a second way you can shelter your interest income from Series EE bonds for an even longer time. If, instead of redeeming the bonds when they come due, you exchange them for Series HH bonds (that pay interest semiannually), you can avoid recognition of the accumulated Series EE bond interest until the Series HH bonds are redeemed.

*   **Example:** Sam purchases $7,500 worth of Series EE bonds, which pay interest of 4 percent per year. In slightly more than seven years, the bonds will have grown in value to $10,000. Instead of redeeming them at that point,*

Sam exchanges them for $10,000 worth of Series HH bonds, which pay interest at the rate of 4 percent per year. The $2,500 of interest income earned over the years on the Series EE bonds would not be taxable at the date of exchange but would be deferred. Sam will receive $400 of taxable interest income per year on the Series HH bonds. The $2,500 of deferred interest income on the Series EE bonds would not be taxable until the Series HH bonds reach final maturity or are redeemed.

There is, however, a limitation on the purchase of EE bonds. An individual may purchase only up to $15,000 per year.

When held five years or longer, EE bonds become eligible to receive a market-based interest rate, retroactive to the first day of the month of issue. During that time, they receive interest at 85% of the average return on marketable Treasury securities with five years remaining to their maturity.

TAXSAVER

Under current law, interest on EE bonds purchased from January 1, 1990, may be exempt from federal tax, if their redemption proceeds are used for certain educational purposes. To be eligible for the tax exemption, the purchaser of the bonds must be at least 24 years of age, and the proceeds from the sale of the bonds must be used to pay for the qualified higher educational expenses of either the purchaser, his/her spouse, or dependents. The tax break phases out for married taxpayers filing jointly who have adjusted gross income beginning at $65,250 in 1996. For single taxpayers and heads of household filers, the phaseout begins at $43,500. The break is not available if you are married filing separately. Caution: a young couple whose income increases significantly may find that by the time their child is ready for college, they are no longer eligible to claim the tax exemption.

Series HH Bonds. These are current income securities: interest is paid at a fixed rate semiannually. Interest must be reported in the year in which it is received. Since March 1, 1993, new issues have paid a 4% rate of interest. (See discussion above for a tax deferral opportunity using Series EE and Series HH bonds.)

TAXSAVER

Both Series EE and HH bonds are subject to estate, inheritance, gift, or other excise taxes—whether federal or state—but they are exempt from all other taxes imposed on the principal or interest by any state, U.S. possession, or local taxing authority.

TAXSAVER

Millions of dollars worth of Series (single) E and (single) H saving bonds continue to be held by the public. Most are earning interest. Some, however, have reached final maturity and no longer earn interest; others are nearing their final maturity dates. The chart below shows the extended maturities that have been announced by the U.S. Treasury. Series E bonds that have reached final maturity should be redeemed or exchanged for Series HH bonds.

Extended maturities

Series	Date of Issues	Interest-bearing Life
E	May 1941–Nov. 1965	40 years
	Dec. 1965 and later	30 years
H	June 1952–Jan. 1957	29 yrs., 8 mos.
	Feb. 1957 and later	30 years
EE	All issues	30 years
HH	All issues	20 years

Dividends. Dividends are distributions of money, stock, or other property paid to you by a corporation. You may also indirectly receive dividends through a partnership, an estate, or a trust. In most cases, dividends are taxable as ordinary income. Some dividends, however, are treated as capital gain distributions. The distributions are nontaxable if the distribution is considered to be a return of capital or if the distribution is in the form of stock or stock rights. You should be informed by the corporation making the distribution about the nature and amount of the dividends at the time of distribution. Dividend distributions from a mutual fund, such as interest on dividends earned from the fund's investment securities, are generally considered ordinary income for tax purposes. See Chapter 8, Mutual Funds.

Stock Dividends and Stock Rights. Generally, the receipt of stock dividends or stock rights in a company is not taxable, unless the shareholder is permitted to choose between stock (or stock rights) and cash or other property (e.g., a dividend reinvestment plan).

If you receive a nontaxable distribution from a company, the adjusted basis of your old stock must be apportioned between the old and the new stock (or stock rights) based on their relative market values.

Example: If you owned 100 shares of XYZ Company which you purchased at $10 a share and you then received another 100 shares as a stock dividend, your adjusted basis for your 200 shares would be $5 a share. You are not required to allocate basis to nontaxable stock rights received if the value of the rights is less than 15% of the fair market value of the stock on the date of distribution.

Mutual fund dividends declared in October, November, and December to shareholders of record in those months are considered paid on December 31 of that year even if the distribution isn't actually paid until January of the next year. For a further discussion, see Chapter 8, Mutual Funds.

RENTAL INCOME AND EXPENSES

Rental income includes any payment you receive for the use or occupation of property. If you receive property or services as rent, the fair market value of the property or services you receive is income. (See Chapter 4 for a discussion of vacation home rentals and depreciation issues.)

CAPITAL GAINS AND LOSSES

For the most part, everything you own and hold for personal and investment purposes is a capital asset. See Chapter 7, Capital Gains and Losses, for a discussion of how sales of capital assets are taxed.

SELLING YOUR HOME

A gain on the sale or exchange (including condemnation) of your principal residence is taxable. If you have a loss on the sale, under current law you cannot deduct it. (See Chapter 4 for more information about the tax consequences of home ownership as well as for tax-saving strategies that involve your home.)

INCOME FROM BUSINESS AND OTHER INVESTMENTS

Sole Proprietorship, Partnership, and S Corporation Income

In a sole proprietorship, you and your business are the same taxpayer. You report gross profit or loss for the year from the sole proprietorship on Form 1040, and it becomes part of your adjusted gross income. In contrast with a sole proprietorship, a partnership is an entity that is separate from the individual taxpayers that are its owners. While a partnership is not an entity subject to federal income tax, if you are a member of a partnership, you are liable individually for tax on your share of partnership income, even if such income is not distributed to you. S corporations generally do not pay federal income tax. Instead, S corporation income typically is taxed directly to the shareholders based on their respective ownership percentage, regardless of whether such income is distributed to them. Like partnerships, S corporations separately report items of income, gain, deduction, and loss that may be subject to special treatment by their shareholders. For a more complete discussion about the taxation of business income, see Part III, Tax Strategies for Businesses, especially

Chapter 15, Determining Income, Deductions, and Taxes for Your Business.

"At-Risk" Limitation Provisions

The deduction for business and other investment losses held directly or through partnerships or S corporations is generally limited to the amount by which you are considered to be "at risk" in the activity. You are considered at risk for the amount of cash you have invested in the venture and the basis of property invested plus certain amounts borrowed for use in the activity.

Borrowed amounts that are considered at risk are (1) loans for which you are personally liable for repayment or (2) loans secured by property, other than that used in the activity. Generally, liabilities that are secured by property within the activity for which you are not otherwise personally liable are not considered to be at risk. An exception: if nonrecourse financing—financing for which you are not personally liable—is secured against real property used in the activity, you may be considered at risk for the amount of the financing.

If you are a partner in a partnership or a shareholder in an S corporation, you are also considered to be at risk for your undistributed share of partnership or S corporation income. The at-risk provisions apply to individuals and closely held corporations (corporations in which five or fewer individuals own more than 50% of the stock). For S corporations or partnerships, the at-risk rules apply to the shareholder or the partner. An exception: closely held corporations engaged in certain equipment leasing and active qualifying businesses are not subject to the at-risk rules.

The law provides a broad list of activities (including the holding of real estate acquired after 1986) that are subject to the at-risk provisions. Each investment activity is considered separately. However, S corporations and partnerships can aggregate investments in similar activity categories. If the "at-risk" provisions apply to you, you should consult with your tax advisor.

Passive Activity Losses and Credits

Under current law individuals, estates, trusts, closely held corporations, and personal service corporations are generally prohibited from deducting net losses generated by passive activities. (Passive activities are discussed below.) In addition, tax credits from passive activities are generally limited to the tax liability attributable to such activities. Disallowed passive activity losses are suspended and carried forward to offset passive activity income generated in future years. Similar carryforward treatment applies to excess credits.

Defining Passive Activities. A passive activity involves the conduct of any trade or business in which you do not materially participate. You are treated as a material participant only if you are involved in the operations of the activity on a regular, continuous, and substantial basis. If you are not a material participant in an activity, but your spouse is, you are treated as being a material participant and the activity is not considered passive.

Seven Tests. The IRS has seven alternative tests you can meet to be considered a material participant. If you satisfy any one of these tests, you will be considered a material participant in an activity. These tests are:
1. You participate in the activity for more than 500 hours during the taxable year;
2. Your participation during the taxable year constitutes substantially all of the participation of all individuals;
3. You participate for more than 100 hours during the taxable year and no one else participates more;
4. The activity is a significant participation activity (SPA) for the taxable year, and your participation in all SPAs during the taxable year exceeds 500 hours. An SPA is an activity in which an individual participates for more than 100 hours, but does not otherwise meet a material participation test;
5. You materially participated in any 5 of the 10 preceding taxable years;
6. The activity is a personal service activity, and you materially participated for any three preceding taxable years. A personal service activity involves performance of personal services in the fields of health, law, engineering, architecture, accounting, actuarial sciences, performing arts, consulting, or any other business in which capital is not a material income-producing factor; and
7. Based on all the facts and circumstances, your participation is regular, continuous, and substantial during the taxable year.

Defining an Activity. The proper grouping of business operations into one or more activities is important in determining the allocation of suspended losses, measuring your material participation, separating rental and nonrental activities, and determining when a disposition of an activity has occurred. IRS regulations define an activity as any "appropriate economic unit for measuring gain or loss." What constitutes an "appropriate economic unit" is determined by looking at all facts and circumstances. The regulations list five factors that are to be given the greatest weight. They are:
1. Similarities and differences in types of business;
2. The extent of common control;
3. The extent of common ownership;
4. Geographical location; and
5. Interdependence between the activities.
   Generally, taxpayers must be consistent from year to year in determining the business operations that constitute an activity. Furthermore, rental and non-rental activities may only be grouped together in a limited number of circumstances. Consult your tax advisor for more information.

Rental Activities. Rental activities are generally considered passive activities. However, the personal use of a dwelling unit for the greater of 14 days or 10% of the time that it is rented out to others is considered use of a personal residence and is not considered a passive activity.

IRS rules provide other exceptions for which activities involving the use of tangible property are not deemed a rental activity.

TAXALERT

Real estate professionals who meet certain eligibility thresholds and materially participate in rental real estate activities may offset rental real estate losses against all sources of taxable income.

Only individuals and closely held C corporations can qualify for this special rule. An individual taxpayer will satisfy the eligibility requirements for any tax year if more than one-half of the personal services (with more than 750 hours) performed in trades or businesses by the taxpayer during such a tax year are performed in real property trades or businesses in which the taxpayer materially participates. Personal services performed as an employee are not considered in determining material participation unless the employee has more than a 5% ownership in the employer. However, independent contractor realtor services would qualify for this purpose. For closely held C corporations, the eligibility requirements are met if more than 50% of the corporation's gross receipts for the tax year are derived from real property trades or businesses in which the corporation materially participates.

Example: *During 1995, a self-employed real estate developer earned $100,000 in fees from projects the developer spent 1,200 hours developing. In addition, the developer incurred rental real estate losses of $200,000 from properties which the developer spent over 800 hours managing during 1994. The developer performs no other personal services during the year, and has no other items of income or deduction. Because the developer (1) materially participated in the rental real estate activity, (2) performed more than 750 hours in real property trades or businesses, and (3) performed more than 50% of the developer's total personal service hours in real estate trades or businesses in which the developer materially participated, the developer will have a net operating loss of $100,000 to carry back (and the excess to carry forward) to offset any source of income.*

Limited Partnerships. Limited partnership interests are considered passive because a limited partner is generally not a material participant. If you have an interest in a limited partnership, you should check with your tax advisor to see if exceptions apply.

In general, working interests in any oil and gas property that you hold directly or through an entity that does not limit your liability is not considered passive, whether or not you are a material participant.

TAXSAVER

One way to increase the deductibility of your passive activity losses is to convert the interest expense from nondeductible passive activity interest to deductible residential interest. You can accomplish this shift by borrowing against your personal residence and using the proceeds to repay passive activity loans. Interest on borrowings of up to $100,000 secured by your per-

sonal residence is usually fully deductible regardless of how the proceeds are used.

Exception for Active Real Estate Participation. An exception to the passive loss rules applies to real estate rental activities in which you are an active participant. For this purpose, "active" participation requires a significant but lesser amount of involvement than does "material" participation. Active involvement would include making management decisions such as approving "new tenants" or making capital expenditures. You are considered to have not actively participated in the rental activity if, at any time during the tax year, you own less than a 10% interest in the activity. Each tax year, you can deduct up to $25,000 of passive losses (or claim the equivalent amount of credits) arising from real estate rental activities against income from nonpassive sources, such as salary, interest, and dividends. The $25,000 maximum deduction is reduced (but not below zero) by 50% of the amount by which your adjusted gross income exceeds $100,000. Thus, this deduction is completely phased out if your adjusted gross income is $150,000 or more. Adjusted gross income, for this purpose, is figured without taxable Social Security benefits, IRA contribution deductions, and any passive activity loss.

Example: Ron's adjusted gross income, figured without taxable Social Security benefits, IRA contribution deductions, and any passive activity loss, is $120,000. He has rental losses of $25,000. If Ron's income had been less than $100,000, he would have been able to deduct the full $25,000 rental real estate loss. Because his income is over $100,000, Ron's $25,000 loss is reduced by $10,000 [50% × ($120,000 − $100,000)]. The disallowed loss of $10,000 can be carried over to future years and deducted (based on these same limitations).

Dispositions of Passive Activities. If you completely dispose of a passive activity in a fully taxable transaction, you can then claim previously disallowed (i.e., suspended) losses. In addition, for dispositions made prior to January 1, 1995, if you dispose of a "substantial part" of a passive activity in a fully taxable transaction, you also may be able to deduct the portion of your suspended losses attributable to that part of your investment— assuming that you can determine with reasonable certainty the amount of the losses attributable to that part of your investment. For dispositions made after January 1, 1995, you must dispose of "substantially all" of a passive activity in order to deduct that same portion. If you dispose of a passive activity by selling your interest to a related party, you will not be able to deduct any suspended losses until the related purchaser disposes of the interest in a taxable transaction to an unrelated person. You may also be able to deduct suspended losses in a passive activity if your interest is disposed of in various other ways, including abandonment, death of the taxpayer, gifts, and installment sales of entire interests. Special rules may apply. You should consult your tax advisor for further clarification and requirements.

SOCIAL SECURITY AND OTHER BENEFITS

Social Security and Equivalent Railroad Retirement Benefits

A portion of your Social Security benefits may be subject to tax. Whether and how much depends upon the extent to which your *provisional income* (a technical term we will explain below) exceeds certain thresholds:

- $32,000 in the case of a married taxpayer filing a joint return—$0 if married filing separately, unless the spouses lived apart for the entire taxable year.
- $25,000 for all other taxpayers.

Provisional Income is your adjusted gross income **plus** tax exempt interest; income earned in a foreign country, Puerto Rico, or a U.S. possession that is not included in your gross income; plus tax-free foreign housing and one half of the Social Security benefits you received.

For taxpayers with *provisional income* in excess of the thresholds there is a two tier system for determining the amount of the Social Security benefits included in income. How much is included will depend on whether your provisional income is in excess of:

- $44,000 in the case of a married taxpayer filing a joint return—$0 if married filing separately, unless the spouses lived apart for the entire taxable year.
- $34,000 for all other taxpayers.

For married joint filers with *provisional income* between $32,000 and $44,000, and for unmarried taxpayers with *provisional income* between $25,000 and $34,000, the amount of the Social Security benefit that is included in income is the lesser of one-half of the benefits received or one-half of the amount by which the *provisional income* exceeds the applicable threshold.

Example: For 1996, George and Harriet file a joint return. They have an adjusted gross income of $27,000. They received $7,500 in tax exempt interest and $8,000 in Social Security benefits. The amount of Social Security benefits that they included in income is computed as follows:

Adjusted gross income	$27,000
Plus: Tax Exempt Interest	7,500
Plus: One-half of the Social Security benefits received	4,000
Provisional Income	$38,500
Less: Threshold base amount	32,000
Excess of *provisional income* above threshold base	$ 6,500
One-half of the excess	$ 3,250
One-half of the Social Security benefits	$ 4,000
The amount included in income	$ 3,250

(The lesser of one-half of the excess of the *provisional income* over the base amount or one-half of the Social Security benefits)

For those whose *provisional income* is in excess of the $44,000 and $34,000 applicable thresholds, not only does the amount of Social Security benefits included in income increase but the computation of the includible amount becomes more complicated.

For joint filers with provisional income in excess of $44,000 and unmarried filers with provisional income in excess of $34,000 the portion of Social Security benefits received that is included in income is the *lesser* of:

- 85% of Social Security benefits received, or
- the sum of the following amounts:
  a) the smaller of (1) the amount that would have been included in income if the threshold did not apply or (2) $6,000 for joint return filers or $4,500 for unmarried taxpayers; plus
  b) 85% of the excess of the *provisional income* over the higher threshold amount.

Example: Instead of $38,500 *provisional income*, as in the prior example, George and Harriet have $61,000 *provisional income* comprised of $45,000 adjusted gross income, $9,000 in tax exempt interest and $7,000 in Social Security benefits (one-half of the $14,000 Social Security benefits they received).

Provisional Income	$61,000
Threshold amount	44,000
Excess of provisional income over threshold	$17,000
1) 85% of excess	$14,450
2) The amount that would have been included (50% of their Social Security benefits)	$ 7,000
3) Statutory amount for joint filers	6,000
4) The lesser of 2) or 3)	$ 6,000
5) The sum of 1) and 4)	$20,450
6) 85% of Social Security benefits ($14,000 × .85)	$11,900
Amount includible in income	$11,900

For married individuals filing separately, taxable Social Security benefits are calculated as the lesser of 85% of the taxpayers *provisional income*.

The table below shows the portion of $10,000 in Social Security benefits received that would be included in taxable income of unmarried and joint filers at various income levels.

Amount of $10,000 in Social Security Benefits Included in Taxable Income

Provisional Income	*Single*	*Joint*
$25,000	None	None
34,000	$4,500	$1,000
38,000	7,900	3,000
44,000	8,500	5,000
50,000	8,500	8,500

TAX*ALERT*

Tax-exempt income is added to your adjusted gross income for purposes of calculating how much, if any, of your Social Security benefits will be subject to tax. Keep this in mind when evaluating the after-tax rate of return of tax-exempt investments versus taxable investments.

Disability

Generally, you must report as income amounts you receive for your disability through an employer-paid accident or health insurance plan.

TAX*SAVER*

If you pay part of the cost of a disability plan, then any amounts you receive that are attributable to your payments will not be taxed to you. For example, if you pay $25 into a disability plan for every $75 your employer puts into the plan, one quarter of the amounts you receive will not be taxed to you.

Employee Death Benefits

Certain amounts received by a beneficiary from or on behalf of an employer by reason of the death of an employee may be excluded from income. The total amount that can be excluded with respect to an employee who has died may not exceed $5,000, regardless of the number of employers or beneficiaries. This exclusion may not apply if the employee had a nonforfeitable right to receive the amounts while living. Benefits paid in a lump-sum distribution for a self-employed person who was treated as an employee for qualified retirement plan coverage can also be excluded, subject to the same limitation.

TAX*ALERT*

This exclusion does not apply with respect to decedents dying after August 20, 1996.

Pensions or Annuities

As a general rule, if you did not pay any part of the cost of your pension or annuity, and your employer did not withhold part of the cost of the contract from your pay while you worked, the amounts you receive each year are fully taxable. For more information about IRAs, Keoghs, and Simplified Employee Pensions (SEPs), see Chapter 5.

What to Exclude From Income. If you paid part of the cost of your annuity, the portion of an annuity payment representing the return of your "investment in the contract" can be excluded from your gross income. The excludable portion is the payment received times the "exclusion ratio," that is, the investment in the contract divided by the expected return under the contract. The "expected return under the contract" is the total amount that you or someone you designate can expect to receive under the contract based on actuarial considerations. The exclusion ratio is determined as of the first day of the first period for which an annuity payment is received. Once computed, the ratio ordinarily will not change.

TAX**ALERT**

Where the annuity starting date is after November 18, 1996, the excludable portion must generally be determined by dividing the investment in the contract by the number of anticipated payments determined under a table provided in the Internal Revenue Code.

For annuities that began payments before 1987, tax-free recoveries will continue even if the annuity owner outlives his or her life expectancy. However, if your first annuity payment was after 1986, the portion of a payment excluded from your gross income cannot exceed the unrecovered investment in the contract immediately before the receipt of such payment.

If annuity payments (from annuities with starting dates after 1986) cease because the annuity owner dies before his or her total contributions have been recovered, the amount of the unrecovered investment is allowed as a miscellaneous itemized deduction to the annuity owner for his or her last taxable year. However, the deduction is not subject to the 2% floor on miscellaneous itemized deductions. Similar rules apply where the contract provides for payments to be made to a beneficiary.

TAX**SAVER**

Annuities are popular investments to earn income and defer taxes. Earnings accumulate and are not taxed until you receive payments. For more on annuities, please see Chapter 11, Investment Planning.

Lump-Sum Distributions. Lump-sum distributions you receive from a qualified retirement plan—an employer's pension, stock bonus, or profit-sharing plan—may qualify for special tax treatment. A lump-sum distribution is the distribution within a single tax year of an employee's entire balance, excluding certain amounts forfeited or subject to forfeiture, from all of the employer's qualified pension plans, all of the employer's qualified stock bonus plans, or all of the employer's qualified profit-sharing plans. The distribution must have been made:

1. Because of the employee's death,
2. After the employee reaches age 59½,
3. Because of the employee's separation from service (does not apply to self-employed persons), or
4. After a self-employed individual becomes totally and permanently disabled.

As with an annuity, you may recover tax-free your cost basis in the lump-sum distribution. In general, your cost basis is:
1. Your total nondeductible contributions to the plan;
2. The total of your taxable one-year term costs of life insurance;
3. Any employer contributions that were taxable to you; and
4. Repayments of loans that were taxable to you.

You must reduce your basis by amounts previously distributed to you tax-free.

You also may be able to receive special tax treatment on the remainder of the distribution:

Long-Term Capital Gain Treatment. If you were at least age 50 on January 1, 1986, you may choose to treat a portion of the taxable part of a lump-sum distribution as a long-term capital gain taxable at a 20% rate. This treatment applies to the portion you receive relating to your participation in the plan before 1974.

Capital gains treatment is not available for lump-sum distributions received after 1991 by individuals who were less than 50 years old on January 1, 1986, or for lump-sum distributions from an IRA.

Special Averaging Method. You may elect to use a 5-year special averaging method to calculate the tax on the ordinary income portion of a lump-sum distribution, including the capital gain portion for which you did not elect capital gain treatment. To use special averaging, you must be at least age 59½ (unless you were at least age 50 on January 1, 1986), elect to use special averaging for all lump-sum distributions received during the year, and have been a participant in the plan for five or more years. You can make this election only once in a lifetime. (For 5-year averaging, see the tax table in the Appendices.)

If you were at least age 50 on January 1, 1986, the age 59½ requirement does not apply and you may elect to use 10-year averaging rather than 5-year averaging. However, the tax rates used in the 10-year averaging calculation are the rates in effect for 1986. (See Table 1.1.)

To get an idea of how special averaging works, assume that your income was received equally by 5 different persons (10 for 10-year averaging) in the current year and that each of these people had no other income. As a result, most of the income is taxed at the lowest rates on the single taxpayer tax rate schedule. The tax for these fictional individuals is then added up and becomes your tax on the distribution.

TAXSAVER

The 5-year or 10-year averaging method may be so beneficial to you that you elect to have the long-term capital gain portion of the lump-sum distribution included in the 5-year or 10-year averaging computation rather than have it taxed as long-term capital gain. The tax should be figured both ways to see which is the lowest. If you are eligible to elect either 5-year or 10-year

TABLE 1.1 Tax Rate Schedule for the 10-Year Tax Option

If the amount is:		The tax is:		
Over—	But not over—			Of the amount over—
$–0–	$1,190	—	11%	$–0–
1,190	2,270	$130.90 +	12%	1,190
2,270	4,530	260.50 +	14%	2,270
4,530	6,690	576.90 +	15%	4,530
6,690	9,170	900.90 +	16%	6,690
9,170	11,440	1,297.70 +	18%	9,170
11,440	13,710	1,706.30 +	20%	11,440
13,710	17,160	2,160.30 +	23%	13,710
17,160	22,880	2,953.80 +	26%	17,160
22,880	28,600	4,441.00 +	30%	22,880
28,600	34,320	6,157.00 +	34%	28,600
34,320	42,300	8,101.80 +	38%	34,320
42,300	57,190	11,134.20 +	42%	42,300
57,190	85,790	17,388.00 +	48%	57,190
85,790	—	31,116.00 +	50%	85,790

averaging, you should also figure your tax both ways to determine which is most beneficial.

Lump-sum distributions from an IRA do not qualify for the special averaging method.

TaxAlert

The Small Business Job Protection Act of 1996 changed the law governing lump-sum distributions from pension, stock bonus, and profit sharing plans. For tax years beginning after December 31, 1999, the 5-year special averaging method will be eliminated. However, if you are one of those individuals who meets the qualifications for the long-term capital gain method and the 10-year averaging method described above, you will still be able to elect to use those methods.

Individual Retirement Arrangements (IRAs). In general, distributions from an IRA are taxed in much the same way as an annuity. The portion of each distribution that is attributable to nondeductible contributions, if any, is excluded from your taxable income. The portion of each distribution to be excluded is determined by dividing undistributed nondeductible contributions by your total IRA account balance. If no nondeductible contributions have been made, then the entire distribution is considered ordinary income. (See Chapter 5 for more details about IRAs.)

OTHER INCOME

Interest-Free and Below-Market-Rate Loans

Certain interest-free and below-market-rate loans must be treated as loans bearing interest at a statutory rate. This may cause the imputed interest to be treated as a gift, compensation, and so on, as described below.

An interest-free or below-market loan is a loan on which no interest is charged or on which interest is charged at a rate below the applicable federal rate (AFR), set monthly by the IRS. Such a loan is generally treated as an arm's-length transaction in which you, as the borrower, are deemed (1) to have received a loan that requires the payment of interest at the applicable federal rate and (2) to have received an additional payment equal to the difference between the AFR and the no-interest or low-interest rate. The additional payment is treated as a gift, dividend, contribution to capital, payment of compensation, or other payment, depending on the nature of the transaction. In effect, two transactions are deemed to have occurred. One results in interest income to the lender and interest expense to the borrower to the extent that the interest at the statutory rate exceeds the actual interest paid. This is known as "foregone interest." In the second transaction, the lender is considered to have paid to the borrower the amount of "foregone interest" in the form of a gift, dividend, compensation, or other payment, depending on the nature of the relationship between the two parties.

Below-Market Demand Loans. If one party receives a below-market gift demand loan or other demand loan (one payable in full at any time upon the lender's demand), the lender will be treated as having made a transfer to the borrower on the last day of the calendar year of an amount equal to the "foregone interest." This amount will be treated as a gift, compensation, dividend, or other payment as appropriate. An identical amount will be treated as a payment of interest by the borrower at the same time. Therefore, the borrower may be entitled to deduct a part of that amount as interest expense. Loans with indefinite maturities are treated as demand loans.

Below-Market Term Loans. If one party receives a below-market "gift" term loan (one that is not a demand loan), the lender is treated as having made a gift on the loan date equal to the excess of the amount borrowed over the present value of all principal and interest payments required by the terms of the loan. The present value is determined using the applicable federal rate established monthly by the IRS. The borrower is treated as if he or she paid the lender interest on the last day of the calendar year.

If one party receives a term loan (other than a gift term loan), the lender is deemed to have transferred an amount equal to the excess of the loan over the present value of all principal and interest payments to the borrower. The transfer is treated as having occurred on the date the loan was made. The amount will be considered a dividend, compensation, or other payment as appropriate. An amount equal to this excess will be treated as original issue discount. Accordingly, the original discount rules apply. The borrower and the lender will be treated as paying or receiving interest on an economic accrual basis over the term of the loan. (Original issue discount is discussed on page 234.)

The applicable federal rate used in the calculations discussed above is based on the average yield on U.S. Treasury obligations. Different rates will be used for short-, intermediate-, and long-term loans. Semiannual compounding is required for both term and demand loans.

Exceptions: The rules for below-market loans do not apply to:
1. Gift loans between individuals that in the aggregate do not exceed $10,000, provided the loan proceeds are not directly used to purchase or carry income-producing assets;
2. Gift loans between individuals not exceeding $100,000, where the borrower's net investment income does not exceed $1,000 and there is no motive to avoid paying tax;
3. Gift loans between individuals not exceeding $100,000, where the borrower's net investment income exceeds $1,000 and there is no motive to avoid paying tax (the amount of interest income and expense imputed is limited to the net investment income); and
4. Compensation or corporate/shareholder loans that in the aggregate do not exceed $10,000, provided the principal purpose of the loan is not avoiding taxes.

TAX*SAVER*

Imputed interest may result in one or both parties of the transaction recognizing taxable income without an offsetting deduction, even though no money changed hands. To avoid this, be sure that the loans carry an appropriate market interest rate and that interest payments are made when due. For term loans, the interest rate is the applicable federal rate in effect on the date the loan is made; for demand loans the rate is the applicable federal short-term rate in effect on each day the loan is outstanding.

Restricted Property Received for Services

The excess of the fair market value of restricted property received for services performed over the amount (if any) paid for such property should be included in income as compensation in the year your interest in the property becomes transferable or is not subject to a substantial risk of forfeiture. Restricted property includes both real and personal property that is subject to some form of restriction, such as a limitation on transferring the property or a risk of forfeiture upon leaving employment before a specified date. However, restricted property does not include either money or an unsecured promise to pay money or property in the future. Generally, the fair market value is determined at the time the property becomes transferable or nonforfeitable.

Instead of deferring the recognition of income until your interest in the property becomes transferable or is no longer subject to a substantial risk of forfeiture, you may elect in the year of transfer to include in your income the fair market value of the property at the time of receipt (disregarding restrictions other than ones that by their terms will never lapse) minus the amount (if any) paid for such property. Generally, this election must be made within 30 days after the transfer of the property. However, if this election is made and the property is subsequently forfeited, you may only deduct the excess of the amount originally paid for the property (if any) over the amount realized (if any) from the forfeiture.

TAXSAVER

The election to include in your income the fair market value of the property at the time of receipt can produce tax savings if the property appreciates in value by the time the restrictions lapse. This election defers recognizing the gain on the appreciation until the property is sold. However, you need to consider the value of money over time for the taxes you will currently pay as well as the possibility of forfeiting the property.

The holding period for the restricted property begins on the first date on which your rights are either transferable or not subject to a substantial risk of forfeiture. If, however, you elect to include in your income the fair market value of the property, the holding period begins on the date of actual transfer.

If you perform services in return for restricted property, the person for whom you perform such services is allowed a deduction for the same amount and in the same year in which you report income. For transfers to employees, regulations generally require withholding by the employer.

Unemployment Compensation

Generally, unemployment compensation benefits are fully taxable. However, if the unemployed worker contributed nondeductible amounts to the unemployment compensation fund during employment, unemployment compensation is not taxable until an amount equal to those nondeductible amounts has been received.

Health and Accident Benefits

Benefits received under a qualified employer-sponsored health or accident plan for the reimbursement of medical expenses and payments for permanent injury or loss of a bodily function can be excluded from your gross income. Reimbursements for medical expenses that you claimed as an itemized deduction in a previous year must be included in gross income.

Benefits received under an employer-funded self-insured medical reimbursement plan by employees who are officers, shareholders, or highly compensated individuals can be excluded from income only if the plan does not discriminate in favor of these employees.

Life Insurance Contracts

Generally, amounts you receive under a life insurance contract paid by reason of the death of the insured, whether in a single sum or otherwise, are not included in your gross income.

Any interest paid along with life insurance death proceeds is taxable.

Any proceeds received upon the surrender of a life insurance contract by the insured are taxable to the extent that the amount received (including amounts recovered tax-free prior to the exchange) is in excess of the amounts paid in. A loss is not deductible.

TAXALERT

Some insurance companies are providing pre-death payments to terminally ill policyholders. The IRS generally is treating payments to the terminally ill on account of imminent death as insurance proceeds at death. Therefore, they are not includible in the policyholder's income.

Modified Endowment Contracts

In general, a modified endowment contract is one in which the accumulated amount paid by the taxpayer under the contract at any time during the first seven contract years exceeds the sum of the average annual premiums for paid-up insurance that would have been paid within the first seven years. Modified endowment contracts entered after June 21, 1988, are taxable as follows:

1. Amounts received under the contract are treated first as income and then as a recovery of investment in the contract.
2. Loans under the contract, as well as loans secured by the contract, are treated as amounts received under the contract except for certain loans relating to funeral expenses.
3. An additional 10% tax is imposed on amounts received that can be included in income. This additional tax does not apply to any distribution: (a) made on or after you turn age 59½; (b) due to your becoming disabled; or (c) that is part of a series of substantially equal periodic payments made over your life or life expectancy or for the joint lives or life expectancies of you and your beneficiary.

Certain Living Expense Contracts

You can exclude from your gross income amounts received under an insurance contract that pays you for living expenses in excess of your normal living expenses resulting from the loss of the use of your principal residence due to a casualty.

Dividends on Life Insurance and Endowment Policies

Dividends on most unmatured life insurance or endowment policies are treated as a partial return of the premiums paid and are not included in your gross income until they exceed the accumulated net premiums paid for the contract.

Alimony and Similar Payments

If you receive payments of alimony or separate maintenance, you must include them in figuring your gross income. Conversely, if you pay alimony or separate maintenance to a former spouse, you may deduct such payments from your gross income. Payments received from a property settlement or for child support are not considered alimony and therefore are not considered income to the recipient (or deductible to the payor).

TaxSaver

The tax consequences of alimony versus other payments need to be carefully considered in working out divorce or separation agreements. For example, if you receive property with a tax basis that is substantially less than its current value, you will be subject to tax when you sell the property on the difference between the tax basis of the property and what you receive. You should consult your tax advisor on such matters. (See page 36 for a further discussion of alimony.)

Tax-Exempt Interest

Interest on certain obligations of a state, territory, U.S. possession, or any political subdivision can be excluded from gross income. In addition, if you earn interest on tax-exempt bonds issued in your home state, the interest will generally not be subject to state or local tax. Special rules apply to interest on arbitrage and industrial development bonds. Tax-exempt interest on certain municipal bonds issued after August 7, 1986, are tax preference items for AMT purposes. (See discussion on page 145.)

TaxSaver

Higher income tax rates increase the appeal of tax-exempt bonds and mutual funds that invest in these bonds, especially for taxpayers in the 39.6% top marginal tax bracket. As tax rates rise, taxable securities must provide a higher yield in order to match the tax-effected yield offered by tax-exempt bonds of similar quality and time to maturity. For example, to a taxpayer in the 31% bracket, a taxable bond yielding 8.70% is comparable to a municipal bond with a 6.0% tax-exempt yield. However, a taxpayer in the new 39.6% bracket would need almost a 10% yield on a taxable bond to match the municipal bond's 6.0% return. And considering the fact that some states have income tax rates over 10%, the combined federal and state marginal tax rate, taking phaseouts and other back door tax increases into account, can exceed 50%. Thus, an investor living in such a high tax state would need a 12% taxable bond to achieve the same after-tax return as a 6% municipal bond.

The following table demonstrates the yield you would have to earn on a taxable bond in order to generate the same after-tax earnings as a tax-exempt bond would provide at a correspondingly lower yield.

Equivalent Yield Needed from a Taxable Bond

Tax-Exempt Yield	Your Combined Federal, State & Local Marginal Tax Bracket						
	28%	31%	33%	36%	39.6%	42%	46%
4.00	5.56	5.80	5.97	6.25	6.62	6.90	7.41
4.50	6.25	6.52	6.72	7.03	7.45	7.76	8.33
5.00	6.94	7.25	7.46	7.81	8.28	8.62	9.26
5.50	7.64	7.97	8.21	8.59	9.11	9.48	10.19
6.00	8.33	8.70	8.96	9.38	9.93	10.34	11.11
6.50	9.03	9.42	9.70	10.16	10.76	11.21	12.04
7.00	9.72	10.14	10.45	10.94	11.59	12.07	12.96

Group Term Life Insurance Paid by Employers

Generally, the cost for group term life insurance paid by an employer for the benefit of employees can be excluded from your gross income, as long as the premiums do not exceed the cost for $50,000 of life insurance.

If the group term life insurance plan discriminates in favor of highly compensated employees, then the cost of this insurance is fully taxable to such employees. For purposes of this rule, highly compensated employees include certain corporate officers and certain shareholder-employees.

E&Y FOCUS: Employee Stock Options

Many employers grant stock options to employees as a reward for services rendered or to be rendered. Stock options allow an employee to buy a specified amount of stock of his or her employer at some set price, and for a stated period of time. For example, your employer might grant you an option to purchase stock in the company at $10 per share—its market price at the time of the grant. If the market price of the stock rises to, say, $15 per share, you would be able to buy the stock at a discount of $5 per share—that is, at the $10-per-share option price rather than the $15 market value. But if the value of the stock never goes above the $10 exercise price, you would let your option lapse.

Merely holding unexercised options may be viewed as providing the option holder with significant economic benefits. Options can be seen as an opportunity to "ride the market" without committing personal capital to a risk that the value of the stock may fall. If the market price of the employer's stock increases, the holder of unexercised options benefits from this appreciation just as a shareholder would. That's because the option holder can acquire the appreciated stock for a known bargain price simply by exercising the option.

Incentive Stock Options

An incentive stock option (ISO) can be received and exercised without recognition of income if certain requirements are met. An incentive stock option (ISO) has the following tax consequences:

1. No taxable income will be recognized by the employee when the ISO is granted or exercised.
2. The income will be taxed as a capital gain when the employee sells stock acquired under an incentive stock option plan, provided the holding period requirements are met.
3. The employer will not be able to deduct the bargain element of the option as an expense, as long as the gain on the option is treated as a capital gain.
4. The difference between the option price and the fair market value at the time the option is exercised is an adjustment for the alternative minimum tax.

This favorable treatment is available provided that:

1. You do not dispose of the stock within two years after the option is granted and you hold the stock for at least one year from the date the option is exercised. If these requirements are not met, you will recognize ordinary income on the difference between the option price and the fair market value at the date the option is exercised or the sales price on the date the shares are sold, if lower. Any amount realized in excess of the fair market value on the date the option is exercised will be considered a capital gain. In such a case, your employer would be entitled to deduct as a compensation expense the ordinary income portion of your gain.
2. For the entire time from the date the option is granted until three months before it is exercised, you must be an employee either of the company granting the option, a parent or subsidiary of that corporation, or a corporation that has assumed the option of another corporation as a result of a reorganization, liquidation, or similar transaction.

Nonstatutory Stock Options

Nonstatutory stock options (NSOs) are options that do not meet certain requirements and are not afforded the special tax treatment given to ISOs (see the preceding paragraphs). Generally, these options are taxed at ordinary income rates. Depending on the particular characteristics of the option, it may be taxed (1) when the option is granted, (2) when it is exercised, (3) when it is sold, or (4) when restrictions on the disposition of the stock lapse. Typically, most NSOs are taxed when exercised.

Tax Treatment At A Glance This hypothetical example illustrates the tax treatment of nonstatutory stock options (NSOs) versus incentive stock options (ISOs):

Option Granted: 4/30/96	Nonstatutory Stock Option	Incentive Stock Option
Fair Market Value of Stock on 4/30/96:	$30	$30
Option Exercise Price:	$30	$30
Option Exercised: 10/30/96		
Fair Market Value of Stock on 10/30/96:	$50	$50
Option Spread:	$20	$20
Tax Treatment of Spread When Option Is Exercised:	$20 Taxed as Ordinary Compensation Income for Regular Tax Purposes	No Regular Tax Consequences (Spread of $20 Is Adjustment For AMT)
Regular-Tax Basis in Option Stock:	$50	$30
AMT Basis in Option Stock:	$50	$50

Stock Appreciates to $90

Disqualifying Disposition (e.g., sale within 1 year of exercise)	$40 Capital Gain	$20 Ordinary Income $40 Capital Gain for Regular Tax and AMT
Non-Disqualifying Disposition	$40 Long-Term Capital Gain	$60 Long-Term Capital Gain for Regular Tax $40 Long-Term Capital Gain for AMT

E&Y FOCUS: When to Exercise Stock Options

Incentive Stock Options. If you expect your company stock to appreciate over the long term, it generally makes sense to postpone exercising incentive stock options (ISOs) until their expiration date is imminent. By waiting you can watch the stock appreciate as long as possible before having to pay the option price.

In the following situations, however, it may make sense to exercise ISOs before they expire:

- If you believe the company's stock price has peaked and you intend to sell the stock as soon as you can after exercising the options (i.e., before the required long-term capital gain holding period);
- If the annual dividends paid on your company's stock exceed the carrying cost of the funds needed to exercise the options, that is, the option price plus any taxes due (this strategy would, of course, subject you to the risk that the stock price may fall); or

- If you have a need for cash now or in the near future that can be satisfied by exercising the options and subsequently selling the stock. You may not want to take the risk of a lower market price in the future.

Nonqualified Stock Options. Generally, if you expect the company stock to appreciate over the long term, it makes sense to postpone exercising NQSOs until their expiration date is imminent. By waiting, you can continue to benefit from the appreciation on all of the options without having to liquidate other assets or some of the stock. Remember, however, that when the options are exercised, you have to surrender cash (or, in some cases, stock) to pay the option price and the tax on the option spread. By deferring the exercise at the option, you can earn more appreciation before you have to cough up the option price and pay the tax bill.

In the following situations, however, it may make sense to exercise options before they expire:
- If you believe the company's stock price has peaked, and you intend to sell the stock as soon as you can after the exercise;
- If the annual dividends paid on your company's stock exceed the carrying cost of the funds needed to exercise the options; that is, the option price plus any taxes due (this strategy would, of course, subject you to the risk that the stock price may fall);
- If you have a need for cash now or in the near future that can be satisfied by exercising the options and subsequently selling the stock. You may not want to take the risk of a lower market price in the future;
- If you expect that ordinary income tax rates will increase in the future; or
- If you are subject to the alternative minimum tax but will not be entitled to a minimum tax credit carryover for the full amount of the AMT. The ordinary income from exercising the option will be subject to the AMT tax rate of 26 or 28%, which is substantially below the regular tax rate.

Prizes and Awards

Generally, contest prizes and awards are included in gross income. The value of an employee achievement award for length of service or safety performance can be excluded from your gross income to the extent your employer can deduct the expense. Special rules apply to limit the total awards you can exclude from your income in any one tax year. The maximum yearly exclusion is generally $400. However, if the awards received are under a plan that satisfies certain conditions specified by the tax law, you may be able to exclude from income up to $1,600 in total annual awards.

Reimbursements for Moving Expenses

Reimbursements for qualified moving expenses are not included in your gross income. Qualified moving expense reimbursements are those amounts received by an employee from the employer that would have been deductible moving expenses if paid by the employee. The same rule applies if the employer pays the expenses directly. (For a discussion of the qualified deductions allowed for employment-related moving expenses, see page 47.)

Gifts and Inheritances

Your gross income does not include the value of property acquired by gift or inheritance. (See Chapter 13 for a discussion of the gift and estate tax.)

Scholarships and Fellowship Grants

You can exclude from gross income the amount received as a qualified scholarship or fellowship grant provided you are a degree candidate and the monies are used strictly for qualified tuition, fees, books, supplies, and required equipment.

Cafeteria Plans

A cafeteria plan is an employee benefit plan under which a participant may choose between two or more benefits consisting of cash and qualified benefits. You may generally exclude from gross income employer contributions for nontaxable benefits selected under the plan (unless you are a "highly compensated participant" in a discriminatory plan). The exclusion from gross income does not apply to "key employees" where the statutory benefits provided to them exceed 25% of the total nontaxable benefits provided for all employees under the plan.

TAXSAVER

Cafeteria plans can be used effectively to increase the tax benefits of certain deductions and credits. For instance, ordinarily only medical expenses in excess of 7.5% of your adjusted gross income can be deducted. However, if you contribute to your employer's cafeteria plan (in pre-tax dollars), you can then be reimbursed by the plan for certain medical benefits if the employer's plan provides this as an option. You will not be taxed on the reimbursement you receive. There are some risks for employees because money left over at the end of the year is forfeited, so consult your tax advisor.

Similarly, dependent care payments you make qualify you for the dependent care credit. Depending on your income level, you may get a tax credit for at least 20% of the payments you made. However, if your contribution to your employer's cafeteria plan is made in pre-tax dollars, the benefit of reimbursement of child care expenses from the plan can be as high as 39.6%, depending on your tax bracket.

__Example:__ Assume you have medical expenses of $1,000. If your expenses are paid through a cafeteria plan, the cost to you will be $1,000 in reduced wages. If you are in the 31% bracket and pay the medical expenses after tax you will have to earn $1,450 to have enough left over to pay the $1,000 of medical expenses.

2

What You Can Deduct: Exemptions, Adjustments, and Deductions

INTRODUCTION

This chapter discusses most of the deductions and exemptions that you can claim to lower your taxable income. Deductions include non-reimbursed medical and dental expenses, charitable contributions, non-business casualty and theft losses, and home mortgage interest payments, as well as amounts you pay for state and local income and property taxes, certain other interest payments, and a variety of miscellaneous items. Some of these deductions are subject to limits and thresholds. In addition, you are entitled to exemptions for yourself, for children, and for other dependents.

The amount of income tax you owe is figured by taking your gross income and subtracting allowable adjustments, deductions, and exemptions. The adjustment amounts reduce your gross income to arrive at a figure known as *adjusted gross income* (AGI). Then, deductions and exemptions are subtracted from your AGI to arrive at your taxable income, the amount on which income tax is imposed. You may subtract the greater of either the standard deduction (which is explained in this chapter) or you may itemize your deductions. For the most part, itemized deductions are for certain types of personal and investment expenses, which the tax law specifies as deductible.

If your income level is above a specified amount, the tax benefits of some personal and dependent exemptions are phased out. In addition, certain deductions are only available to you if your expenses exceed a certain percentage of your income. This chapter will help you sort out those expenses you can deduct from those you can't. In the process, it will help you focus on possible ways to lower your tax bill.

STANDARD DEDUCTION

Individuals who do not itemize their deductions are entitled to a standard deduction amount. This amount varies according to your filing status. The standard deduction that you are entitled to is subtracted from your adjusted gross income in arriving at your taxable income. You can choose between itemizing your deductions or claiming the applicable standard deduction amount in figuring your taxable income depending on which produces the greatest tax benefit.

The standard deduction amounts available to individuals are listed in Table 2.1, below.

For married individuals (filing jointly or separately where neither spouse itemizes) and surviving spouses, an "additional standard deduction" of $800 is allowed for each spouse over the age of 65 and for each spouse who is blind ($1,600 in the case of an elderly and blind taxpayer). The additional standard deduction is $1,000 for elderly or blind individuals who are unmarried and are not surviving spouses ($2,000 in the case of an elderly and blind taxpayer). These additional standard deductions are changed annually by a cost-of-living adjustment.

If you are eligible to be claimed as a dependent on another taxpayer's return, you may not claim the full standard deduction. Rather, your standard deduction would be limited to the greater of either $650 or your earned income (not to exceed the appropriate standard deduction amount). For taxpayers who are at least age 65 or blind and who are eligible to be claimed as a dependent on another taxpayer's return, the standard deduction is limited to the greater of either $650 or earned income, plus any additional standard deduction available because of age or blindness. In calculating the limitation, earned income includes taxable scholarship and fellowship funds you receive.

The following individuals are specifically excluded from using the standard deduction:
1. A married individual filing a separate return where the other spouse itemizes deductions;
2. A nonresident alien; or
3. An individual whose return covers less than 12 months due to a change in the annual accounting period.

TABLE 2.1   Standard Deductions

Filing Status	1996*
Single	$4,000
Head of household	5,900
Married filing jointly and surviving spouses	6,700
Married filing separately	3,350

These amounts are increased annually by a cost-of-living adjustment.

PERSONAL AND DEPENDENT EXEMPTIONS

Personal and dependent exemptions reduce your taxable income. For 1996, each exemption equals $2,550. (The amount is adjusted annually to reflect increases in the cost of living.) You are entitled to:

1. One exemption for yourself. (This exemption is not available to individuals who can be claimed as a dependent on another taxpayer's return.)
2. One exemption for your spouse if (a) a joint return is filed or (b) a joint return is not filed and your spouse has no gross income and is not the dependent of another.
3. One exemption for each dependent whose gross income is less than $2,550 or who is your child, if he or she is: (a) a full-time student under the age of 24 at the end of the year or (b) not yet 19 years old at the end of the year.

TAXSAVER

You may consider the option of taking a dependent exemption for your married child (if he or she so qualifies) and have the child file "married filing separately." In some cases, the benefit of claiming a dependent exemption may outweigh the benefit of having the child file a joint return with his or her spouse.

Personal and Dependent Exemption Phaseout

The tax benefits of the personal and dependent exemptions are phased out for taxpayers whose adjusted gross income exceeds specific amounts. The phaseout is accomplished by reducing the exemption amount allowed by 2% for each $2,500 (or fraction thereof) of AGI in excess of certain levels. In 1996, the phaseout of personal exemptions begins at an *adjusted gross income* of $176,950 for married taxpayers filing a joint return; $88,475 for married filing separately; $147,450 for head of household; and $117,950 for single taxpayers.

Example: Bill and Martha Brown file a joint return. They have three dependent children. For 1996 they have adjusted gross income of $214,050. The dependency exemption amount for 1996, before any reductions, is $2,550. Because their AGI exceeds $176,950 by $37,100, each of their exemptions will be reduced by $742 [($37,100 ÷ $2,500 rounding up to the nearest whole number) × 2% × $2,500]. Thus, each exemption is only $1,808, or a total of $9,040 for their two personal exemptions and three dependency exemptions.

TAXSAVER

Children cannot claim a personal exemption for themselves if they are eligible to be claimed as an exemption on their parents' return. As discussed earlier, parents with adjusted gross income in excess of $176,950 on joint returns, $88,475 on separate returns, $147,450 for heads of households and $117,950 for single individuals begin to phase out the exemptions. So there may be a point where your dependent child could recognize a greater tax benefit if he or she could claim a personal exemption rather than your taking the exemption on your own return. But to shift the exemption to your child, you will have to take steps to disqualify your child as your dependent. Generally, this can only be accomplished if your child receives less than half of his or her support from you.

Social Security Numbers. Taxpayers must report on their income tax return the Social Security number of any dependent claimed who is age one or older before the close of the tax year.

Definition of Dependents

A dependent is any person listed below who receives more than half of his or her support from the taxpayer and who does not file a joint return with his or her spouse:
1. A son or daughter of the taxpayer, or a descendant of either;
2. A stepson or stepdaughter of the taxpayer;
3. A brother, sister, stepbrother, or stepsister of the taxpayer;
4. A father or mother of the taxpayer, or ancestor of either;
5. A stepfather or stepmother of the taxpayer;
6. A son or daughter of the taxpayer's brother or sister;
7. A brother or sister of the taxpayer's father or mother;
8. A son-in-law, daughter-in-law, father-in-law, mother-in-law, brother-in-law, or sister-in-law of the taxpayer;
9. Any individual (other than the taxpayer's spouse) who for the entire taxable year has as his or her principal place of abode the home of the taxpayer, as a member of the taxpayer's household, unless the relationship is in violation of local law.

Dependents of Divorced or Separated Parents. The dependent exemption for qualifying children of divorced or separated parents is generally allowed to the custodial parent (the parent who has custody of the child for the greater portion of the year) unless: (1) a multiple support agreement exists; (2) a pre-1985 divorce or separation agreement shifted the exemption to the noncustodial parent; or (3) the custodial parent releases the claim to the exemption to the noncustodial parent. To transfer the exemption, the custodial parent must sign a written declaration releasing the exemption to the noncustodial parent. The declaration may be made annually, for one or more calendar years, or permanently.

TaxSaver

In giving up the exemption for a dependent child, the custodial parent does not forfeit the right to claim head-of-household status, the earned income credit, or the child and dependent care credit if the individual otherwise qualifies. These are discussed on pages 141 and 150.

The word "dependent" does not include any individual who is not a citizen or national of the United States, unless the individual is a resident of the United States, Canada, or Mexico. A legally adopted child need not be a U.S. citizen to qualify as a dependent if the child is a member of a household of a taxpaying U.S. citizen.

Multiple Support Agreements

An individual supported by several persons, none of whom alone furnishes more than one half of his or her support, may qualify as a dependent. In this case, the dependency deduction may be claimed by any one individual (otherwise entitled to do so) contributing over 10% of the support, provided that:
1. over one-half of the support was contributed by persons who, except for the support test, would be entitled to claim the supported individual as a dependent, and
2. each other person described in (1) contributing over 10% of the dependent's support files a written declaration (Form 2120) with the return of the person who claims the exemption, stating that he or she will not claim a deduction for the same dependent for that year.

TaxSaver

If two or more individuals provide less than 50% but more than 10% of the support to a dependent (e.g., your parent), it may be more beneficial to give the right to claim the exemption to the supporter to whom it will yield the highest tax benefit.

TaxSaver

If your dependent maintains his or her own home and you paid the mortgage and real estate taxes, neither of you will be entitled to the mortgage interest or real estate taxes deduction. You may consider taking a partial interest in the property in order to secure the deductions subject to the mortgage interest limitation (page 42) on your return. Another option would be to give cash to your dependent so that he or she can pay the mortgage and real estate taxes directly. In turn, the dependent can deduct such payments on his or her own return.

INDIVIDUAL RETIREMENT ARRANGEMENTS (IRAs)

An individual retirement arrangement (IRA) is a personal savings plan that lets you set aside funds for your retirement, using pre-tax dollars. Subject to certain limitations, the amount you contribute to your IRA can be deducted from your taxable income. (See Chapter 5 for details.)

SIMPLIFIED EMPLOYEE PENSIONS

A simplified employee pension (SEP) is a written plan that allows an employer to make contributions toward an employee's retirement without becoming involved in more complex retirement plans. If you are self-employed, you can contribute to your own SEP. Subject to certain limitations, the amounts you contribute to an SEP can be deducted from your taxable income. For more information see Chapter 12, Retirement Planning.

KEOGH (HR 10) PLANS

If you are self-employed and own your own business, you may set up a retirement plan, commonly known as a Keogh or HR 10 plan. You must have earned income from the trade or business for which the plan was established to take a deduction for a contribution to the plan. A Keogh plan may be either a "defined contribution plan" or a "defined benefit plan." Within limits, amounts you contribute to a Keogh plan can be deducted from your taxable income. (For more information on this type of plan, see Chapter 5.)

DIVORCE OR SEPARATION

Alimony

Alimony is an amount paid to a spouse or former spouse under a divorce or separation agreement. You are allowed a deduction for alimony payments you make. (See page 25 for an explanation of how alimony you receive is taxed.)

What Qualifies as Alimony. To qualify for a deduction as alimony, payments stipulated in the divorce or separation agreement should not be designated as something other than alimony. In addition, the parties to the divorce or legal separation must not be members of the same household at the time of payment, and there must be no liability for payments to continue after the death of the spouse receiving the money. Payments made under a divorce or separation decree executed after 1984 must be in cash or its equivalent. For example, transferring securities to satisfy payments due under a divorce or separation agreement does not qualify as alimony. Cash payments made to a third party, however—such as medical expenses paid to doctors or hospitals, on behalf of the spouse or former spouse at his or her request—will qualify as alimony, assuming all other requirements are met.

TAXSAVER

If you pay medical expenses for your separated spouse (under a separation agreement) or your former spouse, you should deduct the payment as alimony, not as medical expenses. Alimony is fully deductible from your adjusted gross income (whether or not you itemize your deductions), whereas only the portion of your medical expenses that exceeds 7.5% of your adjusted gross income will be deductible.

Deductible alimony payments made under divorce or separation agreements executed after 1984 are subject to recapture rules when payments are "front loaded." In other words, if the payments decrease by more than a designated amount during the first three post-separation years, you may be required to recapture and include in your gross income some portion of alimony that you deducted in a prior tax year. On the other hand, if you received the payment, you deduct any recaptured amount from your income in the computation year.

Exceptions to the recapture rules apply when alimony payments end because either party dies, the spouse receiving the payments remarries before the end of the third post-separation year, or the payments are subject to fluctuation because they are tied to the payer's compensation or income from a business or property.

Child Support

Child support payments are neither deductible by the payor nor included as income by the spouse who receives them. If any portion of payments that were agreed to be alimony could be reduced because of circumstances relating to a child (e.g., the child's leaving school or the family household, becoming employed, getting married, or dying), that portion may be reclassified as nondeductible and nontaxable child support. This can occur even when the divorce or separation agreement specifically provides for separate child support payments.

Payments are presumed to be child support if a reduction is scheduled to occur within six months before or after a child reaches age 18, 21, or the local age of majority, or when two or more reductions are scheduled within one year of a child reaching an age between 18 and 24 that is designated in the agreement. Payments that represent property settlements or child support are not treated as alimony.

TAX*SAVER*

Deciding whether payments should be classified as alimony, a nontaxable property settlement, or child support can affect the amount of tax paid if the spouse who will be making the payments will be in a higher tax bracket than the spouse receiving them. The spouse making the payment typically wants it to be tax-deductible alimony to minimize his or her out-of-pocket costs. At the same time, the spouse receiving the payment doesn't want to see it eaten up by taxes.

A reasonable way to resolve the problem is to share the overall tax savings realized by treating the payment as alimony. For example, if the spouse making the payment offered to "gross up" the payment to cover the taxes the recipient would owe, both on the amount of the payment originally expected and the "extra" alimony offered, the payor could wind up paying less out-of-pocket (after deductions) than if the initially-agreed-to level of the payment was treated as a nondeductible property settlement.

Transferring Property

Generally, a transfer of property from one spouse to the other "incident to the divorce" is tax-free—no gain or loss is recognized by the transferor spouse. Such transfers can include sales or exchanges of property between ex-spouses within one year after the marriage ends and transfers pursuant to a divorce or separation agreement generally occurring within six years after the marriage ends. These transfers are treated as gifts for tax purposes even if there were actually a bona fide sale. That is, the transferor spouse's basis in the property carries over to the transferee spouse, who will be required to recognize gain or loss when the property is ultimately sold or otherwise disposed of. (See Chapter 4, Tax Planning and Your Home, for more details.)

TAX*SAVER*

Remember, when dividing up appreciated property in a divorce settlement, that the value of a particular property may be overstated if it does not take into account potential taxes that would be due on the gain incurred on a subsequent sale. The spouse receiving the property should consider having the divorce or separation agreement provide for reimbursement when the property is actually sold or otherwise disposed of.

MEDICAL AND DENTAL EXPENSES

Deductible Expenses

You may claim as itemized deductions certain medical and dental expenses for yourself, your spouse, and your dependents. You may also deduct medical expenses that you pay for any person whom you could have claimed as a dependent on your return if that person had not received

$2,550 or more of gross income or had not filed a joint return. A child of divorced parents is treated as a dependent of both spouses for the purpose of computing medical expenses. However, you may deduct only the part of your medical and dental expenses that is more than 7.5% of your adjusted gross income. Medical expenses are not subject to the reduction in itemized deductions for taxpayers with adjusted gross incomes in excess of $117,950 ($58,975 for married persons filing separately) discussed on page 53.

TAX ALERT

The Health Insurance Portability and Accountability Act of 1996 established tax-favored medical savings accounts (MSAs) to fund uninsured medical expenses. Beginning in 1997 and continuing for four years, self-employed individuals and individuals employed by "small employers" who are covered under a high-deductible health plan will be able to deduct contributions to an MSA. Income earned in an MSA is tax free, as are distributions to pay for medical expenses. To have an MSA, you cannot be covered under a health plan in addition to the high-deductible health plan, unless the additional coverage is for accidents, disability, dental care, vision care, long-term care, or if it is another type of "permitted" insurance. However, the number of eligible individuals who can set up MSAs is capped at a national level of 750,000.

What to Include as Medical and Dental Expenses. Medical expenses include the costs of related transportation, hospitalization insurance, Medicare supplemental insurance, certain capital expenditures if they exceed any increase in property value, and certain expenses incurred by a physically handicapped individual for removing structural barriers to accommodate the disability. You may also include the cost of hearing aids, dentures, eyeglasses, and so on, and wages you paid for nursing services. The cost of elective cosmetic surgery is not deductible. However, cosmetic or plastic surgery to correct a deformity or personal injury or to treat an illness or disease is a deductible medical expense. Prescription drugs and insulin are the only medications that are considered medical expenses.

TAX SAVER

If you make a medically related capital improvement to your home, such as installing an elevator, you should request a written recommendation for the improvement from your doctor. In addition, obtain a reliable written appraisal from a real estate appraiser or a valuation expert. Be prepared to prove to what extent the value of your property was not increased by the expenditure of the improvement, because only that amount is deductible.

TAX ORGANIZER

Certain medical expenses may qualify for the dependent care credit. (See page 150.) However, the same expense may not be used for both benefits.

You should analyze each benefit based on your marginal tax rate and your medical expense deduction limitation (7.5% of adjusted gross income) to determine how best to classify the expense.

When seeking medical care away from home, you can deduct lodging expenses of up to $50 per night per individual as a medical expense. Lodging can include the expenses for the person seeking treatment and other qualified individuals, such as a parent traveling with a sick child.

TAX*ALERT*

Self-employed individuals can deduct 30% of their health insurance premiums directly from self-employment income rather than as a medical deduction.

Separate Returns. If you and your spouse do not live in a community property state and you file separate returns, each of you may claim only the medical expenses you actually paid. Any medical expenses paid out of a joint checking account in which you and your spouse have the same interest are considered to have been paid equally by each of you unless you can show otherwise.

TAX*SAVER*

Because you may deduct only the part of your medical and dental expenses that is more than 7.5% of your adjusted gross income, you should consider filing separate returns whenever the medical expenses of either spouse substantially exceed those of the other spouse. Figure your tax filing jointly and separately before deciding which alternative to choose.

When to Deduct. You may deduct medical expenses only in the year you paid them. If you charge medical expenses to your credit card, deduct the expenses in the year the charge is made even if you pay the charge in a later year.

Reimbursements. You must reduce your total medical expenses for the year by the total reimbursements you receive from insurance or other sources for medical expenses during the year before you apply the 7.5% adjusted gross income limit. Reimbursements include payments received from Medicare.

TAX*SAVER*

If you are reimbursed in a later year for medical expenses you deducted in an earlier year, you must report the reimbursement as income in the later year. However, do not report more than the amount you previously deducted as medical expenses. In making the calculation, you may also exclude the amount of expenses in the previous year that did not reduce the amount of income taxes you paid. For example, if you had a taxable loss in the year of the deduction, you would not have had a tax benefit from your medical deductions and any subsequent reimbursement is not considered income. This same rule would apply if the expenses did not produce any benefit in the earlier year because they did not exceed 7.5% of your adjusted gross income in that year.

TAXES

Deductible Taxes

If you itemize deductions, you can deduct state, local, and foreign income taxes, real property taxes, and state and local personal property taxes. You can generally deduct property taxes only if you own the property.

You may deduct only those taxes paid during the calendar year for which you file a return. Deductible taxes are subject to the overall limit on itemized deductions for taxpayers with adjusted gross income in excess of $117,950; $58,975 for married persons filing separately. See discussion on page 53.

See page 145 for the discussion about how state, local, and foreign taxes affect your alternative minimum tax calculations.

Nondeductible Taxes

Taxes that cannot be deducted are: the federal income tax; state and local sales taxes; Social Security taxes; estate, gift, and inheritance taxes; gasoline, cigarette, and liquor taxes; automobile registration fees (unless based on the automobile's value); and driver's license fees. Certain taxes paid in connection with the acquisition or disposition of property, such as transfer taxes associated with a purchase, must be capitalized.

Half the self-employment taxes you pay may be deducted and treated as attributable to a trade or business that you conduct. Most otherwise nondeductible state, local, foreign, and excise taxes are deductible if incurred in a trade or business or in the production of income.

Deduction vs. Credit for Foreign Income Tax

You may elect to have foreign income taxes (including withholding) on dividends or other income credited directly against your U.S. tax liability (subject to a limitation based on the effective U.S. rate of tax). However, you cannot take a deduction or credit for foreign income taxes paid on tax exempt income under the foreign earned income exclusion.

TAXSAVER

It is usually better to take a credit for foreign taxes than to deduct them as itemized deductions, because credits reduce your U.S. tax on a dollar-for-dollar basis, while a deduction just reduces the amount of income subject to tax. See Chapter 9 for more information about the foreign tax credit.

Refunds of Taxes

If you receive a refund of state or local (or foreign) income taxes in a year after the year in which you paid them, you may have to include all or part of the refund in income in the year you receive it. This includes refunds resulting from taxes that were overwithheld, not figured correctly, or decreased as a result of an audit. If you did not itemize your deductions in the previous year or if the portion of the claimed deduction that is refunded did not provide a tax benefit, you do not have to include the refund in income.

Example: In 1995 you have $4,000 in state income taxes withheld. You claim a $4,000 itemized deduction. In 1996, you file a state tax return and receive a $500 refund. That refund must be included in your 1996 income.

INTEREST EXPENSES

If interest paid during the taxable year is deductible it will be as an itemized deduction, a passive activity deduction, or a business expense. However, several limitations apply. Deductions for personal interest are not allowed. There are also limitations on the deduction of passive activity interest (page 11) and investment interest (page 43). Your deduction for interest paid during the year is limited to the amount that represents the cost of using the borrowed funds for that year or a preceding year. An exception to this rule applies for points paid to obtain a loan to purchase or to improve a principal residence as long as the payment of points is an established business practice in your area.

Interest expense, except for investment interest, is subject to the overall limit on itemized deductions for taxpayers with adjusted gross income in excess of $117,950; $58,975 for married persons filing separately. See discussion on page 53.

Personal Interest

Interest on personal loans is not deductible on your individual tax return. Personal interest generally includes all interest other than:

- Interest incurred in connection with a trade or business (other than the trade or business of performing services as an employee);
- Investment interest;
- Interest taken into account in computing your income or loss from a passive activity;
- Qualified residence interest; and
- Interest on certain estate taxes that have been deferred.

TAXSAVER

You should ordinarily pay off personal debts because the related interest expense, unless qualified residence interest, is not deductible. One way to accomplish this objective is to use a home equity loan to pay off your personal debt. This interest is fully deductible up to certain limits.

Home Mortgage Interest

Generally mortgage interest is any interest you pay on a loan secured by your home. This includes a mortgage, second mortgage, a line of credit, and a home equity loan. Most home mortgage interest is deductible, subject to limitations discussed in Chapter 4, Tax Planning and Your Home.

Investment Interest

There are specified limits on the deduction of investment interest by individuals. Investment interest is interest paid on indebtedness properly allocable to property held for investment. Property held for investment includes any property that produces interest, dividend, annuity, or royalty income not derived in the ordinary course of a trade or business, and any property held by a taxpayer in an activity involving the conduct of a trade or business that is not a passive activity (pages 11–15) and in which the taxpayer does not materially participate. Investment interest does not include qualified residence interest (see above) or interest taken into account in computing your income or loss from a passive activity.

The deduction for interest on investment indebtedness is limited to your net investment income—the excess of investment income over certain directly connected expenses.

Investment interest deductions that are disallowed solely by these provisions may, in most cases, be carried forward and deducted in subsequent years, subject to the annual limits.

TaxAlert

A net capital gain attributable to the disposition of property held for investment is no longer includible in the definition of investment income for purposes of computing the investment interest deduction limitation. However, you may elect to include net capital gain amounts in investment income for this purpose if you also agree to reduce your net capital gain eligible for the 28% maximum capital gains rate by the same amount.

Deciding whether to make the election depends on how long you would otherwise have to wait to take your deduction. Here are some general guidelines:

■ *Take the deduction now if your marginal rate on ordinary income is 28% and is expected to stay at that rate. In this case, waiting won't produce a greater benefit.*

■ *You may be better off waiting and carrying forward the investment interest deduction if your rate may soon increase, and you expect to have more non-capital gain investment income in the short term.*

There is no substitute for running the numbers for your situation.

TAXSAVER

You should regularly review the mix of your investment portfolio to be sure that your assets generate enough investment income so you can deduct all the interest you incur on your margin account. A margin account loan is an amount you borrow from a broker to purchase additional securities.

Tax-Exempt Securities

Interest paid on money borrowed to purchase or carry tax-exempt securities or certain life insurance contracts is not deductible. In addition, the deduction of interest paid for money borrowed to purchase or carry investments in stock of certain regulated investment companies will be limited if the company makes a distribution of tax-exempt interest during the taxable year.

Other Interest

Below-Market Interest Rate Loans. If you are the recipient of an interest-free loan, you can deduct interest imputed on the loan, subject to the applicable interest expense limitations. The interest is calculated using specified rates based on the average market yields of U.S. Treasury obligations. With certain exceptions, interest is imputed on loans payable upon demand of over $10,000 outstanding after June 6, 1984, and on term loans made after June 6, 1984. (For further discussion, see pages 20 and 233.)

Interest to Carry Discount Bonds and Investments. Special rules limit your deduction for interest expense incurred to purchase or carry bonds that were acquired at a market discount (purchased at less than face value). For debt obligations issued after July 18, 1984, the interest expense deduction is limited to the sum of:
1. the interest income received from the bonds during the tax year, and
2. the interest expense that exceeds the sum of the interest income received in item (1) plus accrued market discount.

The disallowed interest is deferred until the bond is sold or matures, and is then deducted. If you elect to include the accrued market discount in your current income, you can fully deduct the interest instead of deferring it.

Example: Tom buys a $100,000, 9% interest-bearing bond for $90,000 on January 2, 1996. The bond was originally issued at face value in 1986. It matures in 2006, 10 years after Tom purchased it. Tom borrowed to acquire the bond. In 1996, Tom paid $10,200 in interest on the loan. The allowable interest deduction for 1995 is figured as follows:

(a) Interest expense	$10,200
(b) Interest income ($100,000 × 9%)	(9,000)
(c) Net interest expense	1,200
(d) Accrued market discount ($10,000 ÷ 10 yrs.)	(1,000)
(e) Net interest expense in excess of the interest income received plus accrued market discount	$ 200

Total allowable interest expense deduction is $9,200 [(b) + (e)]. The remaining $1,000 will be allowed as a deduction in the year the bond matures or is sold.

The same limitation applies to interest expense arising from the purchase of short-term obligations. The interest deduction for an amount equal to the daily accrual of the obligation's discount income will be deferred until the short-term obligation is redeemed or sold. If you elect to include the accrued discount in income, you can fully deduct the interest instead of deferring the interest deduction.

TAXORGANIZER

How you characterize interest expense depends on how you used the debt proceeds. You must keep detailed records so that the IRS can trace the ultimate use of borrowed dollars that give rise to each dollar of interest expense.

__Example:__ You purchase through your broker $40,000 worth of stock. Several months later you need $20,000 to purchase a car. You borrow the $20,000 by collateralizing your stock. The interest on that loan is considered to be consumer interest (generally non-deductible). On the other hand, if you had purchased the stock on margin for $20,000—that is, you borrowed the money for the purchase from your broker—and spent your remaining personal funds of $20,000 on the car, the interest attributable to the margin debt is investment interest and potentially deductible.

Qualified mortgage interest is deductible in full, regardless of how the loan proceeds are actually used.

CHARITABLE CONTRIBUTIONS

You are allowed to take a tax deduction for contributions you make to qualified charitable organizations, provided you satisfy detailed rules that require you to substantiate your gifts. (See Chapter 6, pages 98–113.)

CASUALTY AND THEFT LOSSES

A casualty is the damage, destruction, or loss of property resulting from an identifiable event that is sudden, unexpected, or unusual. A sudden event is one that is swift, not gradual or progressive. An unexpected event is one that is ordinarily unanticipated and one that you do not intend. An unusual event is one that is not a day-to-day occurrence and one that is not typical of the activity in which you were engaged.

Defining a Loss. A deduction is allowed for losses of business property, investment property, or nonbusiness property caused by fire, storm, or other casualty, including theft. Generally, the deduction is the lesser of either the adjusted basis of the property before the casualty or the actual loss measured by its fair market value before and after the casualty. If you recover any amount of the loss by insurance, you must reduce the deduction you take accordingly. A special rule applies to business or income-producing property that is completely destroyed because of a casualty loss. Your loss is your basis in the property (without regard to fair market value), less any amount you receive from insurance payments. If your personal casualty losses exceed your personal casualty gains in a taxable year, your casualty loss deduction is limited to the sum of your personal casualty gains and any amounts that exceed 10% of your adjusted gross income.

Deductions for casualty losses of nonbusiness property are limited to the amount of each loss in excess of $100. A husband and wife filing a joint return are treated as one individual for purposes of the $100 limitation. If each spouse sustains a loss from the same casualty, only one $100 limitation will apply. After considering the $100 floor applicable to each separate loss, your total personal casualty losses are deductible in full to the extent they are offset against any casualty gains. A casualty gain occurs when your insurance reimbursement is more than your basis in the property, even if the decrease in the fair market value of the property is more than its basis.

Example:

Value of the property before the casualty	$100
Value after the casualty	75
Loss	25
Insurance reimbursement	20
Basis in property	15
Gain	$ 5

Any excess loss is deductible as an itemized deduction only for the amount that exceeds 10% of your adjusted gross income. If casualty gains exceed casualty losses, the 10% floor is not imposed, and the gains and losses are treated as arising from the sale of capital assets. You are not permitted to deduct nonbusiness casualty losses unless an insurance claim for the damage to the insured property is filed on a timely basis.

Casualty losses occurring in federally declared disaster areas at any time during the taxable year may be deducted on the tax return for the year preceding the year of the loss. This may enable you to get an immediate refund of taxes you already paid.

If you have a casualty or theft on nonbusiness property, you must use Section A of Form 4684, *Casualties and Thefts,* to figure and report your gain or loss. Be sure to attach Form 4684 to your return.

TAXORGANIZER

If you are going to claim a casualty or theft loss, it is important that you gather as much supporting evidence as possible. Newspaper clippings about a storm, police reports, and insurance reports may all be helpful in proving the nature of the casualty or theft loss and when it occurred. You have the burden of proof to establish that a casualty occurred and that your loss was a direct result of a casualty.

Establishing the amount of your loss may be difficult, but the time you spend documenting the loss may help reduce your tax. You should make a list of all lost, damaged, or destroyed items as soon after the disaster or casualty as possible. IRS Publication 584, Nonbusiness Disaster and Casualty Loss and Theft Workbook, *may be useful. It has schedules to help you figure a loss on your home and its contents and on your car, van, truck, or motorcycle.*

Casualty and theft losses are not *subject to the overall 3% limit on itemized deductions for individuals with adjusted gross income in excess of $117,950; $58,975 for married persons filing separately. See discussion on page 53.*

MOVING EXPENSES

Under certain circumstances, expenses you incur in connection with changing the location of your employment are deductible. The expenses can be deductible if the distance between your new job and your residence is at least 50 miles more than the distance between your old job and your residence. In addition, if you are an employee, you must work full-time during at least 39 weeks of the 12-month period after relocating. If you are self-employed, the standard is stiffer. You must work full time at least 78 weeks during the 24-month period after relocating. In addition, you must work full-time for at least 39 weeks during the immediate 12-month period after relocating.

If you are fired or laid off, involuntarily lose your job (for other than willful misconduct), or are required to move again by your employer before the 39 weeks are up (or 78 weeks, if applicable), you can still deduct your moving expenses. You may also be exempted from the 39-week or 78-week requirement because of death and disability.

TAXSAVER

If you file a joint return, the time test may be met by either spouse. However, weeks worked by both husband and wife cannot be added together to meet the time test.

The deduction for moving expenses is allowed for the following:
1. Travel expenses (including lodging) for an employee or self-employed person and his or her family to the new residence
2. Expenses for moving household goods and other personal effects

The deduction for expenses that fall into categories (1) and (2) is unlimited. Expenses that qualify as moving expenses that are not paid or reimbursed by the taxpayer's employer are allowable as a deduction in calculating adjusted gross income (AGI). Thus, moving expenses are no longer an itemized deduction. Reimbursement or payment of moving expenses by an employer is excludable from gross income of the employee, and is not included in the employee's Form W-2.

Use Form 3903, *Moving Expenses,* to report your moving expenses if your move was within or to the United States or its possessions.

TAXALERT

Deductible moving expenses do not include the following:
- *the cost of meals;*
- *the cost of pre-move house-hunting trips;*
- *the cost of temporary living expenses;*
- *the costs incident to the sale or lease of the old residence, including settling of an unexpired lease; and*
- *the costs incident to the purchase or lease of a new residence.*

EMPLOYEE BUSINESS EXPENSES AND OTHER EXPENSES

This section covers a variety of expenses that you are allowed to deduct on your individual return. These personal business expenses can be broken down into three broad categories: deductible employee expenses, deductible expenses of producing income, and other deductible expenses. Business-related travel and entertainment expenses are discussed in Chapter 3.

The general rule is that you may deduct any business expense incurred by you personally that is related to your trade or business, connected with producing income, or paid to determine your tax. Expenses other than these are generally considered personal and typically may not be deducted. But, with careful and proper planning, you may be able to deduct more than you think.

Deductions Subject to the 2%-of-Adjusted-Gross-Income Limit

Most miscellaneous itemized deductions are deductible only to the extent the total of all these deductions is more than 2% of your adjusted gross income. Miscellaneous deductions that are not subject to this limitation are discussed later in this chapter.

Your deduction is the excess of the total of the allowable deductions over 2% of your adjusted gross income. The 2% limit is applied after any other deduction limit (such as the 50% limit on meals and entertainment) is applied.

Unreimbursed employee business expenses are also subject to the overall limit on itemized deductions for taxpayers with adjusted gross income in excess of $117,950; $58,975 for married persons filing separately. See discussion on page 53.

Employee Business Expenses

If you are an employee, including an outside salesperson, you may deduct as an adjustment to *gross* income only the amount reimbursed by your employer for work-related business expenses. Any expenses that are not reimbursed by your employer are deductible only as a miscellaneous deduction (subject to the 2% limit) on Schedule A, Form 1040.

If you claim a deduction for any employee business expenses, you must complete Form 2106 and attach it to your Form 1040. You do not have to complete the form if your business expenses were equal to the reimbursements you received from your employer, the reimbursements were not included in your W-2 form, and you adequately accounted to your employer for those expenses. If none of your employee business expenses are reimbursed by your employer, however, and you are not claiming any meal, entertainment, travel, or transportation expenses, you do not have to complete Form 2106. Instead, list your employee business expenses on Schedule A.

TAXSAVER

If you can get your employer to reimburse you for what would otherwise be unreimbursed business expenses in lieu of an equal amount of salary, you should do so. You gain at no additional cost to your employer. Reimbursed employee business expenses are not subject to the 2% floor that might otherwise limit their deductibility.

Business Gifts

Deductions for business gifts are limited to $25 per individual recipient per year.

TAXSAVER

When there is an overlap, in fact, it is usually to your advantage to treat a particular item as an entertainment expense rather than as a gift. Although entertainment expenses are subject to a 50% limitation and must be considered ordinary and necessary, there is no fixed dollar limitation on the deduction.

Club Dues

No deduction is allowed for dues or assessments paid for membership in a business, social, athletic, luncheon, sporting, hotel, or airport clubs including dues and fees paid to a country club. However, dues paid to professional or service organizations, such as the ABA, AICPA, Kiwanis or Rotary clubs are deductible if paid for business reasons and the organization is not principally an entertainment organization. Specific business expenses, such as meals and entertainment that may occur at a club, would be deductible to the extent that they otherwise satisfy the standard for deductibility.

Educational Expenses

In general, educational expenditures, such as tuition, books, supplies, lab fees, and certain travel and transportation costs, are deductible (whether or not the education leads to a degree) if the education (1) maintains or improves skills required in your employment or business or (2) meets the express requirements of your employer, or applicable law, imposed as a condition of employment. However, educational expenditures that are made to meet minimum educational requirements or that qualify you for a new trade or business, such as a law degree, are not deductible. Therefore, only expenses for education relating to your present work are deductible.

TAX ALERT

Employer-Provided Educational Assistance. *Until the provision lapsed on December 31, 1994, up to $5,250 of employer-provided tuition reimbursement for undergraduate and graduate education was excludable from an employee's income each calendar year. The educational assistance exclusion is reinstated retroactively to December 31, 1994, and through May 31, 1997 (for courses starting before July 1, 1997). The exclusion will not apply to expenses for graduate courses beginning after June 30, 1996.*

TAX SAVER

Employers that included educational assistance in employee income in 1995 will need to issue corrected Forms W-2 and file for refunds of employment taxes. It is expected that the IRS will issue an expedited procedure for obtaining refunds.

Home Office Expenses

The IRS rule is that no deduction is allowed for home office expenses unless the portion of the residence used in connection with your trade or business is used exclusively on a regular basis (1) as your principal place of business, (2) as a place of business for meeting or dealing with patients, clients, or customers in the normal course of business, or (3) is a separate structure that is not attached to your residence and is used in connection with your trade or business. (For more details, see Chapter 4.)

Computers. You may be able to claim an accelerated depreciation deduction and a Section 179 first-year expensing deduction (page 231) for your home computer provided you use the computer over 50% of the time for business (in your work as an employee) and the computer was placed in your home for the convenience of your employer, as a condition of your employment, so that you can properly perform your duties as an employee. Your employer does not have to explicitly require you to buy the computer provided its purchase spares the employer the cost of providing suitable equipment with which to perform your job responsibilities.

Expenses to Produce Income and Other Expenses

You may deduct certain other expenses as miscellaneous itemized deductions to the extent that the total amount of these deductions exceeds 2% of your adjusted gross income. These include expenses you pay:
1. To produce or collect income,
2. To manage, conserve, or maintain property held for producing income, or
3. To determine, contest, pay, or claim a refund of any tax.

These expenses must be ordinary and necessary and bear a reasonable and proximate relation to the income or income-producing property, and the income must be taxable to you.

Indirect Deductions of Partnerships and S Corporations. Deductions of pass-through entities, such as a partnership or S corporation, are passed through to the partners or shareholders. If the deductions are miscellaneous itemized deductions, they are usually deductible only to the extent that they exceed 2% of your adjusted gross income.

Investment Counsel Fees. Amounts paid for managing your investments are deductible subject to the 2% limit if they relate to investments that produce taxable income.

Trustee's Administrative Fees. Fees that are billed separately and that you paid in connection with your Individual Retirement Account or Arrangement (IRA) are deductible, subject to the 2% limit, provided that they are ordinary and necessary.

TAXSAVER

If the trustee of your IRA takes his or her fee out of your $2,000 contribution, there will be less money in your IRA account that can be invested. You should *consider paying the fee separately from your IRA contribution. For more about IRAs see Chapter 5.*

Legal Expenses.   Legal fees that you pay to produce taxable income are usually deductible subject to the 2% limit. You may deduct legal expenses for tax advice related to a divorce if your lawyer's bill specifies how much is for tax advice and if the amount is determined in a reasonable way. Generally, legal expenses of a personal nature are not deductible.

Safe Deposit Box Rent.   If you use a safe deposit box to store taxable income-producing stock, bonds, or investment-related papers or documents, the rent is deductible subject to the 2% limit.

Tax Preparation Fees.   Amounts paid for tax preparation are usually deductible in the year you pay them. Thus, you may deduct, subject to the 2% limit, your fees paid in 1995 for preparing your 1994 return.

Deductions Not Subject to the 2% Limit

Some expenses can be deducted as miscellaneous itemized deductions whether or not the total of your miscellaneous expenses exceeds 2% of your adjusted gross income. Some of the expenses not subject to the 2% limit include the following:

Federal Estate Tax on Income in Respect of a Decedent.   You may deduct the federal estate tax attributable to "income in respect of a decedent" that is ordinary income and that you, as a beneficiary, include in your gross income. Income in respect of a decedent is gross income that the decedent had a right to receive, could have received had death not occurred, and that could not have been properly included in the decedent's final income tax return.

The deduction for Federal estate tax attributable to income in respect of a decedent is subject to the overall limit on itemized deductions for high-income taxpayers.

Gambling Losses to the Extent of Gambling Winnings.   While gambling losses are not subject to the overall limit on itemized deductions, you may not deduct more gambling losses than the gambling winnings you report.

Other Adjustments to Income

Early Withdrawal from Savings Accounts.   Penalties paid because of the premature withdrawal of funds from time savings accounts or certificates of deposit are allowed as a deduction against your total income in figuring your adjusted gross income.

Forestation/Reforestation Amortization Expenses.   If you can claim an amortization deduction for the costs of forestation or reforestation but you do not have to file the *Business Income Form* (Schedule C) or *Farm Income Form* (Schedule F), you can claim such deductions as an adjustment to income in figuring your adjusted gross income.

Supplemental Unemployment Benefits. If, during the tax year, you repaid supplemental unemployment benefits that you have previously reported as income because you became eligible for payments under the Trade Act of 1974, you can deduct the repayment as an adjustment to your gross income. Alternatively, if the amount you repay is more than $3,000, a tax credit is available.

Net Operating Loss Deduction

The net operating loss (NOL) deduction permits a taxpayer to use a loss from one year against income from another year. A net operating loss is determined by making specific adjustments to eliminate certain nonbusiness items in the loss year.

NOLs incurred in taxable years ending after 1975 may be carried back 3 years and then forward 15 years. You may also elect to forgo the carryback period for NOLs incurred in taxable years ending after 1975 and only carry the loss forward for 15 years. Special rules apply to the determination of the NOL deduction under the alternative minimum tax. (See page 140.) Net operating loss for businesses is discussed in Chapter 14.

OVERALL LIMIT ON ITEMIZED DEDUCTIONS

Itemized deductions—i.e., deductions claimed on your return—are phased out by 3% of the excess of your adjusted gross income over $117,950 (married filing separately, $58,475), adjusted annually for inflation. This means, for example, that a taxpayer with AGI of $184,617 would lose $2,000 [($184,617 − $117,950) × 3%] of itemized deductions.

This overall limitation is imposed *after* any other limitations affecting specific categories of itemized deductions are applied. For example, miscellaneous itemized deductions will be subject to both the 2% floor discussed on page 51 and the additional 3% phaseout.

Medical expenses, casualty, theft, and gambling losses, and investment interest expenses are not subject to this limitation. And in no case can the reduction be more than 80% of your otherwise allowable deductions. Also, the limitation does not apply if you are subject to the alternative minimum tax.

TAXSAVER

If you can reduce your 1995 AGI to below $117,950 you will avoid having your itemized deductions reduced at all. For every $1,000 of AGI in excess of $117,950 your itemized deductions are reduced by $30.

3

Travel and Entertainment Expenses

INTRODUCTION

Travel and entertainment expenses that are directly related to your business and income-producing activities are usually deductible whether you are an outside salesperson or an employee.

Travel expenses include transportation fares, automobile expenses, costs of meals and lodging, baggage charges, and miscellaneous business expenses (e.g., telephone charges) incurred while away from home. The cost of transportation (including automobile expenses) between your home and your regular place of business is not deductible, but the cost of local transportation between business locations during the day is generally deductible. You cannot deduct travel expenses when the sole purpose of the travel is educational.

There are limits, however, on the deductibility of certain expenditures for travel, business meals, entertainment activities, and entertainment facilities. In addition, special record-keeping requirements are imposed on taxpayers claiming deductions for these items. Additional special rules apply to deductions for cars and other property used for transportation, foreign travel, and attendance at foreign conventions. This chapter spells out what is deductible and what isn't and the limits that apply.

THE 50% DEDUCTION LIMITATION

Your allowable deduction for business-related meals, entertainment, and entertainment facilities is limited to 50% of the amount spent, including taxes and tips.

Example. A self-employed individual pays $50 for a business meal, plus $4 in tax and $10 in tips for a total of $64. The allowable deduction after the 50% deduction limitations will be $32 (64 × 50%).

Expenses subject to the 50% rule include: cover charges, room rentals for a dinner or a cocktail party, and parking for an entertainment activity.

The 50% limitation generally applies to any deduction for food or beverages, including meals an employee consumes while traveling "away from home" on business. However, the 50% rule does *not* apply to the otherwise deductible costs of transportation to and from a business meal (e.g., cab fare).

Exceptions. The 50% deduction limitation does *not* apply in the following cases:

- Reimbursed expenses (in which case the person making the reimbursement is generally subject to the 50% limitation).
- Ticket packages for certain charitable fundraising sports events.
- Expenses excludable from employees' incomes as *de minimis* fringe benefits (e.g., a holiday turkey, ham, or fruitcake).

Conventions and Investment Seminars

You can deduct travel expenses for attending conventions, seminars, sales meetings, or similar meetings in connection with the active conduct of a trade or business. However, you cannot deduct such expenses if the purpose of attending investment seminars, conventions, or similar meetings is for the production or collection of income, or the management, conservation, or maintenance of property held for the production of income.

Unreimbursed Employee Travel and Transportation Expenses

Unreimbursed employee travel and transportation expenses are deductible only as a miscellaneous itemized deduction (with an exception for certain performing artists). Total miscellaneous itemized deductions are deductible only to the extent they exceed 2% of your adjusted gross income. See Chapter 2, What You Can Deduct, for a further discussion of unreimbursed business expenses.

Example

Adjusted gross income	$75,000
Unreimbursed T&E expenses	2,300
Other miscellaneous itemized deductions	200
Total miscellaneous expenses	2,500
2% of adjusted gross income floor	$ 1,500
Deductible amount	$ 1,000

TaxAlert

An expense item exempted from the travel and entertainment rules still must meet the regular tax requirements to be deductible. This means that the item must be an "ordinary and necessary" expense in carrying on a trade or business, or qualify for a deduction under some specific provision of the IRS code.

TRAVEL AND TRANSPORTATION

Domestic Travel (Away from Home Overnight)

Expenses incurred in traveling away from home overnight on business are generally deductible. Travel expenses include fares, meals, and lodging. However, expenses incurred for meals and entertainment while away from home are subject to the 50% deduction limitation discussed above. To be deductible, domestic travel must be primarily related to business, and certain record-keeping requirements must be satisfied. *If you fail to properly substantiate your expenses, they may be disallowed.*

TAXALERT

A deduction is allowed for travel expenses paid or incurred with respect to a spouse, dependent, or other individual accompanying a person on business travel only if the spouse, dependent, or other individual is a bona fide employee of the person paying or reimbursing the expenses and the following apply:

- *The travel of the spouse, dependent, or other individual is for a bona fide business purpose.*
- *The expenses incurred would otherwise be deductible.*

*   **Example:** *Mrs. Smith, an employee of an investment advisory firm, is accompanied on a business trip by her husband Mr. Smith, who is not a firm employee. Because Mr. Smith assisted his wife on the trip by entertaining clients, helping her conduct a seminar, and performing other substantial business services, Mr. Smith's presence on the trip had a bona fide business purpose. The firm paid all of Mrs. and Mr. Smith's travel expenses. Under the prior law, the firm may have been able to deduct the costs of Mrs. and Mr. Smith's travel as an ordinary and necessary business expense. Under the new law, the company may not deduct the costs of Mr. Smith's travel because he is not a company employee.*

Travel by Water

Your allowable deductions for travel by ocean liner, cruise ship, or other form of "luxury water transportation" cannot be more than twice the highest federal *per diem* amount for travel in the United States multiplied by the number of days of such transportation. (For example, the highest federal per diem amount at the time of travel was $204 on March 15, 1996.) The cost of on-board meals and entertainment, if separately stated (or clearly identifiable) would be subject to the 50% deduction limitation discussed above (before applying the *per diem* limitation).

The luxury water travel limitation does not apply to expenses of a convention, seminar, or other meeting held on a cruise ship.

Conventions on Cruise Ships

No deduction is allowed for the expenses of a convention, seminar, or other meeting held on a cruise ship, unless:
- The meeting directly relates to the active conduct of the taxpayer's trade or business.
- The ship is registered in the United States.
- All ports of call are in the United States or its possessions.

Deductions for such cruises are also subject to a special $2,000-per-year limitation.

TAXALERT

If you claim a deduction for the expense of attending a convention on a cruise ship, you must attach two statements to your tax return. One statement, signed by the person attending the convention, must include the total number of days on board the ship, total number of hours per day devoted to meetings of the convention, and a schedule of the meeting program. The other statement, signed by an officer of the sponsoring organization, must include a program schedule detailing each day's activities and a statement of attendance detailing the number of hours each day you attended program activities. Be aware that these statements function as a red flag to the IRS in selecting returns for audit.

Foreign Business Travel

If your travel outside the United States is devoted to business activities (for more than 75% of the time), or if the business trip is for seven days or less, all related expenses generally are deductible (subject to the 50% deduction limitation on meals). However, foreign conventions are subject to special rules, which are discussed in the following section. If nonbusiness activity accounts for 25% or more of the total time spent out of the United States, or the trip is for more than seven days, the expenses allocable to the nonbusiness activity will not be deductible. However, these limitations will not apply if either:
- The individual had no substantial control over arranging the trip.
- The individual can establish that a personal vacation was not a major consideration in making the trip.

An individual is considered to have no substantial control over the arranging of the trip if he or she traveled under a reimbursement or other expense allowance arrangement and is neither a managing executive of, nor related to, the employer.

Example. Assume an executive attends a business negotiation in London for six days and sightsees for six more days. His employer reimburses the executive for all airfare and for six days of meals, lodging, and incidental costs related to the business portion of the travel. Unless an exception is met, one-half of the airfare cost is allocable to the personal portion of the trip and must be reported on the executive's tax return as an excess reimbursement. (*Note:* The employer, however, can claim the entire reimbursement as a deduction, subject to the 50% deduction limitation.)

Foreign Conventions

With certain exceptions, the expenses of attending a foreign convention are deductible only when the meeting is directly related to the active conduct of a trade or business and it is as reasonable for the convention to be held in a foreign country as in the North American area. Among the factors to be considered in determining the reasonableness of a foreign convention are:

- The purpose of the meeting and the activities being conducted.
- The purpose and activities of the sponsoring organization.
- The residences of active members of the sponsoring organization and where these meetings have been or will be held.

Any convention, seminar, or similar meeting held outside the United States, its possessions, Trust territories, Canada, Mexico, and certain Caribbean countries is generally considered a foreign convention.

Meetings of Stockholders, Employees, Directors, Business Leagues

Certain types of business meetings are subject to less restrictive rules than those that apply to foreign conventions. Deductions are generally allowed (subject only to the record-keeping requirements) for:

- Business meetings of your employees, stockholders, agents, or directors.
- Meetings of tax-exempt business leagues, chambers of commerce, real estate boards, boards of trade, and professional football leagues.

However, any meal or entertainment expenses would be subject to the 50% deduction limitation.

Special Rules

Here are some special rules for deducting certain travel expenses.

- No deduction is allowed for travel as a form of education.
- No deduction is allowed for travel expenses (including meals and lodging) incurred in performing services "away from home" on behalf of a charitable organization unless *no* significant element of personal pleasure, vacation, or recreation is involved in the travel. The limitation

applies whether the expenses are paid directly by the individual or indirectly by the charitable organization (e.g., through reimbursement).

Automobile Expenses

The deduction for automobile expenses can be calculated in one of the following two ways:

- *Actual expenses:* Automobile depreciation is added to the actual expenses related to use of the automobile. Depreciation deductions for certain luxury automobiles may be limited. For automobiles first placed in service in 1996 and for which business use exceeds 50%, the depreciation deduction is limited to $3,060 in the first year, $4,900 in the second year, $2,950 in the third year, and $1,775 for each succeeding year. These amounts will be indexed annually for inflation.

Maximum Depreciation Deduction Allowed (business use >50%)

Year placed into service	Tax Year			
	1st	2nd	3nd	4th + +
1987	$2,560	$4,100	$2,450	$1,475
1988	2,560	4,100	2,450	1,475
1989	2,660	4,200	2,550	1,475
1990	2,660	4,200	2,550	1,475
1991	2,660	4,300	2,550	1,575
1992	2,760	4,400	2,650	1,575
1993	2,860	4,600	2,750	1,675
1994	2,960	4,700	2,850	1,675
1995	3,060	4,900	2,950	1,775
1996	3,060	4,900	2,950	1,775

These amounts are further limited if the auto is used for both business and personal use. If a vehicle is used for business 50% or less of the time, the alternative depreciation system (ADS) must be used.

- *Standard rate:* The deduction is computed using the standard mileage rate of 31 cents per mile for all miles of business use. The basis of the vehicle must be reduced (but not below zero) by 12 cents per mile for all miles for which the standard mileage rate is used.

TAX*ORGANIZER*

If you own a luxury business car, the standard mileage rate is probably inadequate to cover your operating costs. You should keep detailed records of your total expenses so that you may claim a larger deduction than you would be able to by using the standard mileage rate.

TAX*SAVER*

Interest paid on loans to purchase a car—even if used by an employee for business—is considered personal interest and is not deductible. However, if you finance the car by taking out a home equity loan, the interest will be fully deductible as home mortgage interest. The after-tax cost of home equity payments will often be lower than the best car loan available. If you don't own a home or have enough equity available, consider leasing because to the extent the car is used for business, the deductible portion of your lease payments includes the implicit financing costs as well as depreciation.

E&Y FOCUS: Leasing a Car

If you lease a car, you can deduct the part of each lease payment that is for the use of the car in your business or work. Normal operating costs and maintenance may also be deducted. Special rules apply to reduce the annual lease deduction for leased cars similar to the limitations of depreciation that apply to luxury automobiles.

Should you buy or lease a car?

Here are some of the things you need to know before deciding:

1. What are the costs of buying a car including the financing cost and monthly payments on a loan? (Can you finance with a home equity loan and deduct the interest? See TaxSaver above.)
2. The monthly payments on the lease.
3. How many miles you expect to drive the car and the additional charges at the end of the lease term if your actual mileage exceeds the amount set out in the contract. How much more would your monthly payment be if you increased the annual mileage allowance?
4. An estimate of the car's value when you would normally sell or trade it in.
5. What you think you could earn on your payments if it were available for investment.

You would then compare the costs of buying versus leasing a car in today's dollars. To do that you need to calculate the present value of the payments on the lease or on a loan if you decide to borrow some or all of the purchase price. Present value is the financial term for what a dollar paid or received in the future is worth to you today ($1,000 paid five years from today effectively costs you less than if you paid the $1,000 today. That's because you could earn money with that $1,000 during the five years before you pay it.)

A few other points should be noted:

■ Know your obligations under a lease contract for early termination and wear and tear to the car. Leasing car companies will generally make you pay dearly if you want out of your lease early, or if you don't return the car in good shape.
■ Know whether insurance will cover your remaining contract obligation if the car were totally destroyed during the lease term.

Most often the purchase price of a car is negotiable, and so are the lease terms. Shop around.

Purchasing a car outright should be the least expensive way to go if you can't earn more on your money than you would have to pay in finance charges. Purchasing the car with financing is usually next, and leasing (other than a lease with a single, front-end payment) is generally the most expensive. However, these generalizations will vary depending on dealer incentives, interest rates, and other factors applicable to your situation.

Record-Keeping. You must meet the same record-keeping requirements for automobiles as for other travel and entertainment expenses.

TaxOrganizer

Adequate records include a written log, diary, account book, expense statement, trip sheet, or similar record maintained for each expenditure or use. However, in some cases, you may substantiate the business and investment use of automobiles (except pooled vehicles) by keeping records on a sample basis.

Example. You can substantiate the business use of a car by keeping an adequate record of business use during the first week of each month. If this sampling method is used, you must be prepared to demonstrate that the periods for which an adequate record is maintained are representative of the use for the year.

A record should be kept of *each* separate expenditure or use. However, certain expenditures such as fuel or repairs for automobiles may be aggregated. For these costs, only the date and amount (and not the business purpose) need be recorded. These expenditures are then prorated based on the total business use of the property. Similarly, multiple uses that are part of a single business use (such as an uninterrupted business trip) may be recorded by a single record.

Example. A salesman's use of a car during a business trip away from home over several days can be accounted for by a single record of miles traveled.

Exceptions. Certain vehicles, because of their nature—a hearse, for example—are not likely to be used more than minimally for personal reasons. These vehicles are exempt from the record-keeping requirements. Other examples include vehicles designed to carry cargo with a loaded gross vehicle weight over 7 tons, police and fire vehicles, and certain buses and delivery trucks.

Employer-Provided Cars. Employees need to keep the necessary records to substantiate the property's business use for their employers. However, in some situations, the record-keeping burden may be eliminated. If your employer has a written policy generally prohibiting personal use of the car, for example, or includes the full annual value of the automobile in your wages, records do not have to be kept.

TAXORGANIZER

If you claim a deduction for automobiles, you must answer certain questions and provide specific information regarding their use (on Form 2106). For automobile expenses claimed by employees, requested information includes personal, business, and total mileage; total commuting miles and average commuting distance; and a "yes" or "no" response as to whether written evidence exists supporting the deductions or credits. Special rules and questions apply to employers providing vehicles to employees. These information-reporting requirements highlight the importance of maintaining adequate written records.

Entertainment Activities

Though there are some notable exceptions, you are not allowed a deduction for any expense item relating to an entertainment activity unless:

■ The expenditure is *directly related* to the active conduct of your trade or business or

■ The expenditure directly precedes or follows a substantial and *bona fide* business discussion, and it is *associated with* the active conduct of your trade or business.

For this purpose, "entertainment" means any activity generally considered entertainment, recreation, or amusement. An activity may be considered entertainment even though it could be otherwise characterized as something else—advertising, for example.

Examples: Entertaining includes activities at nightclubs, cocktail lounges, theaters, country clubs, and sporting events.

In addition, in order for the expenditure to be deductible, the purpose of the entertainment has to be to obtain income or some other specific business benefit (other than goodwill). Of course, all entertainment expenditures are subject to the 50% deduction limitation, discussed above.

TAXORGANIZER

Additional substantiation requirements. If the business discussion took place before or after a meal or entertainment, the following information about the discussion is required in addition to the general record-keeping requirements for the expenditures:

■ Date and duration of the business discussion.

■ Nature of the discussion and the business reason for the entertainment, or nature of the business benefit derived or expected to be derived.

■ Identification of the persons entertained.

Tickets

The deduction for the cost of a ticket for an entertainment activity (before applying the 50% rule described above) is limited to the face value of the ticket.

Example: A payment to a "scalper" or ticket agency is *not* deductible to the extent the cost of the ticket exceeds its face value.

This limitation does not apply, however, to any ticket to a sports event organized primarily to benefit a tax-exempt charitable organization if all net proceeds are donated to the organization and substantially all work performed in carrying on the event is provided by volunteers. An example would be a golf tournament that donates all net proceeds to charity.

Luxury Skyboxes

Deductions for the cost of leasing private luxury boxes ("skyboxes") *for more than one event* at the same arena are limited to the face value of the highest price nonluxury box seats offered for sale to the general public multiplied by the number of seats in the box. This limitation does not apply if you rent a skybox for only one event at the arena. Rentals by related parties are taken into account in applying these rules. Separate meal and beverage charges are normally not covered by the skybox limitation, but they are subject to the business meal deduction limitations.

Business Meals

No deduction is allowed for the portion of any business meal considered lavish or extravagant under the circumstances. Business meal deductions are restricted in a number of other ways:

- To be deductible, expenditures for business meals (like other entertainment expenses) must meet either the "directly related to" or "associated with" tests discussed on page 62. Quiet business meals or other "goodwill" meals are not deductible unless they satisfy one of these two tests. However, if you eat alone while away from home overnight on business, you will not fail the "directly related to" or "associated with" tests solely because of the absence of a business discussion.
- Business meals are deductible only if either you or your employee is at the meal. For this purpose, an independent contractor who performs significant services for you is treated as an employee if he or she attends the meal in connection with performance of such services.

After the above determinations are reached, only 50% of business meal expenses is allowed as a deduction.

TAXALERT

Congress has instructed the IRS to adopt stricter substantiation requirements for business meals to ensure that they clearly serve a business purpose.

Entertainment Facilities

Deductions for expenses paid or incurred for a facility used for entertainment, amusement, or recreation are generally not allowed. Entertainment facility expenses include depreciation and operating costs such as rent, utilities, and maintenance, and salaries or other compensation paid to caretakers. Interest, taxes, and casualty losses relating to an entertainment facility are, however, deductible.

Any real or personal property—whether owned or leased—may be considered an entertainment facility if used during the year for entertainment. Entertainment facilities can include country clubs, athletic clubs, yachts, hunting lodges, fishing camps, swimming pools, tennis courts, bowling alleys, automobiles, airplanes, hotel suites, apartments, and vacation homes. However, a facility is not considered an entertainment facility if used only incidentally for entertainment, and such use is insubstantial in relation to its other business use, or if such facility is used exclusively by one's employees.

Club Dues

Dues paid for membership in professional organizations such as the AICPA (the American Institute of Certified Public Accountants), AIA (the American Institute of Architects), or the ABA (American Bar Association), or public service organizations such as the Rotary or Kiwanis, are deductible if paid for business reasons and the organization's principal purpose is not the conduct of entertainment activities. Dues or assessments paid for membership in a social, athletic, or sporting club, including dues and fees paid to a country club, are not deductible.

General Travel and Entertainment Record-Keeping Requirements

Travel and entertainment expenses are an ordinary and necessary part of doing business, but they may not be deducted unless you meet specific substantiation requirements, some of which have already been described above. The law specifically disallows any deduction for travel and entertainment expenditures unless you substantiate these expenses through (1) "adequate records" or (2) "sufficient evidence corroborating the taxpayer's own statement." This rule also applies to deductions for entertainment facilities. Maintaining "adequate records" is clearly the preferable approach.

To claim a deduction under either method, you must substantiate the following:

Required Elements
- The *amount* of such expense or other item.
- The *time and place* of the travel, entertainment, amusement, recreation, or use of the facility or property; or the *date and description* of the gift.
- The *business purpose* of the expense or other item.
- The *business relationship to the taxpayer* of the person or persons entertained, using the facility or property, or receiving the gift.

Adequate Records

A diary, log, statement of expense, account book, or similar record of the necessary information should be maintained. Canceled checks, credit card receipts, hotel bills, and other documents must be kept to corroborate any expenditure for lodging and any other expenditures of $75 or more (except transportation charges for which such documentary evidence is not readily available). However, such documents by themselves—without a diary noting business purpose and business relationship of the person entertained—may not adequately support a deduction.

The records must be prepared or maintained so that each entry is recorded "at or near the time of the expenditure or use." A log maintained on a weekly basis will normally be adequate.

TaxSaver

Any expenditure or use not documented by adequate records must be substantiated by "sufficient evidence corroborating" your own written or oral statements. Such evidence may ultimately be accepted by the IRS, but attempting to substantiate T&E expenditures in this manner is not recommended because it may cause unnecessary and time-consuming disputes.

TaxAlert

Claiming a credit or deduction without adequate records (or sufficient corroborating evidence) may result in a negligence or fraud penalty in certain cases.

TaxOrganizer

An IRS agent might request the following information when examining your travel and entertainment deductions in connection with a business meeting:
- *The exact nature of business conducted.*
- *The time actually spent on business.*
- *The social events included in the agenda.*
- *Whether the site and time of the meeting were primarily vacation-oriented (such as at a resort area in season).*

Expense Account Allowances

If your reimbursements for travel and entertainment expenses from your employer equal your expenses, and you are required to make an adequate accounting to your employer, then neither the reimbursement nor the expenses need to be reported on your tax return. (Your employer, however, will be subject to the 50% deduction limitation unless an exception applies.)

If reimbursements exceed your deductible expenses, the excess must be included in your taxable income. If expenses exceed your reimbursements, and you wish to deduct the excess expenses on your tax return, you must substantiate to your employer all the expenses and show the reimbursed portion on IRS Form 2106. You will be subject to the 50% deduction limitation, and excess expenses would be allowable only as a miscellaneous itemized deduction subject to the 2%-of-adjusted-gross-income floor, discussed in Chapter 2.

Adequate Accounting

To adequately account for your expenses you should submit to your employer a written account book, diary, expense statement, trip sheet, log, or similar record—along with receipts and other supporting documentation—sufficient to substantiate each element of an expenditure. You must also account for all amounts received as advances or reimbursements, including amounts charged directly to the employer through credit cards.

An employee who has adequately accounted to the employer will not be required to substantiate business expenses to the IRS unless (1) the employee claims deductions for business expenses in excess of reimbursements, (2) the employee is "related" to the employer or (3) the IRS determines that the employer's accounting procedures are inadequate. (Generally, an employee is considered to be related to the employer if he or she is more than a 10% shareholder or a member of a family owning more than 10% of the stock of the employer.)

Standard Reimbursement Arrangements

According to IRS rules, you do not have to document incurring certain expenses if you are reimbursed for these expenses at (or below) a standard *per diem* rate. However, the time, place, and business purpose of the expenses still must be substantiated. Standard reimbursement rates have been established for (1) overnight travel (including meals and incidental expenses); (2) meals and incidentals only; and (3) mileage.

If the standard federal *per diem* rate exceeds your actual deductible business expenses, the excess need not be reported as income. If the standard reimbursement rate is less than your deductible business expenses, and you wish to deduct the excess, you must claim deductions for the expenses on Schedule A of Form 1040. The unreimbursed expenses will be treated as a miscellaneous itemized deduction subject to the 2%-of-adjusted-gross-income floor and the 50% deduction limitation rule (for meals and entertainment).

If your employer's *per diem* rate exceeds the allowable amount and the reimbursement plan does not require employees to return any amount in excess of the substantiated expenses to the employer, you may have to report the full reimbursement as income and deduct any expenses as a miscellaneous itemized deduction. If the plan does require repayment of the excess *per diem* amount to the employer, but you do not return such amount, you also may have to report the excess amount as income.

Overnight Travel Allowances. You can satisfy the "adequate accounting" requirements for overnight travel expenses if your employer reimburses you for not more than (1) the maximum *per diem* rate established periodically by the federal government for "subsistence" in the travel locality or (2) the high-low substantiation rate ($152 for any "high-cost locality" or $95 for any other locality within the continental U.S.). "Subsistence" for purposes of this rule means expenses for meals and lodging, laundry, and tips, but not taxicab fares or telephone costs, which can be separately reimbursed.

TAXALERT

The IRS has indicated it will generally require the entire amount of subsistence for meals, lodging, laundry, and tips to be treated as an expense for food and beverages, and thus subject to the 50% deduction limitation.

Meal Allowance. An employer may wish to use a flat allowance for meals only to reimburse you for these expenses. Under a special meal allowance rule, an employer can presently reimburse an employee not more than $28 or $36 per day (depending on the locality of travel) for meals and certain incidental expenses for a "full day of travel." The amount deductible by the employer is subject to the 50% deduction limitation.

Mileage Allowance. You can satisfy the "adequate accounting" requirement, if you are reimbursed by your employer for local travel and transportation costs at no more than the standard mileage rate determined periodically by the IRS. The rate for 1996 is 31 cents per mile for *all miles of use for business*. Additional amounts can be deducted for tolls and parking expenses incurred for business purposes.

However, some related rules and limits apply. The standard mileage rate cannot be used if (1) you did not claim the mileage allowance in the first year you used the car for business; (2) the car has been depreciated using a method other than straight-line; or (3) additional first-year depreciation has been claimed. Deductions are not allowed for commuting to a "regular" place of business. However, if you are an employee with a regular place of business, you may deduct daily transportation expenses incurred while working at a "temporary" business location. However, if your reimbursements from your employer exceed the standard mileage rate multiplied by the number of business miles you substantiate, the excess may be considered income to you, unless you are required to return it.

Fixed-Amount Reimbursement Arrangements

If your employer does not require you to account for your travel and entertainment expenses, you can deduct reimbursements received only as a miscellaneous itemized deduction, subject to the 50% deduction limitation rule for meals and entertainment expenses and the 2%-of-adjusted-gross-income floor. Reimbursed expenses that do not exceed the standard-mileage and *per diem* rates set by the IRS may be deducted directly from your gross income.

Disallowed Expenses

If an employer bears the cost of travel or entertainment expenses reimbursing you for your expenses, the rules governing the deduction of these expenses generally apply to the employer, not the employee. However, if you are reimbursed for an entertainment expense, and that expense is subsequently disallowed by the IRS on a subsequent audit of your employer, you may have to treat the reimbursed amount as income paid to you on which you will owe tax. Your employer will not, however, automatically be able to deduct the amount paid to you as compensation. Regulations provide that, to be regarded as deductible compensation, the disallowed expenditure must have been treated as compensation on your employer's income tax return as originally filed.

Payments to reimburse expenses of shareholder-employees may be treated as dividends if the corporation's deduction is disallowed. In this situation, the reimbursed shareholder would have to include the amount in income, and the employer corporation would not be allowed a deduction. However, if a preexisting agreement requires the shareholder-employee to repay the amount of any nondeductible item to the employer, the shareholder-employee then can deduct the amount repaid and the corporation is restored to the position it was in before making the disallowed payment. There's one catch: the IRS could view such an agreement as an indication that the company may have taken some questionable deductions.

Entertainment Expenses Treated as Compensation or Income. An employer is not subject to travel, entertainment, and record-keeping rules if the expenses of providing goods, services, or facilities to an employee are treated as compensation to the employee on the employer's tax return as originally filed and income tax is withheld on the compensation.

Expenses for goods, services, or facilities provided to non-employees are exempt from the special travel, entertainment, and record-keeping rules to the extent that the expenses are includable in the income of the nonemployee recipient either as compensation or as a prize or award. However, this exemption applies only if the taxpayer includes the amount on an information return (Form 1099), if such a return is required.

4

Tax Planning and Your Home

INTRODUCTION

Your home is often your most significant asset. For this reason, if no other, you will want to do everything you can to maximize your after-tax return on this investment. Fortunately, your home can also be your biggest tax shelter. The tax code allows you to deduct interest paid on a home mortgage, within certain limits, from your adjusted gross income. This chapter discusses numerous tax-saving strategies that involve your home. It discusses ways you can maximize your deduction for home mortgage interest; ways to minimize the gain and recognize loss when you sell your residence; and what tax deductions you may be able to take if you own a second home. It suggests different methods by which you may divide jointly owned property because of a divorce, what you can deduct if you have an office at home, and ways you may generate charitable contributions using your home.

Selling Your Home

A gain on the sale or exchange (including condemnation) of your principal residence is taxable. If you have a loss on the sale, you cannot deduct it.

TAX*SAVER*

If you believe your home will decline in value before you sell it, you may want to convert it to rental property before the value declines so that the loss, if any, may be deducted.

TAX*ORGANIZER*

Selling expenses and any home improvements you've made over the years will reduce the amount of gain that is taxable, thereby reducing any taxes you might owe. You need to keep good records of such expenses in order to figure the lowest taxable gain you must report.

If certain conditions are met, however, the tax on the gain from the sale or exchange of your principal residence is postponed. For you to be eligible to postpone the tax, the cost of your new residence must exceed the adjusted sales price of your old residence, and the new residence must be purchased and occupied within a period beginning two years prior to the date of the sale of the original residence and ending two years after such date. For certain members of the armed forces and individuals whose tax home is outside of the United States, the time period is longer.

TaxSAVER

If you want to defer tax on the gain from the sale of your old home, make absolutely sure you occupy the new home as your principal residence in time. You are not allowed any additional time even if conditions beyond your control keep you from moving in. This is a hard-and-fast rule.

When Your New Home Costs Less than the Sales Price of Your Old One. If the two-year rule is met, but the cost of the new residence is less than the adjusted sales price of your old residence, you may have to recognize gain to the extent that the adjusted sales price of the old residence exceeds the cost of the new residence. Any gain not recognized on the sale of the old residence reduces the tax basis of the new residence.

The term "adjusted sales price" means the selling price minus the sales expenses of the sale and fixing-up expenses incurred in putting the residence into condition for sale. For example, expenses of sale could include broker's fees, fees for drafting a contract of sale, fees for drafting the deed, escrow fees, and mortgage title insurance. Fixing-up expenses include decorating and repair expenses you have incurred to sell the old home and must be for work done during the 90 days prior to signing the sale contract and paid within 30 days after the sale.

Example: Your old home had a basis of $75,000. On January 5, 1996, you signed a contract to sell the old home for $160,000 and on January 6, 1997, you purchased a new home for $138,000. You incurred selling expenses of $8,000 and fixing-up expenses of $3,000 on the sale of your old home. Your calculations would be:

1.	Selling price of old home	$160,000
2.	Minus: Selling expenses	(8,000)
3.	Amount realized	$152,000
4.	Basis of old home	(75,000)
5.	Gain on old home [(3) minus (4)]	$ 77,000
6.	Amount realized on old home	$152,000
7.	Fixing-up expenses	(3,000)
8.	Adjusted sales price	$149,000
9.	Cost of new home	138,000

10. Gain not postponed [(8) minus (9)]	$ 11,000
11. Gain postponed [(5) minus (10)]	$ 66,000
12. Cost of new home	$138,000
13. Minus: Gain postponed (11)	(66,000)
14. Basis of new home	$ 72,000

One-Time Exclusion for Taxpayers 55 and Older. If you are age 55 or older, you are allowed a one-time exclusion of a gain up to $125,000 ($62,500 in the case of a married individual filing a separate return). To qualify, you must be age 55 before the date of the sale and must have owned and occupied the residence for three out of the previous five years.

There is an exception to the three-out-of-five-year rule for certain incapacitated taxpayers. If you are physically or mentally incapable of self-care during the five-year period, time that you spend in a licensed facility (including a nursing home) can qualify as use of the residence for up to two of the three required use years as long as you own the property during the period of incapacitation. Because this exception only applies for two years of the three-year period, you must still use the property as a residence for a period of at least one year.

Special rules also apply when the property sold was acquired as a result of an "involuntary conversion" of a former residence—the forced disposition of property as a result of condemnation. In such cases, the holding period of the former residence is added to the holding period of the property sold to determine whether the three-out-of-five-year test is satisfied.

Married individuals are entitled to only one lifetime exclusion per couple. For example, if you are married and you and your spouse own your home as joint tenants, tenants by the entirety, or as community property, and if you file a joint tax return for the year of sale, then you and your spouse are treated as one person for purposes of taking the one-time exclusion. Thus, only one spouse is required to meet the qualifications for claiming the one-time exclusion. However, you are only entitled to the $125,000 election once during your lifetime; and since a married couple is treated as a single individual, the couple is entitled to take only one $125,000 exclusion, not two (one for each spouse). If one spouse took the exclusion prior to the marriage, either as an individual or with a prior spouse, then neither spouse can exclude the gain. This is true even if it results in one spouse being prevented from ever using the election. However, if each spouse had made an independent election prior to marriage, neither spouse has to repay the tax on the gain previously excluded by the other spouse.

Any gain in excess of $125,000 may be deferred if you reinvest the money in a new residence within a certain period, as explained above. ($62,500 in the case of a married individual filing a separate return).

Example: A 55-year-old taxpayer sells his residence for $250,000 on July 21, 1996, and purchases a smaller home. The original residence was purchased more than three years ago for $120,000. The new home is purchased by July 10, 1998, and costs $160,000. There is no tax on the $130,000 gain, and the basis of the new residence is $155,000, computed as follows:

Gain Realized and Not Excluded:

Sales price	$250,000
Basis of original residence	(120,000)
Realized gain	$130,000
One-time exclusion (55 years old)	(125,000)
Gain not subject to exclusion	$5,000

Gain Recognized:

Sales price	$250,000
One-time exclusion	(125,000)
Adjusted sales price	$125,000
Cost of new residence	(160,000)
Gain recognized (not less than zero)	$0

Basis of New Residence:

Cost of new residence	$160,000
Gain not excluded and not recognized	(5,000)
Basis of new residence	$155,000

E&Y FOCUS: The Split-Gain Technique

A married couple that plans to sell their jointly owned principal residence and plans to buy a replacement residence that costs less than the adjusted sales price of their former home—e.g., they are retiring and moving to a lower-cost area or downsizing after the children have moved out—can reduce the amount of capital gain recognized on the sale of the former home by a planning approach known as a "split-gain technique." In essence what is done is that the ownership of the residence is changed from joint ownership where the two own all of the property to an ownership structure in which each owns one half. When the property is sold each one takes their half of the proceeds. Then one spouse purchases a new replacement residence with his or her half of the proceeds. The other spouse does not purchase a replacement residence but reports all the gain from the sale of their old home. This technique is best understood through the following simplified example:

> A husband and wife jointly own their principal residence, which is worth about $800,000 and cost them $400,000 when they bought it. They plan to sell their house and purchase a retirement home that will cost them $400,000. They have a $400,000 gain on the sale of the first house. Because the cost of the new house is much less than the proceeds from sale of the old house, they will recognize a $400,000

gain and pay a capital gains tax of about $112,000. If, instead of their owning the property jointly, they each own one-half, each will get $400,000 from the sale, and each will have a $200,000 gain. If the wife purchases the replacement residence, her $200,000 gain will not be recognized. The husband's $200,000 gain will be recognized. His capital gains tax will be $56,000 (28% of $200,000).

The wife's basis in the new house will be only $200,000. If she sells the house in the future, she may have to pay taxes on that deferred gain. However, deferring the payment of tax is better than paying taxes currently.

This technique to reduce the amount of gain that a married couple would have to recognize currently is effective only if the excess of the adjusted sales price of the former home over the cost of the replacement residence is greater than one-half of the realizable gain.

Example: Assume in the example above that the replacement residence cost $700,000. If the couple purchases the new home jointly, only $100,000 of the gain would have to be currently recognized. However, if the wife purchases the home alone, then the husband's entire $200,000 share of the gain would have to be recognized.

If you are thinking of taking advantage of the "split-gain" technique, you should consider the following preparatory steps:

- Converting title in your residence from joint tenancy to tenants in common before selling the old home;
- Having the settlement attorney issue separate Forms 1099 reporting one-half of the gain to each spouse;
- Filing as married filing separately for the year of sale with each spouse completing a Form 2119 (*Sale of Your Home*); and,
- Having the spouse that takes title individually to the new home (or, in a community property state, as separate property) use only his or her sale proceeds and other separate funds, if necessary, to purchase the new home.

Real Estate Taxes. The deduction for real estate taxes on any real estate sale is apportioned between the seller and the buyer based on the number of days in the real-property tax year that the property is owned by each.

Below Market Interest. In certain instances the seller of a personal residence may be required to acknowledge additional interest income for debt obligations issued with a below-market interest rate. (See page 44.)

Home Mortgage Interest

Generally, mortgage interest is any interest you pay on a loan secured by your home. This includes a mortgage, a second mortgage, a line of credit, and a home equity loan. Most home mortgage interest is deductible, subject to the following limitations:

The loans secured by your principal residence and a second residence cannot exceed $1 million. In addition, in order to be deductible, the debt has to qualify as "acquisition indebtedness." Acquisition indebtedness is debt incurred in acquiring, constructing, or substantially improving a qualified residence. Acquisition indebtedness is reduced by principal payments made on such debt. If you have repaid some of your "acquisition debt" (most commonly by making mortgage payments), it cannot be restored through refinancing. You can refinance your mortgage up to the balance remaining on the old mortgage and still deduct the interest. If you refinance in an amount in excess of the balance remaining on the old mortgage, the interest allocable to the excess is not deductible unless the excess was used to substantially improve your home or it qualifies as home-equity indebtedness (discussed below).

Acquisition indebtedness that was incurred prior to October 14, 1987 is not subject to the $1 million limitation. However, the amount of such debt reduces (but not below zero) the $1 million limitation on subsequent acquisition debt. Such debt includes that which was incurred on or before October 13, 1987, and was secured by a qualified residence as of that date and at all times thereafter.

Home mortgage interest is deductible on a home-equity loan if the loan does not exceed $100,000. The home-equity debt must not exceed the fair market value of a qualified residence that is reduced by the amount of acquisition indebtedness for that residence. Home-equity loans may provide you with deductible interest on debt incurred for personal purposes, such as the purchase of a family car. (See Chapter 2, page 31.)

TaxSaver

If you own more than two homes, you may not deduct the interest on more than two of these homes as home mortgage interest during any one year. You must include your main residence as one of the homes. You may choose any one of your other homes as a qualified residence and may change this choice in a different tax year.

However, you cannot choose to treat one home as a second residence for part of a year and another home as a second residence for the remainder of the year if both of these homes were owned by you during the entire year and neither was your main residence during that year.

TaxSaver

Generally, costs for your children's dormitory space at college are not deductible. However, if you purchase a condominium in which your college-age dependent child lives while at school, you may be able to generate a deduction. This is possible because the interest expense for a qualified second residence is deductible. The interest portion of the mortgage and any related property taxes would be deductible. Obviously, appreciation or depreciation potential and other factors must be considered when looking at this idea, but under the right circumstances it could make sense.

E&Y FOCUS: Before You Refinance

Here are some questions you should consider when you are thinking about refinancing your mortgage:
1. What will it cost to refinance the mortgage?
2. How much longer do I plan to own my home?
3. Will my financial condition in the future allow me enough cash flow to continue paying the mortgage?
4. Should I consider an adjustable rate mortgage (ARM), or a fixed rate mortgage? Because of current low interest rates, ARMs may require smaller monthly payments than a fixed rate mortgage. However, monthly payments on an ARM will increase if interest rates go up and could, at some time, exceed the amount of a fixed rate mortgage.

If the rates stay low you can be ahead with an ARM. However, if you are on a fixed income there is always a risk that rates will go up beyond what you can afford.

Points

"Points" are certain charges sometimes paid by a borrower. They are also referred to as loan origination fees, maximum loan charges, or premium charges. If the payment of any of these charges is only for the use of money, it is interest.

Because points are, in effect, interest paid in advance, generally you may not deduct the full amount for points in the year paid. Points that represent prepaid interest generally must be deducted over the life of the loan.

Exception: You may deduct the entire amount you pay as points in the year of payment if the loan is used to buy or improve your principal residence and is secured by that home. This exception will apply only if:
1. The payment of points is an established business practice in the area where the loan was made, and
2. The points paid do not exceed the number of points generally charged in this area.

Furthermore, the points charged on a mortgage obtained to purchase your principal home are immediately deductible whether paid out of separate funds or, if the following additional conditions are satisfied, incorporated into the mortgage note. These additional requirements are:
1. Your lender prepares a Form HUD-1, *Uniform Settlement Statement*, that explicitly states the points incurred on the loan. Points may be identified as "loan origination fees," "loan discount," "discount points," or simply, "points."
2. The points must be computed as a percentage of the principal amount of the loan.

3. The total of your down payment plus other cash paid by the time you close is at least as much as the amount of points charged.

To be immediately deductible, points paid on home improvement loans must be paid from separate funds at closing—that is, they cannot be included in the borrowed amount.

Points paid on a loan to purchase or improve your second home do not qualify for full, immediate deduction. Generally, points paid on the refinancing of a principal residence must be spread over the life of the loan.

TAXALERT

If a buyer does not have enough cash to close the purchase of a house and pay points, the mortgage lender will very likely require a higher interest rate. But, the purchaser might not be able to afford payments with the higher interest, so the seller pays the points. The question then is "if there is a deduction who gets it?"

The IRS decided in 1994 that a borrower (the purchaser) may treat amounts paid by the seller in connection with the acquisition of a principal residence as mortgage points that are deductible in the taxable year paid. The new rule applies back to points paid after December 31, 1990. If you are affected by this new rule, you may file amended returns deducting the points paid during years beginning after December 31, 1990 and before January 1, 1994.

TAXSAVER

A borrower may deduct points paid by the seller if the following conditions are satisfied:
- *The rule only applies to points—that is, to financing costs described on the HUD-1 or similar settlement statement as "loan origination fees," "loan discount," "discount points," or "points."*
- *Points must be described as a percentage of the loan amount.*
- *The amount of the points must be reasonable for the local market.*
- *Points are only deductible to the extent of the amount of funds brought to the table by the buyer. Furthermore, the buyer's basis in the home must be reduced by the amount of seller-paid points deducted.*

As noted above, this rule is retroactive and applies to all primary residences purchased since January 1, 1991 that involved seller-paid points.

TAXSAVER

Generally, each point adds about 1/8% to the interest rate on a 30-year mortgage. However, the effect is much greater if the loan is for a shorter period of time. Therefore, if you expect to sell your property well before the mortgage is paid off, it could be better to pay a higher interest rate and fewer points.

Alternative Minimum Tax Consequences. Home mortgage interest is allowed as a deduction for AMT purposes. However, the definition of such interest is narrower than that of "qualified residence interest" for regular tax purposes. Refinanced home mortgage interest that is applicable to any mortgage in excess of the outstanding mortgage before refinancing is not deductible for AMT purposes. (See page 73 for further discussion.)

Second Homes

Vacation Homes and Other Dwellings. Benefits may be derived from the ownership of a second home. You may significantly reduce your taxable income by increasing your home mortgage interest deduction, subject to certain limitations (see pages 73–74). If you rent your property, you may reduce your taxable income further through the deduction for rental expenses (see page 10).

Residence and Domicile. Residence and domicile are different concepts. They may be the same or they may be different. Your residence is where you currently live. Your domicile is where you are permanently established. The home you may be residing in may be your vacation home while your domicile is somewhere else. You can have many residences but only one domicile. Where your domicile is located can have a significant effect on your income and estate taxes. For a further explanation see Chapter 13, Estate and Gift Taxes, on page 195.

TaxSaver

When considering retirement, you should try to establish your domicile in a state where the income and estate taxes will be the lowest.

Example: A New Yorker who has a residence in New York City retired to Florida for five years before his death. The man kept an office in New York but spent most of his time (more than six months) in Florida. New York claimed that the man was a resident of New York because he died there and was buried there. The New York estate taxes would have equaled $4 million. However, the man had arranged his will through a Florida attorney and took numerous steps to declare Florida as his new domicile. It was determined that he was, indeed, a resident of Florida and a nonresident of New York. As a nonresident, his estate taxes in New York were less than $20,000.

E&Y FOCUS: Establishing Your Domicile

Where you actually establish domicile can have a tremendous impact on your tax bill. For instance, New York and Massachusetts have significant state income taxes while Florida and Texas have none. States also have differing rules governing certain estate matters, such as the division of property when someone dies without a will.

To Establish Your New Domicile

- Register and vote in your new state whenever possible. Advise the Board of Elections where you formerly voted that you have moved, and cancel your old registration.
- File a declaration of domicile. Some states, such as Florida, have a special form you can file to establish permanent residency.
- File, as a resident, all state and local tax returns required by your new state—and use your new address on all future tax returns.
- Change your car's title and registration.
- Obtain a driver's license in your new state.
- Take advantage of homestead exemptions if your state offers them—they're an excellent way to help establish a change of domicile and reduce real estate taxes.
- Open bank accounts in your new state.
- Become a member of organizations in the new state, rather than continue memberships in the old state.
- Execute a new will in which you refer to your domicile.
- Spend more time in your state of domicile than in any other state.
- Declare your new state as your domicile on all forms that require a statement of residence. Examples are passports, contracts, credit applications, and hotel registrations.
- Use your new address in all formal agreements.
- Register securities at your new address.
- Change insurance policies that do not relate specifically to property located outside your new state.
- Change your address with the Social Security Administration.
- Change credit cards, particularly those which are national in scope.

Rental Income and Expenses

Rental income includes any payment you receive for the use or occupation of property. For example, if you rent the loft above your garage or a room in your house, you will have rental income. If you receive property or services as rent, the fair market value of the property or services you receive is rental income.

Deductible Rental Expenses.   Repairs, advertising, janitorial and maid service, rental of equipment, utilities, fire and liability insurance, taxes, interest, commissions for the collection of rent, and travel and transportation expenses—all of these expenditures, if they are incurred in renting property, may be deductible. Repairs are expenses incurred to keep your property in good operating condition. Repair expenses include repainting property inside or out, fixing gutters or floors, and fixing leaks. Repairs are different from improvements. Improvements must be "capitalized" and depreciated—that is, the cost of the item is written off as a business expense over a period of years. (See the discussion of depreciation later in this chapter.) Improvements are expenditures that either add to the value of your property or prolong the property's useful life. Improvements include such items as building an addition, putting in new plumbing or wiring, and installing a new roof.

TAX*ALERT*

The Small Business Job Protection Act of 1996 provided that if you dispose of improvements to rental property after June 12, 1996, you are able to take the adjusted for depreciation basis into account for purposes of determining a gain or loss. Prior to the new law, you would usually continue to depreciate the cost of the improvement, and you would not take it into account when calculating a gain or loss on the property.

TAX*SAVER*

You may deduct expenses on your rental property during a period in which it is not being rented as long as it is actively being held out for rent. This rule applies to a period between rentals as well as to the period during which a property is being marketed as a rental property for the first time. The IRS can disallow these deductions if you are unable to show that you were actively seeking a profit and had a reasonable expectation of achieving one. However, the deduction cannot be disallowed merely because your property was difficult to rent.

Rental of Vacation Homes and Other Dwellings. If you rent out part or all of a vacation home or other dwelling unit, and you also use any part of the unit for personal purposes during the year, you must divide your expenses between the rental use and the personal use.

TAX*SAVER*

When Rental Income Isn't Taxed. *If a residence is rented out for fewer than 15 days during the taxable year, the rental income is not taxable. This is one of the few instances in which the IRS considers rental income to be nontaxable. Consequently, if you live near the site of a major annual sporting event—say, The Masters Golf Tournament in Augusta, Georgia—and you rent out your residence during the event (for 14 days or less), any income you receive will be tax-free. However, expenses attributable to the rental of your residence, such as depreciation, insurance, and so on, are not deductible except for interest, taxes, and casualty losses that are deductible on Schedule A, Form 1040, if you itemize.*

Figuring Rental Expenses. If you rent out a dwelling unit for 15 days or more, the income you receive is taxable. Expenses related to the property rental are deductible, subject to certain limitations based on the number of days you personally use the dwelling unit. Generally, your deductions can be found by applying this formula: Expenses × rental days ÷ total days used for all purposes.

Example: You own a ski chalet that is used only during the winter ski season. During the year, the dwelling unit is rented out for 80 days and used personally by you for another 10 days. Total utility expenses are $1,800. You can deduct $1,600 of the utility expenses against rental income ($1,800 × 80 ÷ 90). The remaining $200 is considered a nondeductible personal expense.

If You Use a Rental Property for More Than 14 Days. When you use a dwelling unit for personal purposes for more than the greater of 14 days or 10% of the number of days that the dwelling unit was rented at a fair market rate during the year, a further restriction applies to the deduction for rental expenses. In this case, the dwelling unit is treated as a residence. The rental expense deductions are limited to the amount of gross rental income, reduced first by any allocated expenditures that would otherwise be deductible, such as interest and taxes, and then by other deductible expenses, such as allocated utilities and depreciation.

Generally, a dwelling unit is used for personal purposes only on days that it is:

- used by you or by any other person who has an interest in it;
- used by a member of your family or by a family member of any other person who has an interest in it, unless that family member uses the dwelling unit as his or her main home, pays a fair rental price, and arranges the rental pursuant to a shared equity financing agreement. For purposes of this rule, your family includes only brothers and sisters, spouses, ancestors (parents, grandparents, etc.) and lineal descendants (children, grandchildren, etc.);
- used by another under an arrangement that lets you use some other dwelling unit; or
- used by anyone at less than a fair rental price.

TAX*SAVER*

The rule relating to personal use does not apply to use by an in-law of the taxpayer who owns the property. Thus, a son-in-law could lease property at a fair value to his mother-in-law, and it would not be treated as personal use.

Some days that you spend at the dwelling unit are not counted as days of personal use. For example, any day that you spend repairing and maintaining your property on a full-time basis is not counted as a day of personal use. In addition, the fact that family members used the dwelling for personal purposes on the same day that you are repairing or maintaining it does not make the day a personal day. You also do not have to count days on which you used the property as your main home as days of personal use, if you used the property as your main home before or after renting it or offering it for rent, and either (1) you rented or tried to rent the property for 12 or more consecutive months, or (2) you rented or tried to rent the property for a period of less than 12 consecutive months and the period ended because you sold or exchanged the property.

TaxSaver

The IRS method for allocating expenses between personal and rental use requires a strict allocation between the total number of days the unit was used during the year and the number of rental days. Taxpayers, however, have successfully challenged this method in a number of Tax Court cases. Using the Tax Court method, you can allocate interest and taxes based on the number of days in the year rather than the number of days rented as prescribed by the IRS. Depending upon the method you chose for allocating expenses between personal and rental use, you may be able to increase your total expense deductions.

Vacation Homes and the Passive Activity Rules

Vacation homes and other rental properties considered rental activities are subject to the passive activity rules discussed on page 11. Consequently, when making decisions regarding renting, financing, and selling properties, you must consider the impact of rental losses being disallowed and the $25,000 rental loss limitation deduction that is applicable to certain taxpayers. (See discussion of exception for active real estate participation in Chapter 1.) Losses that are not deductible as a result of the passive activity rules can be carried forward to later years and, subject to the same income limitations, deducted in those years.

TaxSaver

When the cash flow from your rental property is not enough to meet your operating costs, you should reconsider your reasons for owning the property. You should determine if the expected growth in the value of the property will make up for the losses you are incurring each year. Remember, what has to be made up includes what you could earn on the proceeds from the sale if the property were sold today.

Depreciation

Depreciation is the annual deduction you are entitled to take to cover the cost of certain capital expenditures for property held for business or investment purposes. The depreciation deduction is claimed over "the recovery period" of the property, which varies depending upon the type of property. For example, the recovery period for the cost of a new roof on a rental home is longer than the recovery period for furniture bought for the home. Depreciation is calculated in the same way whether you report income on the cash or accrual method.

Several factors determine how much depreciation you can deduct. The main factors are: (1) your cost basis in the property and (2) the recovery period for the property.

The total of all your annual depreciation deductions cannot be more than your cost or other basis in the property. For this purpose, the total depreciation must include any depreciation that you were allowed to claim, even if you did not claim it.

For more information about depreciation see Chapter 14, Some Basic Planning Strategies for Businesses.

Contributions to Charitable Organizations

Contribution of Property. A transfer of an undivided interest in property qualifies as a charitable contribution and may be deducted. You may deduct the fair market value of the property at the time of contribution if the property would qualify for long-term capital gain treatment if sold. Generally, the contribution of your residence will qualify for such treatment. However, if you have owned your residence for less than a year, your deduction is its fair market value minus the amount that would be ordinary income or short-term capital gain. See page 103 for a discussion of charitable contributions.

Contribution of Property Subject to a Mortgage. If you contribute your residence to a charity and it is subject to a mortgage, you will be allowed a partial deduction. In determining the amount of the contribution, the contribution will be treated as a bargain sale—the amount of the charitable deduction is the difference between the fair market value of the property and the amount of the mortgage. Further, you must include the full amount of the mortgage as income when you make the charitable gift.

Partial Interest in Property. Generally, no deduction is allowed for a charitable contribution of less than your entire interest in property. For example, the owner of property will not get a deduction for giving a "life estate interest" in a property to charity. (A life estate interest is an interest in property that terminates upon the death of the life estate's owner.) A contribution of the right to use property is a contribution of less than your entire interest in that property and is not deductible.

Exceptions: There are some situations in which you may claim a deduction for a charitable contribution that is less than your entire interest in the property:

1. *Undivided part of your entire interest.* A contribution of an undivided part of your entire interest in property must consist of a part of each and every substantial interest or right you own in the property. It must extend over the entire term of your interest in the property.
2. *Remainder interest in a personal residence or farm.* You may take a charitable deduction for an irrevocable gift to a qualified organization of a remainder interest (i.e., the donor retains an interest for his or her lifetime) in a personal residence or in a farm.

If you give a remainder interest in a personal residence (or a farm) to a qual-
ified charity, the present value of the remainder interest is deductible as a
charitable contribution. One significant advantage of such a gift is that you
suffer no loss of income or increase in expense from the gift, but you still
gain a current income tax deduction. The gift may be made without the use
of a trust. In addition, you continue to use and enjoy the home for life.

To qualify for the deduction, the gift must be a gift of your personal resi-
dence. The home does not have to be your principal residence. Thus, the gift
may be your vacation home.

The charity receives no immediate benefit; however, the opportunity for
future benefits can be substantial.

Example: *A 62-year-old woman owns a personal residence with a fair*
market value of $162,000. The land on which the residence is located is
valued at $42,000. The residence has a remaining useful life of 35 years and
an estimated salvage value of $30,000. According to IRS tables, the value of
the remainder interest in the home and the land is approximately $40,000,
which is currently deductible as a donation of the interest. Besides a sub-
stantial income tax deduction, the donor will receive an estate tax deduction
for the value of the interest that passes to charity at her death.

Divorce and Separation

The tax effects on the sale or transfer of one's residence incident to a
divorce can vary substantially depending on whether the couple retains
ownership, sells, or transfers the property.

If title is given to your spouse or former spouse, incident to divorce, no
gain or loss is recognized on a transfer. A transfer of property is incident
to divorce if the transfer occurs within one year after the date on which
the marriage ends, or if the transfer is related to the ending of the marriage. The spouse receiving the property takes the basis of the transferring spouse. This result occurs even if the spouse that retains the residence pays cash and the transaction mirrors the form of a sale.

Alternatively, couples may decide to sell the house to a third party and
split the proceeds. In this circumstance, both parties will recognize gain
upon the sale of the house unless they qualify for the rollover exception
or the $125,000 exclusion (see page 71).

If both of you are over age 55, and if you choose to sell your property, you
should wait until after the divorce to do so. At that time, you and your former
spouse each may elect the $125,000 exclusion, if applicable (see page 71).
If you sell the property while you are still married, the IRS requires that if you
make the election you must do so as a couple, and you will not each receive
the $125,000 exclusion.

Yet another alternative is to retain your interest in the residence even though you no longer live there. This option may be attractive if there are not enough assets to compensate you for your interest in the residence. Under this alternative, you and your spouse could agree, pursuant to the settlement, that the residence subsequently will be sold (for example, when the children no longer live there) and the proceeds from the sale divided between the two of you. However, when the residence is later sold, you may not qualify for the $125,000 exclusion, and you may not be able to roll over any gain from the sale into the purchase of another residence because at the time of the sale, the home is no longer your principal residence.

TAX*SAVER*

If you decide to retain your interest in the residence, you should consider transferring it to your spouse and *as part of the divorce settlement require him or her to divide the proceeds upon sale. Consequently, any applicable exclusions may be used toward the entire proceeds.*

Home Office Expenses

To qualify for a deduction for home office expenses, you must use the home office exclusively as an office and it must be your primary place of business. In determining whether you meet this standard, you must look at: (1) the relative importance of the activities performed at each business location; and (2) the amount of time spent at each location. The IRS has indicated that it will first look to the "relative importance" test. If this test does not produce a definitive answer, then the amount of time spent at each location is the determining factor. This test may result in a taxpayer having no specific office which can be deemed the principal place of business and, thus, being denied a deduction for home office expenses.

The allowable deduction is limited to the gross income generated from the use of the residence, reduced first by any expenditures otherwise deductible, such as taxes and interest, and then reduced by other deductible trade or business expenses, such as prorated utilities and depreciation. Any disallowed expenses can be carried forward to future years, subject to the gross income limitation in those years.

You are not entitled to home office deductions for expenses attributable to the rental of all or part of your home to your employer for performing services as an employee. An independent contractor is treated as an employee under these rules.

5

IRAs, 401(k) Plans, and Other Retirement Plans

INTRODUCTION

Ask a financial planner what's the best way to save money for your retirement, and chances are he or she will recommend that you contribute as much as you can to a 401(k) plan, an individual retirement account or annuity (IRA), a Keogh plan, a Simplified Employee Pension (SEP)—or some combination of the four, if you're eligible. Within certain limitations, all these retirement plans give you the ability to contribute before-tax dollars to an account or trust and receive a tax-deferred accumulation of funds, which will not be taxed until the amounts are withdrawn—generally, when you are retired and quite possibly in a lower tax bracket. This chapter will explain in more detail what these retirement plans are and how they operate. In addition, it will suggest strategies you can use to make the most of your retirement funds.

IRAs

An IRA is a personal savings plan that lets you set aside funds for your retirement. Subject to the limitations discussed below, you may be able to make and deduct from your gross income on your tax return a cash contribution paid to an IRA.

Your annual IRA contribution is limited to the lesser of $2,000 or 100% of your compensation (or earned income from self-employment). Alimony is treated as compensation for this purpose. The amount you can contribute to your IRA is determined on an individual basis. Therefore, if you and your spouse each receive compensation over $2,000, then each of you can contribute $2,000 to your respective IRAs. Earnings in your IRA are not taxable until they are distributed to you.

Although anyone with compensation or earned income may contribute to an IRA, a full deduction is not permitted on your tax return if:

1. You or your spouse is an active participant in a qualified retirement plan provided by one of your employers, and
2. Your adjusted gross income exceeds $50,000 ($35,000 for single filers and $10,000 for married persons filing separately).

If you or your spouse is an active participant in an employer's qualified retirement plan, you can claim a reduced IRA deduction if your adjusted gross income is less than the dollar amount described above but more than $40,000 ($25,000 for single filers and $0 for married filing separately). For married couples filing separately, if one spouse is an active participant in a qualified retirement plan, then the other spouse will also be treated as a member of the plan, unless the couple has lived apart throughout the entire year.

TaxSaver

Contributing before-tax earnings to an IRA account can make a big difference in your retirement savings. For example, assume you are in the 36% tax bracket and that you are earning 8% interest on your savings. You can earn approximately 1.4 times more money after paying taxes on the distribution (payable at the time of withdrawal) on a $2,000 IRA contribution held for 20 years than if you did not make that before-tax contribution. If your tax rate drops after your retirement because you have less income, your savings could amount to an even bigger nest egg.

__Example:__ If you contributed $2,000 a year to an IRA for 20 years and the IRA earned 8% each year, at the end of 20 years you would have about $91,500. If you deposited $1,280 ($2,000 less $720 in tax) each year in an account earning 8% and paid tax on the interest you earned each year, you would have about $43,000 in the account at the end of 20 years. Even paying 36% tax on the $91,500, you would have about $58,600 left as opposed to $43,000 without the IRA. If after retirement your tax rate is 28%, you would have about $65,897 left from the IRA as opposed to $43,000 without an IRA. As the following table on page 87 shows, the compounding effect in your IRA increases your balance disproportionately as the return on your investments increases.

Nondeductible IRA Contributions.   Even if you do not qualify for a tax-deductible contribution to your IRA, you can still make an after-tax contribution. The earnings on these contributions accumulate tax-deferred until you withdraw the money from your IRA. The maximum nondeductible contribution you can make to your IRA is determined as though the contribution were deductible, minus the amount of any deductible contribution you may make. See Table 5.2.

Spousal IRAs.   If you can make a contribution to an IRA and are married, you can also establish an IRA for a non-working spouse. The spousal IRA must be kept separate from your IRA, that is, one for you and one for your spouse or one IRA with separate subaccounts, one for you and one for

TABLE 5.1   Investing in Your IRA

	8% Annualized Return		14% Annualized Return	
	IRA Account	Savings Account	IRA Account	Savings Account
Annual Contribution	$2,000	$2,000	$2,000	$2,000
Less Tax @ 36%	$0	$720	$0	$720
Net Contribution	$2,000	$1,280	$2,000	$1,280
Amount After 20 Years	$91,524	$42,865	$182,050	$65,192
Less Taxes Paid on Withdrawal @ 36%	$32,949	$0	$65,538	$0
Amount Remaining	$58,575	$42,865	$116,512	$65,192

TABLE 5.2   IRA Deductions

Adjusted Gross Income (In $) Allowable Deduction

Married Filing Jointly*	Single	Not an Active Participant	Active Participant
0–39,999	0–24,999	2,000	2,000
40,000– 48,999	25,000– 33,999	2,000	200– 2,000**
49,000– 49,999	34,000– 34,999	2,000	200***
50,000 and over	35,000 and over	2,000	0

*A married couple filing separately is subject to a special limitation (see above).
**The $2,000 amount is reduced by a percentage equal to your adjusted gross income in excess of the lower adjusted gross income limits divided by $10,000. For example, a single individual with an adjusted gross income of $32,000 is allowed an IRA deduction of $600.
***The IRA deduction will not be reduced below $200 until it is reduced to $0 at $50,000 (married filing jointly) and $35,000 (single) of adjusted gross income.

your spouse. For calendar year 1996, the most you can contribute to a spousal IRA is the *lesser* of $2,250 or 100% of your compensation. And, you can allocate the contribution in any way you want as long as not more than $2,000 is allocated to one person.

For example: Joe and Joan have a spousal IRA to which $2,250 is contributed. The contribution can be divided $2,000 for Joe and $250 for Joan, $250 for Joe and $2,000 for Joan or any combination in between such as $1,125 for Joe and $1,125 for Joan.

TaxAlert

The Small Business Job Protection Act of 1996 changed the law governing spousal IRAs. Beginning in 1997, deductible IRA contributions of up to $2,000 can be made for each spouse. In order to receive the deduction, the combined compensation of both spouses must be equal to or greater than the contributed amount. If you are a homemaker who does not work outside the home, the new law will increase the amount you can deduct for contributing to an IRA from $250 to $2,000.

When to Make Your IRA Contributions. Contributions to an IRA can be made starting from the first day of the tax year through the due date (without extensions) of your tax return for that tax year. This means that IRA contributions can generally be made until April 15 of the year following your tax year.

TaxSaver

You can maximize your savings by funding your IRA as early as possible for any given tax year. By contributing to your IRA at the beginning of a tax year instead of waiting until April 15 of the following year, your contribution can earn as much as 15 1/2 months' worth of additional interest. The interest earnings will not be taxed until the money is withdrawn from the account.

IRA Custodial Fees. Annual custodial fees paid to maintain an IRA, as well as the initial fee to establish an IRA, may be deductible if you pay for the fees separately rather than having the costs charged to the IRA account itself. Such IRA expenses are only deductible as miscellaneous itemized deductions subject to 2% of the adjusted gross income floor.

401(k) Plans

If your employer has a 401(k) plan or another plan that allows you to set aside income (e.g., a tax-sheltered annuity or 403(b) plan, which is generally available to employees of tax-exempt and educational organizations), you can elect to defer a certain amount of your salary on a before-tax basis. Such amounts are withheld from your salary and are not reported as income until withdrawn from the plan. Income earned on your 401(k) investment is also tax-deferred. Unlike an IRA, you may be able to borrow from your 401(k) plan without penalty. Subject to nondiscrimination tests which apply to 401(k) plans, you can elect to defer your wages up to a maximum of $9,500 in 1996. Also, many employers provide a matching contribution in their 401(k) plans. For example, a 401(k) plan may provide that for each $1 you contribute, the employer will contribute 50¢. With this kind of plan, you would receive an immediate return on your investment of 50%.

Because funds in a 401(k) plan accumulate tax-free, it is usually a good idea to make as large a contribution to your 401(k) plan as possible. In addition, because contributions to your 401(k) plan are made on a before-tax basis, any contributions made to the plan reduce your adjusted gross income.

TAXSAVER

Although the funds in your 401(k) plan are meant to be set aside for your retirement, you may still have access to them if you need money at an earlier time. Your plan may permit you to borrow from your account, subject to strict rules. Despite the restrictions, you may be better off borrowing from your retirement fund than getting a loan from your bank. If the loan from the bank is for personal purposes, it will result in nondeductible interest. A loan from your 401(k) plan does not generate deductible interest, but the interest you pay is allocated directly back to your account.

In addition to the general qualified plan distribution rules discussed below, 401(k) plans are also subject to special rules regarding certain distributions. Specifically, employee deferrals cannot be distributed prior to one of the following events:
- retirement
- death
- disability
- separation from service with the employer
- attainment of age 59½
- termination of the plan
- disposition of corporate assets or disposition of subsidiary
- hardship

SIMPLE PLANS

TAXALERT

For tax years beginning in 1997, your employer can establish a new type of retirement plan called the savings incentive match plan for employees (SIMPLE). Employers with 100 or fewer employees earning at least $5,000 and who do not maintain another employer-sponsored retirement plan are eligible to set up SIMPLE plans, which were created by the Small Business Job Protection Act of 1996. SIMPLE plans, which are not subject to some of the complicated rules that apply to other types of retirement plans, can be adopted as an IRA or as a part of a 401(k) plan. All employees who earn more than $5,000 a year must be eligible to participate, and self-employed individuals may also participate in SIMPLE plans. In general, contributions to a SIMPLE plan are not taxable until withdrawn.

The employer generally must either match elective employee contributions (limited to $6,000 annually) dollar-for-dollar up to 3 percent of compensation or make a "nonelective" contribution of 2 percent of compensation on behalf *of each eligible employee. No other contributions may be made to a SIMPLE account. Contributions to a SIMPLE account generally are deductible by the employer; however, matching contributions are deductible only if made by the due date (including extensions) of the employer's tax return.*

Employers are given a 2-year grace period to maintain a SIMPLE plan once they are no longer eligible to participate.

Distributions From IRAs and 401(k) Plans

The rules governing the taxation of distributions from IRAs and 401(k) plans are very complex. Not only can the tax rules for ordinary retirement withdrawals be confusing, but the tax law also provides for complicated penalty taxes if distributions are received too early (generally before age 59½), if distributions exceed an annual allowable amount, or if distributions begin too late (generally after April 1 of the year following the year you turn age 70½).

Tax Rules for Ordinary Withdrawals. In general, distributions from IRAs and 401(k) plans are taxed as ordinary income. If nondeductible contributions have been made to an IRA, however, distributions are taxed in much the same way as an annuity. The portion of each distribution that is attributable to nondeductible contributions, if any, is excluded from your taxable income. The ratio of each distribution to be excluded is determined by dividing undistributed nondeductible contributions by your total IRA account balance. If no nondeductible contributions have been made, then the entire distribution is considered ordinary income. (Nondeductible contributions to IRAs have only been allowed since 1987.)

With 401(k) plans, lump-sum distributions may qualify for special tax treatment. A lump-sum distribution is the distribution within a single tax year of an employee's entire balance, excluding certain amounts forfeited or subject to forfeiture, from all of the employer's qualified pension, stock bonus, or profit-sharing plans. The distribution must have been made:
1. Because of the employee's death;
2. After the employee reaches age 59½;
3. Because of the employee's separation from service (does not apply to self-employed persons); or
4. After a self-employed person becomes totally and permanently disabled.

As with an annuity, you may recover tax-free your cost basis in the lump-sum distribution. In general, your cost basis is:
1. Your total nondeductible contributions to the plan;
2. The total of your taxable one-year term costs of life insurance;
3. Any employer contributions that were taxable to you; and
4. Repayments of loans that were taxable to you.

You must reduce your basis by amounts previously distributed to you tax-free.

If a lump-sum distribution is received from your 401(k) account, two types of special tax treatment may be available. These two types are discussed below.

Long-Term Capital Gain Treatment. If you were at least age 50 on January 1, 1986, you may choose to treat a portion of the taxable part of a lump-sum distribution as a long-term capital gain taxable at a 20% rate. This treatment applies to the portion you receive relating to your participation in the plan before 1974.

Special Averaging Method. You may elect to use a 5-year special averaging method to calculate the tax on the ordinary income portion of a lump-sum distribution, including the capital gain portion for which you did not elect capital gain treatment. To use special averaging, you must: be at least age 59½ (unless you were at least age 50 on January 1, 1986), elect to use special averaging for all lump-sum distributions received during the year, and have been a participant in the plan for five or more years prior to the distribution. You can make this election only once in a lifetime.

If you were at least age 50 on January 1, 1986, the age 59½ requirement does not apply and you may elect to use 10-year averaging rather than 5-year averaging. However, the tax rates used in the 10-year averaging calculation are the rates in effect for 1986.

To get an idea of how special averaging works, assume that your income was received equally by 5 different persons (10 for 10-year averaging) in the current year and that each of these people had no other income. As a result, most of the income is taxed at the lowest rates on the single tax-payer tax rate schedule. The tax for these fictional individuals is then added up and becomes your tax on the distribution.

TAXSAVER

The 5-year or 10-year averaging method may be so beneficial to you that you elect to have the long-term capital gain portion of the lump-sum distribution included in the 5-year or 10-year averaging computation rather than have it taxed as long-term capital gain. The tax should be figured both ways to see which is the lowest. If you are eligible to elect either 5-year or 10-year averaging, you should also figure your tax both ways to determine which is most beneficial.

Lump-sum distributions from an IRA do not qualify for either long-term capital gain treatment or the special averaging method.

TAXALERT

The Small Business Job Protection Act of 1996 changed the law governing lump-sum distributions from 401(k) plans. For tax years beginning after December 31, 1999, the 5-year special averaging method will be eliminated. However, if you are one of those individuals who meets the qualifications for the long-term capital gain method and the 10-year averaging method described above, you will still be able to elect to use those methods.

Penalty Tax for Early Distributions. Most distributions from qualified retirement plans made to employees before they reach age 59½ are subject to an additional tax of 10% on the taxable part of the distribution. For this purpose, a qualified retirement plan means: (1) a qualified employee retirement plan (including a 401(k) plan); (2) a qualified annuity plan; (3) a tax-sheltered annuity plan for employees of public schools or tax-exempt organizations; or (4) an IRA.

This additional tax does not apply, under the following circumstances, to distributions that are:

1. Made to a beneficiary or to the estate of the participant on or after his or her death;
2. Made because the participant is totally and permanently disabled;
3. Made as part of a series of substantially equal periodic (at least annual) payments over the participant's life expectancy or the joint life expectancies of the participant and his or her beneficiary. (This exception does not apply to non-IRA distributions unless the distribution begins after you've left your job);
4. Made to an employee who left his or her job in or after the year in which he or she reached age 55;
5. Paid to the employee, to the extent the employee has deductible expenses for medical care (whether or not the employee itemizes deductions for the tax year);
6. Paid to another person designated in a qualified domestic relations order; and
7. Made to an employee who, as of March 1, 1986, left his or her job and began receiving benefits from the qualified plan under a written election designating a specific schedule of benefit payments.

Exceptions 4, 5, and 6 above do not apply to IRAs.

Penalty Tax for Excess Distributions. There are currently two ways to determine the rate at which excess distributions are taxed.

1. *The general rule:* Under the Tax Reform Act of 1986, annual non-lump-sum distributions from qualified plans (including pension annuities and IRA withdrawals) are subject to a 15% excise tax to the extent that the distributions in total exceed $155,000 in any year. The taxable portion of a qualified lump-sum distribution that exceeds $775,000 will also be subject to this tax. The tax also is applied to excess amounts remaining in a qualified plan or an IRA at death, including the value of payments to any beneficiary after your death.
2. *The grandfather rule:* Anyone whose total accrued taxable benefits and balances in all qualified plans and IRAs were at least $562,500 as of August 1, 1986 could have elected to grandfather (that is, shelter from the excise tax) the total amounts accrued in the plans as of that date. Individuals who did not elect the grandfather rule are governed by the general rule as described above. The grandfather election must have been made on Form 5329 no later than when you filed your 1988 federal income tax return.

Basically, the amount that is covered under the grandfather rule is not subject to the 15% excise tax. If you took advantage of the grandfather rule, the grandfathered amount recovered each year depends on which recovery method you elected: the discretionary method or the attained age method. The grandfathered amount is recovered at a different rate each year under each recovery method.

Under the discretionary method, 10% of the annual distributions you receive are considered to be a recovery of the grandfathered amounts. You may also irrevocably elect to accelerate this percentage to 100% in the future. With this acceleration there will be no 15% excise tax until the grandfathered amount is completely recovered.

Alternatively, under the attained age method, a percentage of your annual distributions is considered the recovery of grandfathered amounts. This method results in a decreasing percentage of annual distributions being treated as the recovery of the grandfathered amounts as you grow older. However, you may not use this method if your 35th birthday is after August 1, 1986.

Under the grandfather rule, annual non-lump-sum distributions are subject to the 15% excise tax to the extent that the distributions in total exceed the greater of the remaining, unrecovered grandfathered amount or $155,000 (as adjusted for annual inflation). For lump-sum distributions, the limit is the greater of the remaining, unrecovered grandfathered amount or $775,000 (as adjusted for annual inflation).

TAXALERT

Under the Small Business Job Protection Act of 1996, the 15 percent excise tax is suspended for distributions received in 1997, 1998, and 1999. Amounts distributed during this period will be considered to consist of non-grandfathered amounts first.

Penalty Tax for Late Distributions. Distributions from qualified pension, profit-sharing (including 401(k)), stock bonus, IRA, and tax-sheltered annuity plans generally must begin by April 1 of the year following the calendar year in which the employee reaches age 70½, without regard to the employee's retirement.

As a minimum distribution, the individual must either: (1) receive his or her entire interest in the plan by the required beginning date, or (2) begin to receive regular partial distributions by the beginning date in an amount large enough to use up the entire interest over the employee's life expectancy or over the joint life expectancies of the employee and a designated surviving beneficiary. The payout can also be over a period that is less than the employee's life expectancy.

If the required minimum distribution is not made, an excise tax, equal to 50% of the amount required to be (but not actually) distributed, is imposed. This excise tax may be waived if you establish that the shortfall in distributions was due to reasonable error and that reasonable steps are being taken to remedy the shortfall.

TAXALERT

The Small Business Job Protection Act of 1996 changed the requirements concerning when distributions from pension plans must be made. Beginning after December 31, 1996, distributions from qualified pension, profit-sharing (including 401(k)), stock bonus, and tax sheltered annuity plans must begin by April 1 of the calendar year following either: (1) the calendar year in which the employee attains age 70½ or (2) the calendar year in which the employee retires, whichever occurs later. (The law has not changed for IRAs.)

Individuals who are 5-percent owners of the employer are required to begin receiving qualified plan distributions no later than April 1 of the calendar year that follows the year in which the 5-percent owner reaches age 70½.

Participants in qualified plans who currently receive distributions, but who do not have to receive distributions under the new law, may, if the plan allows, be able to stop receiving distributions until required to do so under the new law.

Nontaxable Distributions. Some distributions from an IRA or 401(k) plan are not taxed. These include: (1) rollovers (discussed below), (2) withdrawals of IRA contributions by the due date (including extensions) of the return for the year the contributions are made, and (3) withdrawals of excess IRA contributions.

Rollovers. A rollover is a tax-free transfer of cash or other assets from a qualified retirement plan to an eligible retirement plan. An eligible retirement plan is an IRA, a qualified employee retirement plan, or a qualified annuity plan. A rollover may also include a distribution from one IRA and a contribution to another.

The rollover must be completed not later than the 60th day following the day on which you receive the distribution. Generally, only one rollover is allowed per year for rollovers between IRAs. If you transfer funds directly between trustees of your IRAs and you never actually control or use the account assets, however, this is not considered a rollover and you may transfer your account as often as you like.

TAXSAVER

Mandatory Withholding on Rollovers. *A mandatory withholding of 20% is imposed on distributions eligible for rollover unless the plan making the distribution directly transfers the payout to the IRA or other qualified plan that is designated to receive the rollover. Traditionally, distributions have been paid directly to retiring or terminating employees who in turn decided how much of the proceeds should be kept or rolled over. This new rule, however, sets a trap if the distribution check is made out to you. On a $100,000 distribution, for example, you would receive only $80,000 after withholding. If you plan to roll over the entire $100,000 to your IRA, you would have to come up with an additional $20,000 in order for the total amount deposited in the IRA within 60 days of receiving the $80,000 check to equal the original $100,000 distribution. Otherwise, the $20,000 withheld would be treated* *as a taxable distribution subject to ordinary income tax, and, if applicable, the 10% early distribution tax (discussed above). Note that the $20,000 with-held is refundable, but only after you file your Form 1040 after the close of the year. However, a check merely delivered to you will not present a problem, so long as it is not negotiable by you. For example, a check made payable to "ABC Bank as trustee of the IRA of John Q. Smith" is okay.*

TAX*SAVER*

Because of the mandatory withholding rules, if you are going to receive a payment from a qualified plan that is to be rolled over to an IRA, make sure that the plan transfers the funds directly to the IRA through a trustee-to-trustee payment.

You can roll over the otherwise taxable portion of a distribution of any part of your account balance into a qualified retirement or annuity plan. A distribution that is required for an individual who is over age 70½ or that is part of a series of substantially equal periodic payments for life or a term of 10 or more years is ineligible for tax-free rollover.

TAX*ALERT*

For tax years beginning after 1996, a tax-free rollover may also be made between SIMPLE plans. In addition, after two years of participating in a SIM-PLE plan, your SIMPLE account can be rolled over to an IRA tax-free. If you stop participating in a SIMPLE account, such as when you leave your em-ployment, your SIMPLE account will be treated as an IRA.

TAX*SAVER*

If you need money for no longer than 60 days, consider withdrawing the money from your IRA if you are sure you will have the cash to put into another IRA within 60 days. You will not incur any tax or penalties, and you will have the cash for 60 days. You can do this only once in a 12-month period.

SIMPLIFIED EMPLOYEE PENSIONS

A simplified employee pension (SEP) is a written plan that allows an em-ployer to make contributions toward an employee's retirement without becoming involved in more complex retirement plans. If you are self-em-ployed, you can contribute to your own SEP.

The SEP rules permit an employer to contribute and deduct each year to each participating employee's SEP up to 15% of the employee's com-pensation or $30,000, whichever is less. If you are self-employed, special rules apply when figuring the maximum deduction for these contributions. In determining the percentage limit on contributions, compensation is net earnings from self-employment, taking into account the contributions to the SEP.

TAXSAVER

Even if your employer makes contributions to a SEP for your account, you can make contributions to your own IRA. The IRA deduction rules, previously discussed, apply to any amounts you contribute to your IRA.

TAXSAVER

A self-employed person can claim a deduction to a SEP as long as the plan is set up and the contribution made by the due date of the return, including extensions. Even if you failed to set up a Keogh plan by December 31, you can still establish a SEP after the end of the year and make a timely payment.

KEOGH (HR 10) PLANS

If you are self-employed and own your own business, you may set up a retirement plan, commonly known as a Keogh or an HR 10 plan. You must have earned income from the trade or business for which the plan was established to take a deduction for a contribution to the plan. A Keogh plan may be either a "defined contribution plan" or a "defined benefit plan."

Under a defined contribution plan, such as a profit-sharing plan or a money purchase pension plan, the benefit you eventually receive is based solely on the contributions credited to your account and the earning attributable to those contributions. Typically, contributions to a profit-sharing plan are made out of a company's profits, and therefore can vary from year to year. Contributions to a money purchase pension plan are usually calculated as a percentage of self-employed income and must be made whether the company had a profit or loss for the year.

Under a defined benefit plan, you are promised a fixed benefit and the annual contributions are based on the amount that is actuarially needed to provide you that benefit at a normal retirement age.

Deductible contributions to a profit-sharing plan are generally limited to the lesser of $30,000 or 13.043% of earned income for the year; deductible contributions to a money purchase pension plan are generally limited to the lesser of $30,000 or 20% of earned income for the year. If you maintain a combination of a profit-sharing Keogh plan and a money purchase Keogh plan, the maximum combined deductible contributions are limited to $30,000 or 25% of earned income per year.

The current maximum benefit that can be promised at retirement age under a defined benefit plan is generally the lesser of 100% of earned income (determined on a three-year average basis) or $120,000. This dollar limit is adjusted annually for cost-of-living increases. The $30,000 defined contribution plan limit will also be adjusted for cost-of-living increases once the defined benefit dollar limit exceeds $120,000.

Note that, for purposes of these limitations, "earned income" must be reduced by an amount equal to one-half of your self-employment taxes for the year.

Here are a few more rules:

1. A Keogh plan must be established before the end of your tax year.
2. The plan must be written. Prototype plans can frequently be obtained from banks and other financial institutions.
3. A summary description of the plan must be provided to your employees. There are specific definitions of employees who must be covered and specific rules on such items as discrimination and vesting.

COMPANY RETIREMENT PLANS

For a discussion of how company retirement plan benefits are taxed, see Chapter 12, Retirement Planning.

TaxAlert

States Can't Tax Former Residents' Pensions. *A state is now prohibited from imposing income tax on any retirement income collected after December 31, 1995 by an individual who is not then a resident or domiciliary of that state. Retirement income from a broad range of plans and trusts is covered, including:*

- *pension, profit-sharing, and stock bonus plans (such as 401(k) plans),*
- *simplified employee pensions (SEPs),*
- *Code Section 403(b) tax-sheltered annuity arrangements (often available to teachers),*
- *individual retirement account or individual retirement annuities,*
- *eligible deferred compensation plans as defined in Code Section 457 (plans set up by state and local governments and tax-exempt organizations),*
- *any federal government retirement program, and*
- *special employee-funded trusts set up before 1959, as described under Code Section 501(c)(18)).*

In addition, the law exempts from state taxation certain income received from nonqualified deferred compensation plans in the form of an annuity over 10 or more years. It also protects any distribution received from a nonqualified ERISA "excess" plan after termination of employment.

6

Charitable Contributions

INTRODUCTION

Those who do good, should do well. So it is with the tax treatment of charitable contributions. You are entitled to a tax deduction for charitable contributions you make. How you make your contributions and even the type of property used—cash, stock, or whatever—can affect whether you get the maximum tax benefit from your contribution. This chapter discusses some of the tax strategies you can use so that the contributions you make can have the most impact on both the charities you're benefitting and the taxes you're paying.

A charitable contribution is a contribution or gift to, or for the use of, a qualified organization. Although contributions to tax-exempt organizations are generally made for charitable purposes, the potential tax benefits of the contributions should not be ignored. In many cases, the tax benefit can lower the cost of making a gift, perhaps enabling you to give even more generously.

Making the most of your contributions will depend on:

- Who is the recipient—a public charity or a private foundation?
- When will you make the gift—now or later?
- What will you give—cash or property?
- How will you make the gift—outright or deferred?

Which Gifts Qualify?

Only gifts to organizations recognized by the IRS as charities are deductible. You cannot assume that an organization to which you want to contribute is officially recognized as a charitable organization and that your contribution will be deductible for federal income tax purposes. Many tax-exempt organizations are not qualified to receive tax-deductible status. IRS Publication No. 78, which is periodically supplemented, contains a list of qualified organizations.

You may deduct a contribution you make to, or for the use of, the following organizations:

- A state, a U.S. possession (including Puerto Rico), a political subdivision of a state or possession, the United States, or the District of Columbia, if the contribution is made only for public purposes
- A community chest, corporation, trust, fund, or foundation organized and operated only for charitable, religious, educational, scientific, or literary purposes, or to sponsor national or international amateur sports competition, or for the prevention of cruelty to children or animals
- War veterans' organizations, including posts, auxiliaries, societies, trusts, or foundations organized in the United States or its possessions
- Domestic fraternal societies operating under the lodge system, if the contribution is to be used only for charitable, religious, scientific, literary, or educational purposes, or for the prevention of cruelty to children or animals
- Nonprofit cemetery companies, if the contribution can be used only for the perpetual care of the cemetery as a whole, and not for a particular lot or mausoleum crypt

Examples of Qualified Organizations. Qualified organizations include the following:
- Nonprofit volunteer fire companies
- Public parks and recreation facilities
- Nonprofit hospitals and medical research organizations
- Churches and other religious organizations
- Most nonprofit educational institutions
- Most nonprofit charitable organizations, such as the Boy Scouts, CARE, Gifts in Kind, Girls and Boys Clubs of America, Girl Scouts, Goodwill Industries, Red Cross, Salvation Army, United Way, and Volunteers of America.

Deductible Contributions. Only individuals who itemize deductions may deduct charitable contributions. Even then, deductions for charitable contributions are subject to the overall limit on itemized deductions, for example, for taxpayers who file jointly with adjusted gross income in excess of $117,950. See discussion on page 53.

Your total deduction for charitable contributions is limited to 50% of your contribution base, an amount generally equal to your adjusted gross income, but in some cases you may be limited to 20% or 30% of your contribution base. See "Limits on Deductions" later in this chapter, especially the section on "When contributions are more than 20% of your income."

Benefits Received. If you make a contribution to a charitable organization and also receive a benefit from that organization, you may deduct only the amount that exceeds the value of the benefit you receive. If you pay more than fair market value to a qualified organization for merchandise, goods, or services, the amount you pay that is more than the value of the item may be a charitable contribution.

Example: If you contribute $100 to a symphony orchestra and receive a pair of tickets worth $25, your deduction is limited to $75. Generally, the charity will advise you of the value of the benefit and how much you can deduct. The IRS has issued new requirements as to what is needed to document these types of contributions beginning with 1994 donations. See discussion beginning on page 112.

Dues, fees, or assessments are deductible if you pay them to qualified organizations. However, you may deduct only the amount that is more than the value of the benefits you receive. You may not deduct dues, fees, or assessments paid to country clubs and other social organizations.

Athletic Tickets.   If you make a payment to or for the benefit of a college or university that would be deductible as a charitable contribution but for the fact that you receive (directly or indirectly) the right to purchase seating for a sporting event at the school's stadium, only 80% of your payment is treated as a charitable contribution. But there's a catch: the 80% limitation does not apply if you receive tickets or seating (rather than merely the right to purchase tickets) in return for the payment. In that case, the deduction must be reduced by the value attributable to the tickets.

Out-of-Pocket Expenses.   You may deduct certain amounts you pay in the course of providing volunteer services to a charitable organization. You may not, however, deduct the value of your time or services.

Car Expenses.   You may deduct unreimbursed out-of-pocket expenses, such as the cost of gas and oil, that are directly related to the use of your car in giving services to a charitable organization. You may not deduct any part of general repair and maintenance expenses, depreciation, or insurance.

If you do not want to deduct your actual expense, you may use a standard rate of 12 cents a mile to figure your contribution deduction of the use of your car in providing services to the charitable organization. You may deduct parking fees and tolls in addition to the standard mileage rate. However, depreciation and insurance are not deductible.

Travel Expenses.   You may deduct your transportation and other travel expenses while you are away from home performing services for a charitable organization. Deductible travel expenses include: air, rail, and bus transportation; out-of-pocket expenses for your car; parking fees and tolls; taxi fares and other costs of transportation between the airport or station and your hotel; lodging cost; and the cost of meals. Travel expenses are only deductible if there is no significant element of personal pleasure, recreation, or vacation in the travel.

When Deductible.   To deduct your contributions, you must make them in cash or other property before the close of your tax year. If you make a contribution with borrowed funds, a deduction is allowed in the year you make the contribution, regardless of when you repay the loan. Contributions charged on your credit or charge card are deductible in the year you make the charge, not when you pay the bill.

TaxOrganizer

The IRS has said informally that a volunteer's ordinary expense records combined with some substantiation from charities probably would suffice as substantiation for the deduction.

Gifts of properly endorsed stock certificates are deductible in the year you mail or personally deliver the certificates to the charity or to the charity's representative. However, if you give the certificates to your broker or the issuing corporation for transfer to the charity, a deduction is not allowed until the stock is transferred on the corporation's books. If you plan to give stock to a charity, plan far enough in advance to assure yourself of having the certificates. A note or a pledge to a charity is not deductible until it is paid.

TaxSaver

For most people, the simplest approach to gift-giving is to give an outright gift. Even then, proper planning can pay surprising dividends for you.

Consider your tax rates in planning charitable contributions. A $1,000 contribution reduces taxes by $150 for a taxpayer in the 15% bracket, $280 for a taxpayer in the 28% bracket, $310 for a taxpayer in the 31% tax bracket and so forth. The after-tax cost of a contribution decreases as tax rates increase. Thus, if you can control the timing of your charitable contributions, you should consider making larger contributions in years in which you are subject to high marginal tax rates.

Consider also when your contribution is made. A deductible contribution reduces the tax due April 15 of the year following the contribution. A contribution made on December 31 reduces the tax due by as much as the contribution made on the prior January 1, except you have the use of the money from January 2 to December 30. While it is not always practical to defer your giving until the last day of the year, when planning substantial gifts the time value of money should be considered.

Private Foundations

A private foundation is an entity which can be formed and controlled by you or your family to support your charitable activities or to make charitable grants according to your wishes. Once the foundation qualifies for tax-exempt status, your charitable contributions to it are deductible, subject to the limitations discussed later.

TaxSaver

You don't have to be inordinately rich to consider setting up your own private foundation. Private foundations afford you a good deal of flexibility in determining how your charitable contributions will be spent, may be controlled by a single individual or family, and provide some tax benefits, too. The foun-

dation has to be set up according to specific IRS rules and you will need professional advice.

*   **Example:** Suppose you want to commit to making a contribution of $20,000 a year to a charity for the next five years. Assuming you are in the 39.6% tax bracket and can realize an 8% rate of return on your investments, (1) you could contribute about $80,000 to your private foundation, which would make the payments in each of the five years, or (2) you could make these contributions out of your current income. Choosing the latter would cost you more because the tax savings would be spread out over the five-year period as the contributions were made. Your savings may be even greater if you fund the foundation with appreciated stock in December 1996 because you do not have to pay any tax on the unrealized capital gain. Otherwise deductible contributions of appreciated stock that exceeded the 20% of AGI limitation and are carried over to later years and will continue to be deductible—subject to that year's percentage limitation.*

TaxAlert

From December 31, 1994 to July 1, 1996, deductions for long-term capital gain property donated to a private nonoperating foundation are limited to your basis in the property. From July 1, 1996 through May 31, 1997, you can claim a deduction for the appreciated value of the stock—not just your basis.

TaxSaver

The tax benefits from creating a private foundation can also be achieved by contributing to a community trust. A community trust is a public charity in which you may establish a segregated account, thus avoiding the costs of setting up your own private foundation. However, because it is a public foundation, you will not have the same degree of control over the use of the contributed funds as you would with your own private foundation.

Nondeductible Contributions

Some organizations are not qualified to receive tax-deductible contributions. For example, contributions to the following organizations are not deductible:

- Chambers of commerce and other business leagues or organizations
- Civic leagues
- Communist organizations
- Country clubs and other social clubs
- Homeowners' associations
- Political organizations (and candidates)

Contributions used to influence legislation are not deductible. Even if an organization is a qualified organization, no deduction is allowed for contributions to the organization that are earmarked for use in, or in connection with, attempting to influence the general public on legislative matters, elections, or referenda.

Direct contributions to needy or worthy individuals are not deductible. The contributions must be made to, or for the use of, a qualified organization and not earmarked by you for the use of a specific person.

Gifts of Property

If you donate property to a qualified organization, you generally may deduct the fair market value of the property at the time of the contribution. However, if the property increased in value while you owned it, you may have to make some adjustments. (See Giving Property That Has Increased in Value, below.)

Determining Fair Market Value. Fair market value is the price at which property would change hands between a willing buyer and willing seller, neither having to buy or sell, and both having reasonable knowledge of all the necessary facts.

Used Items. The fair market value of used items is ordinarily far less than their original cost. You should claim as the value the price that buyers of used items actually pay in stores where such property is for sale, such as consignment or thrift shops. (See IRS Publication 561, *Determining the Value of Donated Property,* for further details.)

Giving Property That Has Increased in Value. As noted above, if you donated property to a qualified organization, you generally may deduct the fair market value of the property at the time of the contribution. The exception to this rule is when the property you donate has increased in value. In this case, the amount of the deduction is the fair market value of the property minus the amount that would have been ordinary income or short-term capital gain had the property been sold at its fair market value on the date of the gift. (Ordinary income property would include items such as inventory; any property held one year or less is short-term capital gain property.) The following are two examples of these rules.

Example: You donate stock that you held for five months to your church. The fair market value of the stock is $20,000, but you paid $16,000 (your basis). Because the $4,000 of appreciation would be a short-term capital gain if you sold the stock, your deduction is limited to $16,000 (fair market value less the appreciation).

Example: You donate 300 shares of stock to your local charitable hospital on December 15, 1995. The stock has a fair market value of $30,000 on the date of contribution. You acquired the stock in the following three transactions:

Date of Acquisition	Number of Shares	Total Cost
January 15, 1994	100	$5,500
December 1, 1994	100	7,000
January 15, 1995	100	8,500

Your deduction is $28,500. If the stock had been sold for $30,000 on the date of the contribution, the gain from the first two purchases would have been long-term capital gain. However, a sale of the third hundred shares would have generated $1,500 in short-term capital gain. This latter gain must be deducted from the $30,000 fair market value to arrive at the amount of your deduction.

TAXSAVER

If you donate appreciated securities that you have held for the required long-term holding period, you benefit in two ways. First, you are entitled to a deduction based on the fair market value of the securities. Second, you avoid paying tax on the appreciation. Consequently, the real cost to you of your contribution is reduced by the tax benefit of the contribution deduction you claim and the tax you avoided by not selling the appreciated property.

*   **Example:** You have adjusted gross income of $190,000 and are in the 36% tax bracket. If you give stock that cost you $20,000 but is now worth $50,000 directly to a public charity, your taxable income will be reduced by $50,000 and you will have a tax savings of about $18,000 (provided you are not subject to the alternative minimum tax). If you sell the stock first and give the proceeds to the charity, you will still have a $50,000 deduction, but you will also pay tax on the entire $30,000 of capital gain, probably at the maximum capital gain rate of 28%—$8,400. This will reduce your overall tax savings to $9,600 ($18,000 less $8,400). And this simple example does not take into account the fact that the additional capital gain income will increase your overall limit on itemized deductions (see page 53)—reducing your tax savings even more. Thus, the best approach in this example is to give the appreciated stock to charity. You get a $50,000 deduction and recognize no gain.*

*   On the other hand, if the property value has decreased below your cost, it usually is better to sell the property and donate the proceeds. By selling it you will realize a capital loss that may be used to offset other capital gains or—within limits—other income.*

TAXSAVER

To ensure that you get the maximum tax benefit from a contribution of appreciated property, be sure that the property qualifies for long-term capital gain treatment if sold.

Bargain Sales

A bargain sale of property to a qualified charitable organization—that is, a sale at less than the property's fair market value—is partly a charitable contribution and partly a sale. The part that is considered a charitable contribution is the difference between the fair market value at the time of sale and that amount realized. The part that is considered a sale is the amount realized. It may result in a taxable gain. To determine the amount of the gain, you must allocate your adjusted basis in the property between the part that is considered a charitable contribution and the part sold. The adjusted basis of the part sold is figured as follows:

$$\text{Adjusted basis of entire property} \times \frac{\text{Amount realized}}{\text{Fair market value of entire property}}$$

TAXSAVER

Suppose you want to make a $50,000 donation to a public charity but you have no cash. However, you have stock in a publicly traded corporation that cost you $30,000 a few years ago and is now worth $75,000. You plan to sell the stock on the open market for $75,000 (less, of course, transaction costs) and give $50,000 in cash to charity, but that would mean paying a tax on the $45,000 of long-term capital gain. Capital gains can be taxed at a rate up to 28%. In this situation, a bargain sale may help.

If you sell the stock to the charity for $25,000, you will provide it with a $50,000 benefit ($75,000 value − $25,000 cost = $50,000) and generate a $50,000 deductible charitable contribution for yourself. Because you have sold an asset, you do recognize some gain. However, under a special tax rule relating to bargain sales to charity (explained above), the gain realized on the $25,000 bargain sale price is $15,000—or $30,000 less than the taxable gain that would have resulted from your selling the stock and donating the cash. If the tax rate on your gain is at the top 28% capital gain rate, the tax attributable to the gain from the bargain sale ($4,200) would be much less than that of the outright sale ($12,600).

Limits on Deductions

If your total contributions for the year are 20% or less of your adjusted gross income, they are fully deductible (provided they otherwise qualify), and it is not necessary to figure whether the limits discussed below apply.

Partial Interest in Property. Generally, no deduction is allowed for a charitable contribution of less than your entire interest in property. For example, the owner of property will not get a deduction for giving a "life estate interest" in the property to charity. (A life estate interest is an interest in property that terminates upon the death of the life estate's owner.) A contribution of the right to use property is a contribution of less than your entire interest in that property and is not deductible.

Exceptions: There are some situations in which you may claim a deduction for a charitable contribution that is less than your entire interest in the property:
1. *Undivided part of your entire interest.* A contribution of an undivided part of your entire interest in property must consist of a part of each and every substantial interest or right you own in the property. It must extend over the entire term of your interest in the property.

2. *Remainder interest in a personal residence or farm.* You may take a charitable deduction for a gift to a qualified organization of a remainder interest in a personal residence or in a farm, if the gift is irrevocable. A remainder interest in an asset is an interest that takes effect after a specified period of time—often the lifetime of the person giving the interest.

TAX*SAVER*

If you give a remainder interest in a personal residence (or a farm) to a qualified charity, the present value of the remainder interest is deductible as a charitable contribution. One significant advantage of such a gift is that you suffer no loss of income or increase in expense from the gift, but you still gain a current income tax deduction. The gift may be made without the use of a trust. In addition, you continue to use and enjoy the home for life.

To qualify for the deduction, the gift must be a gift of your personal residence. The home does not have to be your principal residence. Thus, the gift may be your vacation home.

The charity receives no immediate benefit; however, the opportunity for future benefits can be substantial.

__Example:__ Assume a 62-year-old individual owns a personal residence with a fair market value of $162,000. The land on which the residence is located is valued at $42,000. The residence has a remaining useful life of 35 years and an estimated salvage value of $30,000. According to IRS tables, the value of the remainder interest in the home and the land (based on the donor's life expectancy) is approximately $40,000—which is currently deductible on a donation of the interest. Besides a substantial income tax deduction, the donor will receive an estate tax deduction for the value of the interest that passes to charity at his or her death.

3. *Interest transferred in trust.* A charitable deduction is available for the transfer of an income or remainder interest in property if the property is held in a qualifying charitable trust.

TAX*SAVER*

Say you may want to make a contribution to charity but you need all your income for current expenses. You have two alternatives. You can either leave the property to charity when you die or give the property to charity now, subject to a retained income interest. Deferred giving, as the latter technique is known, simply involves a present gift to charity of the future use and employment of property. It offers one big advantage: you can get an income tax deduction now. Deferred giving also allows you to satisfy your charitable goals now while continuing to receive needed income. Moreover, you may even be able to enhance your cash flow in retirement years. Following are some deferred giving techniques.

Charitable Remainder Trusts

You transfer cash or income-producing property into a charitable remainder trust. The trust provides that at least annual payments be made to you or any other designated beneficiary that is not a charity either over a term not exceeding 20 years or over the lifetime of the beneficiary or beneficiaries. When the term or lifetime interest ends, the charity will have full use of the entire property. Although actual receipt of the charity's interest is deferred, you receive an *immediate* income tax deduction for the present value of the interest that passes to charity. Later, the trust assets will be included in your taxable estate, but you will also receive an estate tax charitable deduction of an equal amount.

The lifetime gift or the charitable bequest must be in the form of a charitable remainder annuity trust, a charitable remainder unitrust, or a pooled income fund. See explanations below.

Charitable Remainder Annuity Trust. A charitable remainder annuity trust must pay the income beneficiary a fixed *dollar amount* of at least 5% of the initial value of the assets placed in the trust.

Charitable Remainder Unitrust. The charitable remainder unitrust, another type of remainder trust, differs from the annuity trust in that it must pay the income beneficiary a fixed *percentage* of the fair market value of the trust's assets, valued annually. Payments from a unitrust can be limited to trust income with any unpaid amounts carried over to future years, when the trust has sufficient income to pay its current and past obligations. Thus, a charitable remainder unitrust may also be used as a retirement planning vehicle.

Example: Suppose a 55-year-old donor who intends to work for 10 more years transfers $100,000 of appreciated stock to a trust in exchange for annual payments for life equal to 7% of the trust's value. The donor would receive an immediate contribution deduction of about $24,000, the present value of the interest passing to charity. The trust could sell the stock tax-free and invest the proceeds to maximize growth. After 10 years of minimal or zero payout, the trust reinvests its assets to maximize its yield. Payments to the donor could be made of the entire income of the trust until the trust has made up for the 10 years of missed payments. As an added benefit, the donor who, say, is in the 36% income tax bracket could take the $8,640 (36% $\times$ $24,000) of tax savings from the deduction and purchase life insurance that would be owned by and payable to his or her children. The insurance proceeds paid to the children would partially replace the stock transferred to the trust and, with appropriate planning, would not be taxed in the parent's estate.

Pooled Income Fund. A pooled income fund is a large trust maintained by a charity to which you may donate the remainder interest in property while retaining an income interest for the rest of your life. The amount of income you receive depends on the fund's rate of return. The tax consequences are similar to those for charitable remainder unitrusts.

TAXSAVER

The advantages of using a charitable remainder unitrust (CRUT): The table compares the sale of $300,000 of stock ($50,000 basis) with the transfer of stock to two different 20-year unitrusts—one with a 6% payout rate and the other with a 12% payout rate. The table assumes an 8% pretax total return on the reinvestment of the stock sale proceeds, a 36% combined marginal tax rate on current income, and a 33% combined tax rate on capital gains. For comparison, the table assumes that the after-tax portion of the unitrust distributions are reinvested to achieve the same 8% pretax total return earned without a CRUT.

	No CRUT	20-Year CRUT 6% Payout	20-Year CRUT 12% Payout
Current Value of Stock	$300,000	$300,000	$300,000
Tax Basis	50,000	50,000	50,000
Capital Gains Reportable	$250,000	—0—	—0—
Capital Gains Tax	82,500	—0—	—0—
Remaining to Invest	$217,500	$300,000	$300,000
Present Value of Charitable Remainder (Tax Deduction)[1]	—	87,032	23,269
Tax Benefit of Deduction	—	31,331	8,377
Net Assets Received by Beneficiary After 20 Years[2]	590,765	553,406	613,582
Future Value of Charity's Interest at End of Trust Term	—	406,560	106,010
Combined Value Received by Donor and Charity	$590,765	$959,965	$722,592

1. *Assumes an IRS interest rate of 7.2 percent, and annual trust payments made at year-end.*
2. *The CRUT scenarios incorporate tax savings from the charitable deduction and assume the entire amount is deductible without carryover.*

The Charitable Lead Trust. A charitable lead trust is somewhat the mirror image of a charitable remainder trust. If you set up a charitable lead trust, the charity gets the *income* or *lead* interest, and the remainder interest returns to you or passes to beneficiaries of your choice.

If the remainder interest reverts to you, you may claim a current charitable income tax deduction equal to the present value of the income stream. However, the trust income will be included in your income as the charity receives it, and the remainder will be included in your estate. If the remainder interest passes to beneficiaries other than a charity, there may be no up-front charitable deduction, but usually (1) the income will not be included in your taxable income and (2) the remainder will not be included in your estate.

Future Interest in Tangible Personal Property. You may deduct the value of a charitable contribution of a future interest in tangible personal property only after all intervening interests and rights to the actual possession or enjoyment of the property have either expired or been turned over to someone other than yourself or a related party or organization.

A future interest is any interest that is to begin at some future time, regardless of whether it is designated as a future interest under state law. The amount of the deduction is the value of the future interest when you and a related person no longer have an interest in the tangible personal property. When these interests end, you may still claim the deduction even if there are other outstanding interests that must end before the future interest is realized by the qualified charitable organization.

Example: You transferred a sculpture in 1995 to your son to use and enjoy for life. When your son dies the sculpture will go to the local museum of art. If your son irrevocably transfers his life interest to a local college or any other unrelated person in a later year, you may take a charitable deduction in that year, but not sooner. The amount of your deduction is the value of the future interest in the sculpture at the time of the transfer to the unrelated person.

When Contributions Are More Than 20% of Your Income. If your contributions are more than 20% of your adjusted gross income, the amount of your deduction may be limited to 20%, 30%, or 50% of your adjusted gross income.

How much you can deduct depends on three main factors: the type of the charity to which the contribution is given—a public charity or a nonoperating private foundation; the nature of the contribution—cash or property; and the manner of the contribution—to the charity or for the use of the charity. Sometimes the use to which the property will be put also needs to be considered. In addition to the percentage limitation, ordering rules apply. These may limit deductions if multiple contributions are made during the year. You should consult with your tax advisor.

Carryovers

You may carry over your contributions that cannot be deducted in the current year because they exceeded your adjusted gross income limit. You may deduct the excess in each of the next five years until it is used up, but not beyond that time. Contributions limited in the original contribution year will be subject to the same limitation in the carryover years. Excess contributions cannot be carried back and deducted in previous tax years.

TaxSaver

If a gift of long-term capital gain property subject to the 30% limitation is made and, for some unforeseen reason, cannot be used entirely in the current year or in carryover years, you may elect to reduce its value by 100% of the gain and deduct the lower basis on the gift under the 50% limitation.

*   **Example:** John Walsh makes a contribution of long-term capital gain property that cost him $40,000 and now has a fair market value of $50,000. John dies during the taxable year. His adjusted gross income on his final return is $80,000.*

*   Without the election (mentioned above), John's deduction would be limited to $24,000 (30% × $80,000). However, if the value of the property is reduced by $10,000 (the appreciation in the value of the property), the deduction is subject to the 50% limit (50% × $80,000) and is increased to $40,000, his basis in the property.*

TAXSAVER

If you anticipate a decline in your future adjusted gross income and you are subject to the 30% limitation for long-term capital gain property, you may want to consider electing to deduct the property's basis rather than its fair market value.

Record-Keeping and How to Report Charitable Contributions

You are required to keep records to prove the amount of the cash and noncash contributions you make during the year. The kind of records you must keep depends on the amount of your contributions and whether they are cash or noncash contributions.

Cash Contributions

Cash Contributions of Less Than $250. For each cash charitable contribution that is less than $250, you must keep one of the following:
1. A canceled check,
2. A receipt (or a letter or other written acknowledgment) from the charitable organization showing the name of the organization, the date of the contribution, and the amount of the contribution, or
3. Other reliable written records that include the information described in (2). Records may be considered reliable if you keep contemporaneous records, or if, in the case of small donations, you have items such as buttons, tokens, or emblems that have been given to contributors.

Cash Contributions of $250 or More. You must obtain a contemporaneous written acknowledgment from any charitable organization to which a contribution of $250 or more is made in order to deduct that contribution. A canceled check no longer constitutes substantiation for a contribution of money. You must obtain the written acknowledgment on or before the earlier of the date on which your return is actually filed or the due date for the return, including extensions.

The written acknowledgment must contain the following:

1. The amount of cash contributed;
2. Whether the charitable organization provided any goods or services in consideration, in whole or in part, for the contribution; and,
3. A description and good faith estimate of the value of goods or services provided by the charity.

If the goods or services provided as consideration for the contribution consist solely of *intangible religious benefits,* a statement to that effect must be included in the written acknowledgment.

The IRS has not yet indicated whether or not matching contributions made by a third party—say, an employer-sponsored match of an employee's contribution to a university—will count toward the $250 threshold.

You are not required to obtain substantiation for a donation if the charitable organization files a return with the IRS which includes the same information otherwise required from the taxpayer. However, the primary responsibility for requesting and maintaining the required substantiation rests with you, not the charitable organization.

Payroll Deduction Contributions. The IRS allows taxpayers who make contributions to charities through deductions from their paychecks some relief from the strict substantiation requirements for other cash contributions. You may substantiate payroll deduction contributions by a combination of:

(a) A paycheck stub, W-2, or other document from your employer showing the amount withheld from your wages; and
(b) A pledge card or other document from the charity stating that it doesn't provide goods or services in exchange for your contribution.

This substantiation requirement only applies to contributions in excess of $250 withheld from a single paycheck.

Contributions to Charity Dinners, etc.

For any contribution over $75 for which the charity provides goods or services (such as a charity dinner), the charity must provide a statement to the donor that reports the estimated value of the goods or services received by the donor in exchange for the contribution. As under prior law, a payment to a charity is deductible only to the extent that it exceeds the value of any goods or services received in return.

TaxSaver

Raffle Tickets or Door Prizes. *If you purchase a ticket to a fundraising dinner, generally you can deduct the cost of the ticket which exceeds the value of the meal and any entertainment you receive at the event. However, if you are also given the chance to win a prize (say, a trip or car), the IRS will not allow you to deduct any portion of the purchase price of the ticket. If* *you decline to participate in the raffle by notifying the charity that you do not want to participate, you should be able to deduct the purchase price of the ticket less any value of the dinner and entertainment.*

Noncash Contributions

For a contribution not made in cash, the records you must keep depend on whether your deduction for the contribution is:
1. Less than $250,
2. At least $250 but not more than $500,
3. Over $500 but not more than $5,000,
4. Over $5,000.

Deductions of Less Than $250. If you make any noncash contribution, you must get and keep a receipt from the charitable organization showing:
1. The name of the charitable organization,
2. The date and location of the charitable contribution, and
3. A reasonably detailed description of the property.

A letter or other written communication from the charitable organization acknowledging receipt of the contribution and containing the information in (1), (2), and (3) will serve as a receipt.

You are not required to have a receipt where it is impractical to get one (for example, if you leave property at a charity's unattended drop site).

Deductions of At Least $250 But Not More Than $500. If you claim a deduction of at least $250 but not more than $500 for a noncash charitable contribution, you must get and keep an acknowledgment of your contribution from the qualified organization. This acknowledgment must contain the information in items (1) through (3) listed under *Deductions of Less Than $250,* above.

The acknowledgment must also meet these tests:
1. It must be written;
2. It must include:
    (a) An indication as to whether the qualified organization gave you any goods or services (other than token items of little value) in return for your contribution, and
    (b) A description and good faith estimate of the value of any goods or services described in (a);
3. You must get it on or before the earlier of the due date, including extensions, for filing the return, or the date you file your return for the year you make the contribution.

Deductions Over $500 But Not More Than $5,000. In addition to the substantiation requirements listed above under *Deductions of at Least $250 But Not More Than $500,* Form 8283 must be attached to your return if total noncash charitable contributions exceed $500. This form must contain the following information:
- Name and address of the organization receiving the gift;

- A description of the property contributed;
- The date of the contribution;
- The date the property was acquired;
- How you acquired the property (e.g., gift, purchase); and
- Fair market value of the property and the method used to determine such value.

Deductions Over $5,000. The substantiation requirements listed earlier under *Deductions Over $500 But Not More Than $5,000* also apply to deductions in excess of $5,000. In addition, individuals are required to obtain independent qualified appraisals for donations of noncash property if the claimed value of the property exceeds $5,000 or if the claimed value of all similar items donated to one or more charitable organizations exceeds $5,000. Nonpublicly traded securities must be appraised if they are valued at over $10,000. Publicly traded securities are not subject to this requirement.

7

Capital Gains
and Losses

INTRODUCTION

If you are looking for a tax break, generating capital gains could be one of your biggest opportunities. The top tax rate applicable to long-term capital gains is 28% while the rate applicable to ordinary income can go up to 39.6%. That's an 11.6% difference. If you can generate net capital gains, instead of ordinary income, you will save considerably on your taxes. Also, with capital assets you usually have the flexibility to control when you recognize the income or loss, because in most cases you determine when to sell your assets.

HOW CAPITAL GAINS ARE TAXED

Generally, capital gains are taxable, whether the underlying asset is held as an investment or for personal purposes. On the other hand, capital losses are only deductible if the assets were held for investment purposes. Consequently, if you sell your personal residence for a gain, the gain will be considered a capital gain. However, if you sell your residence at a loss, you will not be able to deduct the amount of the loss.

If you incur losses from the sale of investment assets, you can deduct those losses to the extent they equal your capital gains. But if your losses exceed your capital gains, you can only deduct up to $3,000 of those losses in a given tax year against ordinary income. Any excess will be carried over until it can be offset against future capital gains or be deducted as a loss against your ordinary income up to $3,000 a year. (See Deducting Capital Losses on page 116 for more details.)

TAXSAVER

Generally it is preferable to defer gains and accelerate losses for the simple reason that the later the taxes are paid, the longer you have the use of the money. In addition, when you recognize a gain or loss it can also affect the tax benefits of your itemized deductions and exemptions. That's because capital gains and losses are included in figuring your adjusted gross income. Therefore, your capital gains and losses affect the calculation of your itemized deductions and personal exemptions which are phased out after your income reaches a certain level. Further, miscellaneous itemized deductions are deductible only to the extent that they exceed 2% of your adjusted gross income. Medical expenses are deductible only to the extent that they exceed 7.5% of your adjusted gross income. Capital gains income therefore also has an impact on both of these calculations. Depending on your itemized deductions, the time at which you recognize a capital gain or loss can have a significant impact on your taxes.

Defining a Capital Asset

For the most part, everything you own and hold for personal or investment purposes is a capital asset. Examples of capital assets include stocks and bonds, your house or other residence, household furnishings, automobiles and boats, jewelry, and gold, silver, or other metals. Capital assets do not include inventory; notes and accounts receivable acquired in the ordinary course of a business for services rendered or from the sale of inventory; or, in certain cases, copyrights or literary, musical, or other artistic compositions. Letters and memorandums prepared by or for you also are not classified as capital assets. Gains on sales of certain assets used in a trade or business are taxed at capital gains rates; however, you may have to pay ordinary income tax rates on a portion of the gain resulting from the sale of such property.

Capital Gains Tax Rates

The top tax rate on net capital gains is 28%. The 39.6% tax rate for individuals does not apply to net capital gains—that is, the net long-term capital gain for the year over the net short-term capital loss for the year. A long-term capital gain or loss results from the sale of an asset held for over one year. Sales of assets held one year or less produce a short-term capital gain or loss.

TaxSaver

If you are a high-income individual, the different tax rates for capital gains and ordinary income may encourage you to favor certain investments geared toward appreciation. Capital gains are taxed at a maximum rate of 28%; current interest and dividends generated by investments are taxed at ordinary income rates as high as 39.6%.

Calculating a Gain or Loss

You calculate the gain or loss on a sale or trade of property by comparing the amount you realize with the adjusted basis of the property. The adjusted basis of a property is your original cost or other basis, such as "carryover basis" if the property was acquired by gift, or a "stepped-up" basis, if the property was acquired by inheritance—properly increased or decreased for items such as purchase commissions, legal fees, capital improvements, and depreciation. "Carryover basis" is the basis of the donor whereas "stepped-up basis" generally is the fair market value of the property on the date the person from whom the property was inherited died. The amount you realize from a sale or trade is the total of all money you receive, plus the fair market value of all property or services you receive. An indebtedness against the property, or against you, such as a mortgage, that is paid off as a part of the transaction or that is assumed by the buyer must be included in the amount realized.

Deducting Capital Losses

Capital losses are deductible to the extent that they do not exceed certain limitations. If your capital losses are more than your capital gains, up to $3,000 ($1,500 if you are married and file a separate return) of losses may be deducted provided your taxable income is at least equivalent to the amount of the deduction.

Example: You have capital gains and losses for the year as follows:

	Short-Term	Long-Term
Gains	$700	$ 400
Losses	800	2,000

Your deductible capital loss is $1,700, calculated as follows:

Short-term capital losses	$800	
Minus: Short-term capital gains	700	
Net short-term capital loss		$100
Long-term capital losses	$2,000	
Minus: Long-term capital gains	400	
Net long-term capital loss		$1,600
Deductible capital loss		$1,700

Your deduction in this example (assuming you are not married, filing a separate return) is limited to this $1,700 or your taxable income, whichever is smaller.

Carrying Forward Capital Losses

If your capital loss is more than the yearly limit, you may carry over the unused part to the next tax year and treat it as if it occurred in that year.

A net loss may be carried forward until it is exhausted or until you die. This carryforward may be used to reduce your tax when you have a capital gain in the future. If you do not have future capital gains, you may nonetheless use the carryforward loss to offset taxable income up to $3,000 per year.

TAX*SAVER*

You may save taxes by carefully planning major sales and exchanges. It may be better to wait until after the end of the year before finalizing a sale so that a gain may be deferred until the next year or so that more losses may be realized in the current year. Remember, too, capital gains increase your adjusted gross income (AGI). If your AGI is above $117,950 (on a joint return), a portion of your itemized deductions will not be allowed. Furthermore, if your AGI is above $176,950 (on a joint return), your personal exemptions are decreased.

Worthless Securities. Stocks, stock rights, and corporate or government bonds with interest coupons or in registered form, which became worthless during the tax year, are treated as though they were capital assets sold on the last day of the tax year if they were capital assets in your hands. To determine whether they are long-term or short-term capital assets, you are considered to have held the stocks or securities until the last day of the year in which they became worthless.

TAX*SAVER*

The deduction for a worthless security must be taken in the year in which it becomes worthless, even if it is sold for a nominal sum in the following year. If you do not learn that a security has become worthless until a later year, you should file an amended return for the year in which it became worthless. Since it may be difficult to determine exactly when a stock becomes worthless, the capital loss deduction should be claimed in the earliest year in which such a claim may be reasonably made.

TAX*ORGANIZER*

You should keep any documents indicating the date on which the security becomes worthless. Examples of sufficient documentation are bankruptcy documents and financial statements.

Qualified Small Business Stock. An individual taxpayer who holds *qualified small business stock* (QSBS) for more than five years can exclude from gross income 50% of any gain realized from the sale or exchange of the stock. The rules for determining whether stock is "qualified small business stock" are summarized on page 120.

Strategies for Individuals Selling Securities

Specify Shares to be Sold

If your broker holds your securities that you purchased at different prices and dates, you must tell him or her which shares you are going to sell. If you don't, the shares you purchased first generally will be considered the shares sold. This rule can result in a different gain or loss than you intended. See Chapter 11, Investment Planning, for further discussion.

> **TaxSaver**
>
> *If you have excess gains over losses, you should sell property on which you have losses to offset your gains and eliminate the tax on them.*
>
> *If you have already realized more than $3,000 of capital losses over and above your realized capital gains, and you want to sell an appreciated asset that you think has gone up as far as it will go, sell that asset and use your accumulated losses to offset the gain.*

Selling Shares in Mutual Funds.   See Chapter 8.

Put Options

Acquiring a put option means buying an option contract to sell 100 shares of stock at a set price (the "strike price") during a specific time period. Put options can be used as a means of protecting and deferring your capital gain. While deferring a sale to a subsequent year, put options protect against a decline in value.

> **TaxSaver**
>
> *Investors who own appreciated securities that they are not yet ready to sell because of tax reasons can buy put options as a way of protecting their gains against possible price declines. If the price of the stock goes above the strike price, you get the benefit of the increased price less the cost of the put, which you let expire. If the stock price declines, you may either sell your shares at the strike price or sell the put option separately. Either way, the sale and your capital gain have been deferred to next year. However, the premium you pay for the option contract must be factored into your consideration for using this planning technique.*

Selling Short Against the Box

Selling short is not a hedge but rather a bet that the security price will drop. Selling short against the box means selling borrowed securities while owning substantially identical securities that you later deliver to close the short sale. That allows you to lock in a profit while delaying the recognition of a gain. Many investors with unrealized profits may want to consider a short sale against the box to postpone recognizing a gain until a later tax year.

Wash Sales

Suppose your objective is to take a tax loss this year while preserving your investment position. It can be done as long as you don't run afoul of the wash sale rule. A wash sale occurs when you sell stock or securities and within 30 days before or after the sale you buy, acquire in a taxable exchange, or acquire a contract or option to buy substantially the same stock or security. To the extent that the same number of stocks or securities sold are replaced in a wash sale, the loss will not be recognized for tax purposes.

TAXSAVER

The easiest way to maintain your investment position in a security, recognize a loss, and avoid the wash sale rule is to buy identical securities 31 days before or after you sell your old securities at a loss. Another possibility is to reinvest in a similar security that would not be considered "substantially identical" and therefore would not violate the wash rule. For example, if you sold your investment in a mutual fund that invests in bonds, you could reinvest in another fund that owned bonds of a similar grade and yield.

Installment Sales

You can defer recognition of a gain from the current year by structuring the sale of the investments on an installment basis. In an installment sale, only part of your gain will be recognized at the time of the sale. The rest of the gain will be recognized as subsequent installments are received. Such sales need to be carefully evaluated. Stock or securities traded on established markets cannot be reported for tax purposes on an installment basis.

Like-Kind Exchanges

Generally, the tax on the gain from any real estate held for investment or business reasons can be deferred if the property is traded for similar real estate. However, if you received "boot" (that is, cash or unlike property) in addition to the like-kind property, you may have to recognize a gain up to the value of the money or unlike property received. The rules for like-kind exchanges are complicated, and you should consult with your tax advisor in order to properly structure this transaction.

OTHER OPPORTUNITIES FOR INDIVIDUALS

Qualified Small Business Stock

An individual taxpayer who holds qualified small business stock (QSBS) for more than five years can exclude from gross income 50% of any gain realized from the sale or exchange of the stock. This exclusion is limited to the greater of:

1. 10 times the taxpayer's basis in the stock; or
2. $10 million in gain from all of the taxpayer's transactions in stock of that corporation (held for more than five years).

These rules apply to stock issued after August 10, 1993.

The rules for determining whether stock is "qualified small business stock" can be summarized as follows:

- The stock must be newly issued stock.
- The stock cannot be acquired in exchange for other stock.
- The issuing corporation must be a "C" corporation (i.e., not an "S" corporation that passes its income and losses directly on to the shareholders), but may not be a cooperative, Domestic International Sales Corporation (DISC), former DISC, Foreign Sales Corporation (FSC), Real Estate Investment Trust (REIT), Regulated Investment Company (RIC), Real Estate Mortgage Investment Conduit (REMIC), a corporation having a possessions tax credit election in effect, or a corporation owning a subsidiary who has a possessions tax credit election in effect.
- At least 80% of the corporation's assets must be used in the active conduct of a *qualified trade or business,* or in the start-up of a future *qualified trade or business.*
- A qualified trade or business is any business other than one involving the performance of services in the fields of health, law, engineering, architecture, accounting, actuarial science, performing arts, consulting, athletics, financial services, brokerage services, or any other trade or business where the principal asset of the business is the reputation or skill of one or more employees. A qualified trade or business also cannot involve the businesses of banking, insurance, financing, leasing, investing, or similar businesses, farming, or certain businesses involving natural resource extraction or production, and businesses operating a hotel, motel, restaurant, or similar business.
- The corporation may not have greater than $50 million in gross assets (i.e., sum of cash plus the aggregate fair market value of other corporate property) at the time the qualified small business stock is issued. If the corporation meets this test at the time of issuance of the stock, a subsequent event that violates this rule will not disqualify stock that previously qualified.

Rolling Gain Over into a Specialized Small Business Investment Company

Under certain circumstances, gain on the sale of publicly traded securities will not be taxed if the proceeds from the sale are used to acquire common stock in a specialized small business investment company (SSBIC) within a 60-day period.

Special Treatment for Lump-Sum Distributions

If you were at least age 50 on January 1, 1986, you may be able to elect to treat a portion of the taxable part of a lump-sum distribution as a long-term capital gain taxable at a 20% rate. This treatment applies to the portion you receive relating to your participation in the qualified plan before 1974. Capital gains treatment is not available for lump-sum distributions received after 1991 by individuals who were less than 50 years old on January 1, 1986.

Donating Appreciated Assets

When making a charitable contribution, it may be tax-wise to donate appreciated marketable securities instead of cash. You may be able to avoid the capital gains tax on the property, and the charity generally sells the stock or securities, receiving cash but not paying any tax due to their tax-exempt status. If you want the stock or securities you donated in your portfolio, then take the cash you were originally planning to give to charity and repurchase the identical investment. Your investment now has a new, increased cost basis.

If you plan to make a charitable contribution of an investment asset, follow these two rules:

Rule 1

If you have appreciated property that you have held for more than a year, donate it—don't sell it and donate the cash. The following example explains why.

Example: Let's assume that you are going to donate $30,000 to your favorite charity. You have stock that you bought for $6,000 several years ago; it now has a market value of $30,000.

If you give the stock directly to the charity you don't report any capital gain and you can deduct $30,000 as a charitable contribution. Assuming you are in the 39.6% tax bracket, the charitable contribution would reduce your taxes by $11,880.

Here's what happens when you sell the stock and give the proceeds to charity. First, you have a gain of $24,000 on which you pay a 28% capital gains tax of $6,720. You would, however, be able to claim a charitable contribution deduction of $30,000 that would normally reduce your taxes by $11,880, assuming you were in the 39.6% tax bracket. Adding the taxes you pay on the gain to the taxes you save from the deduction, your net tax benefit is $5,160.

Rule 2

If you have property that has depreciated in value, sell it and give cash— don't donate the property directly. Here's why.

Example: Let's suppose that you own stock that cost $33,000 a few years ago. The stock is currently worth $30,000. If you donate it to a charity, you will get a deduction of $30,000, its fair market value. If you sell it you will have $30,000 in cash. You can give the cash to a charity and claim a charitable deduction. You will also have a capital loss on the sale of your stock of $3,000. The capital loss is also deductible.

Stock Options

The wide gap between the top tax rates on ordinary income and capital gains (11.6%) is likely to enhance the attractiveness of incentive stock options (ISOs) to executives compared to nonqualified stock options (NSOs). ISOs generally do not trigger taxable income until the stock received from exercising the option is sold. Exercising an ISO does, however, result in income for alternative minimum tax purposes and, therefore, may trigger the alternative minimum tax (see discussion on page 145). Careful planning should be undertaken in this regard. Further, if ISO stock is sold at least one year after the date of exercise and two years following the date the ISO was granted, the difference between the sale price and exercise price is taxed as a long-term capital gain at the 28% rate. By contrast, the recipient of an NSO generally will recognize ordinary income when the NSO is exercised, which could be taxed at a rate of as much as 39.6%. See Chapter 1 for more about stock options as an employee benefit.

Concerns Regarding Community Property

Community property is most often property acquired by spouses while they are married and domiciled in a community property state. But not *all* property acquired during the marriage is community property. If one spouse individually receives a gift or inheritance, it is not community property but rather is "separate property" owned solely by the recipient. Property acquired or otherwise owned by each spouse prior to marriage is also considered separate property.

Community property and marital property are treated differently from noncommunity property when someone dies. In a noncommunity property state, the basis of the decedent's property is increased or decreased for tax purposes to fair market value as of the date of the decedent's death. However, when one spouse in a community property state dies, the basis of *both* spouses' interest in *every* piece of community property is stepped up or down, that is, increased or decreased to the fair market value at date of death.

8

Mutual Funds

INTRODUCTION

Currently, Americans have over $3 trillion invested in mutual funds, making them the most popular investment vehicle in the country. There are now more mutual funds than there are companies on the New York Stock Exchange. They come in all shapes and sizes but share a common purpose. All mutual funds receive money from many investors, pool the funds, and use them to purchase investments that the funds' professional investment managers select. Since the investor owns shares in the investment company—mutual funds are technically known as open end *regulated investment companies*—he or she indirectly owns a share of its investments.

Generally mutual funds are classified according to their investment objectives. Aggressive growth funds, for example, are characterized by high risk and high return. These funds typically seek capital appreciation and do not produce significant interest income or dividends. The objectives of balanced funds, on the other hand, are to conserve investors' initial principal, pay high current income through dividends and interest, and promote the long-term growth of both principal and income. While aggressive growth funds generally invest only in stocks, balanced funds typically invest in both bonds and stocks. There are many other kinds of mutual funds—growth and income funds, bond funds, sector funds, index funds, etc.—all with differing investing objectives and different strategies to achieve them. A general rule to keep in mind: the higher the potential reward from your investment, the greater the risk that you may not achieve the expected return.

Which mutual fund or funds you choose will depend largely upon your own investment objectives. But, one factor you should definitely consider is how your mutual fund investment will be taxed. Generally a mutual fund is a conduit for tax purposes—that is, the fund does not ordinarily pay income taxes, but its shareholders do. Gains are generally passed through to shareholders in a fund in the form of dividends and capital gains distributions. As a shareholder, you are liable for any taxes due on these distributions. Consequently, it can matter enormously how those gains are taxed.

Dividend distributions from a mutual fund, such as distribution of interest or dividends earned from the fund's investment securities, are generally considered ordinary income for tax purposes. Ordinary dividend distributions also can include any net short-term capital gains—short-term capital gains minus short-term losses—realized by the fund when it sells securities. A capital gains distribution from a fund represents net long-term capital gains realized by the fund. While a fund may also realize net long-term losses from the sale of securities, it is not permitted to "pass through" these losses to shareholders. Instead, the fund must carry net capital losses forward to offset any future capital gains. Generally, all dividend and capital gains distributions from a fund are subject to federal and state income taxes. Dividends from municipal bond or municipal money market funds are one exception. These dividends are usually exempt from federal income tax and may also be exempt from state and local income taxes, depending upon where you live and your state's tax law. A second exception is dividends derived from interest earned by the fund on U.S. Government Bonds. These dividends are exempt from state but not federal tax.

This chapter explains in detail how different distributions from mutual funds are taxed, as well as the different methods by which you may calculate your gain or loss upon the sale of your shares in a mutual fund. It also discusses some of the expenses you may incur when investing in mutual funds.

DIVIDENDS

A distribution by a mutual fund of money or property to you generally will qualify as an ordinary income dividend. These dividends must be reported on your Form 1040. The mutual fund making the distribution will send you a Form 1099-DIV indicating how much dividend income you have received.

Dividends Declared One Year but not Paid Until the Next. Often a mutual fund will declare a dividend at the end of the calendar year but not pay it until January of the following year. Nevertheless, you are treated as having received the dividend in the year in which it was declared. This rule is unique to mutual funds dividends. It does not apply to regular corporate dividends which are taxable to cash basis taxpayers in the year in which the dividends are received.

TAXSAVER

You should pay close attention to the timing of your purchase of a mutual fund. For example, if you invest in a fund near the end of the year and the fund shortly thereafter makes a year-end distribution, you will have to pay tax on the distribution even though from your point of view you are simply getting back the capital you just invested in the fund. In effect, all you've done is "bought" taxable income that the fund earned earlier in the year but had not yet paid out to shareholders. Typically, the fund's share price drops by the amount of the distribution. Your cost basis in the mutual fund however, will be the pre-distribution price you paid for the shares.

There is one consolation. Your higher basis will reduce any capital gain on a later sale. However, if you sell the fund at a loss, it will increase your capital loss. If you want to limit your tax liability and lower your basis in the shares, you should delay your purchase of fund shares until after the record date for the distribution. Usually a fund can tell you when distributions, if any, for the year are expected. Alternatively, you can consult investment publications, which indicate distribution dates for the previous year.

Example: ABC Fund declares and distributes a $1 dividend on December 1. If you had purchased 1,000 shares at $10 per share on November 30, you will have to report $1,000 of income for 1995. If instead you bought the shares on December 2, after the record date, you will pay $9 per share and have no taxable income to report. Of course, for the shares bought on November 30, your basis would be $10 per share instead of $9.

TAX SAVER

If you are thinking of selling shares in a mutual fund, particularly near the end of the year when many funds pay dividends, you should consider redeeming your shares before any upcoming dividend payments are made by the fund. If your shares are worth more than you paid, you can take a capital gain on the redemption and avoid paying the higher tax rate on ordinary income that you would pay on an ordinary dividend. If your shares are worth less than you paid for them, you can minimize your capital losses by selling before the dividend. Remember, the net asset value per share of the fund (that is, the amount you would receive on the redemption of your shares) decreases by the amount of the dividend.

Some dividends may be treated as a tax-free return of capital. This occurs when the mutual fund does not have enough current or accumulated earnings and profits to cover the distribution. In this situation, the distribution is considered to be a "return of capital" (the amount you originally invested) and is nontaxable to the extent of the basis in your shares. (Your basis is generally the price at which you bought the shares plus or minus any adjustments.) This amount will be shown in Box 1d of Form 1099-DIV. Although the distribution is tax-free, it will reduce your basis in the mutual fund shares. To the extent that the distribution is greater than your basis in your shares, you will be treated as having a gain from the sale or exchange of the shares. This gain must be reported on Schedule D (Form 1040).

Tax-Exempt Interest Dividends

Funds that invest in municipal bonds may pay dividends which are exempt from federal taxes. In order for such dividends to qualify for tax-free status, the fund must invest at least 50 percent of the value of its assets in tax-exempt municipal bonds at the end of each quarter. If you invest in such a fund and receive tax-exempt income, you must report such amounts on your tax return even though you do not need to include such amounts in income. The fund will send you a statement within 60 days of the close of the year indicating whether you have received such tax-exempt interest income. These amounts will not appear on your Form 1099-DIV.

Reinvestment of Dividends

Many mutual funds offer dividend reinvestment plans in which you may use your dividends to buy more shares of stock in the mutual fund instead of receiving the dividends in cash. If you reinvest your dividends, you still must report the dividends. Whether you include the reinvested dividends in income depends on the nature of the dividend. For example, if you reinvest your tax-exempt dividends, you do not have to include them in income. For further information, see Chapter 11, Investment Planning.

TaxOrganizer

If you participate in a dividend reinvestment plan, you should keep a record of the dividends and of the shares purchased with the reinvestment. The reinvested dividends are part of your cost basis for the shares. You will need these records to figure your cost basis when you sell all or some of your shares.

Capital Gains Distributions

Mutual funds may make capital gains distributions from their net realized long-term capital gains. Even funds that invest in municipal bonds may make taxable capital gain distributions. No matter how long a time—or more to the point, how short a time—you may have owned shares in the mutual fund making the distribution, these distributions will be treated as long-term capital gains and taxed at the preferential long-term capital gains rates. In addition, these long-term capital gains may be offset by unrelated capital losses you may have. Form 1099-DIV will indicate the amount of the long-term capital gain you must include in your income.

TaxSaver

Before you invest in a mutual fund, you should consider the rate at which the fund turns over its assets. A fund with a high turnover rate will generate frequent gains and losses, increasing the chances that capital distributions will be short-term, rather than long-term. Short-term capital gain distributions are taxed as ordinary income dividends; long-term capital gains are eligible for the lower long-term capital gain rate.

In addition to the amounts you receive from a fund, you must report and include in your income any amounts that the mutual fund credited to you from its undistributed capital gains, even though you did not actually receive such amounts. Undistributed capital gains are taxed at the corporate tax rate of 35 percent. The mutual fund will pay the capital gains tax, and those taxes may then be claimed by you as a credit on your return.

TAX*ORGANIZER*

A mutual fund will report the amount of undistributed capital gains to you on Form 2439, not on Form 1099-DIV.

A special rule exists for capital gain distributions you receive when you sell your shares in the fund at a loss within six months from the date of original purchase. In this case, the portion of your capital loss attributable to the capital gain dividend is treated as a long-term—not a short-term—capital loss.

TAX*SAVER*

Potential Capital Gains Exposure. *One of the most revealing indicators of a mutual fund's future tax liability is its potential capital gains exposure. It tells the percentage of a fund's total assets that is made up of unrealized capital gains. These gains represent the growth in the securities in the fund's portfolio which will be distributed and taxed to future shareholders. Such gains are not taxable until the fund sells the appreciated securities and distributes net capital gains to shareholders. When all else is equal, a higher level of potential capital gains exposure means that owning the fund could result in a higher tax bill down the road.*

On the flip side, a fund with negative capital gains exposure gives new shareholders the potential for turbocharged returns. These funds have accumulated net capital losses prior to new shareholder ownership. Unlike net capital gains, these cannot be distributed to shareholders. Instead, the losses can be used to offset future gains realized by the fund.

As a result, the cost basis inside a fund with negative capital gains exposure exceeds the fair market value of its assets. This gives the fund the ability to shelter future gains, which can boost the net asset value of the fund without triggering a taxable event for shareholders. Thus, you can control the taxation of this type of growth while the fund eats through its losses, since no taxes are due until you sell your shares.

Foreign Tax Credit

Some mutual funds invest in foreign corporations. If a mutual fund owns securities of foreign corporations, it may have to pay foreign taxes on the income it earns from those securities. However, if the fund holds more than 50 percent of its total assets in foreign securities at the close of its tax year, the fund can pass through to its shareholders the foreign tax credit it receives for taxes paid at the fund level. For a discussion of the foreign tax credit and whether you should claim the credit or a tax deduction, see Chapter 9, Filing Status and How to Calculate Your Tax.

Investment Expenses

Investment expenses that you incur in the production of income generally are deductible subject to certain limitations. Investment expenses include expenses for counseling and advice, legal and accounting fees, and any investment newsletters. See Chapter 2, What You Can Deduct, for more information.

TAXSAVER

If you own shares in a publicly offered mutual fund, you do not have to pay tax on your share of the fund's expenses. There should be no entry in Box 1e of the form 1099-DIV. However, expenses of a non-publicly offered fund are taxable. You should consult your tax advisor for details.

Fees

Front-End Fees.   "Front-end," or purchase, fees (also known as "load charges") reduce your investment in a mutual fund, but they are still considered part of your cost basis for tax purposes.

Example: You invest $10,000 in a fund that charges a 1 percent load on portfolio transaction (purchase) fee. Your account statement reports a net balance of $9,900 ($10,000 minus the 1 percent fee). For tax purposes, however, your cost remains at $10,000.

TAXSAVER

Your basis in mutual fund shares does not include load charges (sales fees) paid after October 3, 1989, on the purchase of shares if you held the shares for 90 days or less and then reinvested the proceeds in a fund within the same fund family with a reduced load charge. Instead, the load charges become part of your basis in the shares of the new fund into which you put your investment.

TAXSAVER

Before you buy a mutual fund, you should examine the sales charges and redemption fees it charges, if any. No-load funds do not have a sales charge. Mutual fund listings in newspapers generally indicate whether there is a sales charge. No-load funds have the same purchase and redemption price for fund shares. Your broker should be able to tell you which funds charge commissions.

E&Y FOCUS: Ongoing Fund Expenses

Regardless of any sales charges, all funds have ongoing expenses for administration and management that are charged as an annual percentage of the assets under management. These fees are deducted from the portfolio's investment earnings before the income is distributed to shareholders.

Management fees typically make up the majority of a fund's ongoing expenses. They represent the cost of portfolio management, which is charged by the fund's investment advisors. Managers in investment markets that require more specialized research skills—such as the small-cap and international equity markets—typically command higher fees. Also, equity funds generally charge higher management fees than fixed-income funds.

12b-1 fees are named for the Securities and Exchange Commission rule that allows funds to charge shareholders for "distribution and marketing" expenses. These fees are often used to pay "trailing commissions," which brokers receive in addition to any front-end sales charge. In other words, the sales representatives receive an incentive to help maintain investors after the initial sale. The average 12b-1 fee among U.S. stock funds is about 0.3%, although it can run as high as 1%.

Back-End Fees.   Fees may also be deducted from your fund when you redeem or sell shares. These are generally called redemption or "back-end" fees. (Certain back-end fees called "contingent deferred sales charges" or "contingent deferred sales loads" typically decline and eventually disappear over a set period of time.) If your mutual fund reports all proceeds net of redemption fees on your Form 1099-B, you do not need to adjust your tax cost. However, if your mutual fund reports gross proceeds before any redemption fees on Form 1099-B, you should increase your cost basis by the amount of the fee you paid when calculating your capital gain or loss.

Other Fees.   Custodial and account maintenance fees are deductible as "investment expenses" on Schedule A of your income tax return, subject to certain limitations. See Investment Expenses, above, and Chapter 2.

SALE OF MUTUAL FUND SHARES

If you sell, exchange, or have shares redeemed (when a mutual fund reacquires its shares), you may have a capital gain or loss. You will have a short-term capital gain or loss if you held your shares for one year or less. You will have a long-term capital gain or loss if you held the shares for more than a year. The gain or loss on the sale, exchange, or redemption of mutual fund shares is the difference between the amount of the proceeds you receive and your adjusted tax basis in your shares.

TaxSaver

You will have a capital gain or loss when you exchange shares of one mutual fund for another mutual fund in the same mutual fund family. So, for example, if you exchange shares in ABC Growth Fund for shares in ABC Technology Fund, you may have to recognize a capital gain or loss. Generally, any service fee charged for the exchange may be added to your basis of the shares you acquired.

You will not have to recognize a capital gain or loss, however, if the shares in one mutual fund are converted to the shares of another or if the redemption of your shares is treated as a dividend.

The Wash Sale Rule for Mutual Funds

The wash sale rule (see Chapter 7, Capital Gains and Losses) prevents you from selling shares of stock, taking a loss on your tax return, and buying back the substantially identical stock within the 30 days before or after the sale. The wash sale rule also applies to mutual funds. You can sell mutual fund shares at a loss and take the loss on your tax return as long as you do not repurchase shares in the same fund. You can, however, purchase the shares of a different fund with similar investment objectives and holdings.

Losses on Municipal Bond Funds

If you have held the shares of a tax-exempt fund for six months or less and you redeem the shares at a loss, you will not be able to claim the loss on your tax return to the extent you have received any tax-exempt dividends paid by the fund during the time you owned the shares.

Calculating Your Gain or Loss on Mutual Funds Sales

Determining Your Basis. Your basis in your mutual fund shares is extremely important since it allows you to determine how much of a gain or loss you will have upon the sale of your mutual fund shares. But determining your basis can be tricky—especially because investors often acquire mutual fund shares at different dates, in various quantities, and at various places. Therefore, it is imperative that you retain all records concerning your acquisition of mutual fund shares.

Determining your original basis will vary depending upon whether you have purchased shares, received them in a reinvestment plan, inherited them, or received them as a gift:

- If you purchased shares, your basis will equal your purchase price. Any commission fees may be added to the basis of the shares you acquired.
- If you acquire shares through a reinvestment plan, your basis of the shares will equal the cost at the time of the reinvestment.
- If you inherit mutual fund shares, your basis in the shares will equal the fair market value of the shares at the date of the decedent's death or valuation date. The fair market value is the last quoted redemption price, commonly referred to as the "bid price" or "net asset value."
- If you acquire mutual fund shares through a gift, your basis in the shares may vary depending upon whether you have a gain or loss when you sell the shares. To determine your basis, you will need to know (1) the donor's basis in the shares, (2) the fair market value of the shares at the time they were given to you, and (3) whether any gift tax was paid on the shares.

When the fair market value of the shares is less than the donor's adjusted basis, your basis in the shares, if you have gain on their sale, is the same as the donor's adjusted basis. However, if you have a loss when you sell the shares, your basis in the shares is the fair market value of the shares at the time you received the gift. If the fair market value of the shares is equal to or greater than the donor's adjusted basis, your basis is the same as the donor's adjusted basis at the time you received the gift.

You must increase your basis by all or part of the gift tax paid, depending on the date of the gift. If you received the gift after 1976, you must increase your basis in the gift by the part of the gift tax paid that is due to the net increase in the value of the gift.

Once you have determined your original basis, you must determine your adjusted basis. Your basis must be reduced if you receive a return of a capital dividend (see Dividends, earlier in this chapter). On the other hand, if you had to pay tax on an undistributed capital gain, your basis must be increased by the difference between your share of the undistributed capital gain you reported and the tax paid for you by the fund.

TaxOrganizer

You should keep all confirmation statements for purchases of mutual fund shares as well as records of dividends that are automatically reinvested in your account. Your basis is increased by amounts reported to you by the fund on Form 2439 as undistributed capital gains you are required to report as income less the tax paid by the fund on the undistributed gains. Your basis is reduced by nontaxable dividends that are a return of your investment.

Identifying Which Shares Are Sold

To calculate your gain or loss, the IRS permits you to use either the cost basis of your shares or the average basis of your shares. The different methods can result in differing amounts of taxes owned. Consequently, it is important to assess which method is best for you.

If you use the cost basis of your shares, you can figure your basis by (1) the identified cost method, or (2) the first-in, first-out method (FIFO). Alternatively, if you use the average basis of your shares, you can determine your average basis using (1) the single-category method or (2) the double-category method. All of these methods are described below and the advantages and disadvantages of each method are discussed in Table 8.1 below.

The Identified Cost Method. Using this method, you use the adjusted basis of the specific shares that you identify to be sold to calculate your gain or loss.

Example: Assume that you have six shares of Widget Fund, a mutual fund, and they have a fair market value equal to $50. You purchased two shares for $10 in 1986, two shares for $20 in 1990, and two shares for $40 in May 1995. You decide to have the fund redeem three shares of stock. Under the identified cost method, you may elect to sell the portion of your shares with the highest basis to minimize your gain—and your taxes— on the sale. Consequently, you decide to sell two shares with a $40 basis, thus recognizing a $10 short-term gain on each share. (The gain would be short-term if you sold the shares before May 1996.) You also sell one share with a $20 basis, recognizing a $30 long-term gain.

To qualify for this method you must be able to identify the shares you have sold. To do so, according to IRS regulations, you need to: (1) Specify to your broker or fund the specific shares that you want sold, and (2)

TABLE 8.1 Choosing a Cost Basis Method

Cost Basis Method	Advantages/Disadvantages
Specific identification	The most flexible way to determine your gain and losses. But there are important restrictions governing its use.
FIFO	The simplest approach. But it may mean a large gain if your shares have appreciated significantly and you are redeeming only part of your account.
Average cost (single category)	The middle ground. A more modest tax burden than the FIFO method but more tedious calculations if you sell shares frequently.
Average cost (double category)	Only makes sense if (1) you have elected it in the past and are required to continue using it and (2) there is a tax benefit from maintaining separate short- and long-term average costs.

receive a confirmation statement detailing that you asked to sell specific shares.

First-In, First Out Method (FIFO). Generally, if you cannot adequately identify the specific shares you want sold, and you do not make an election to average your cost basis, the IRS requires the FIFO method to be used. Under the FIFO method, the shares sold are assumed to be the earliest shares purchased or acquired.

Example: Assume the same facts as in the example above. Under the FIFO method, the three shares sold would be the first three you purchased—two shares with a $10 basis and one share with a $20 basis. Assuming you sell the shares for $50 each, you will have a long-term gain of $110—a considerably greater gain than if you had used the identified cost method.

Average Basis Method. If you chose to use either the single or double category average basis method, you must elect to do so on your income tax return for the first taxable year in which you use the method. Once you elect to use the average basis method for some shares of a mutual fund you sell or transfer, you must use the method for all the shares of that fund that you hold. However, you can use a different cost method when you sell shares of another mutual fund in the same fund family. The average basis method cannot be applied to shares purchased from other shareholders or to shares you inherit or acquire as a gift.

Double-Category Average Basis Method. If you use this method, all of your shares of a mutual fund are divided into two categories at the time of each sale or transfer. The first category includes all shares which you have held for a year or more. The second category includes all shares which you have held for one year or less. The basis of each share in each category is equal to the adjusted basis of all shares in that category at the time of the sale or transfer divided by the aggregate number of shares in the category.

If you use the double-category method, you specify from which category the shares are to be sold or transferred. Your choice must be confirmed in writing within a reasonable time after the sale. If no written confirmation is made, it is assumed that the shares sold were from the long-term category.

After a year, shares from the short-term category are transferred to the long-term category. If none of the short-term shares have been sold, the basis of the transferred shares is their cost (not the average basis). If some of the short-term shares have been sold, the basis of the unsold transferred shares is the average basis of the shares in the short-term category at the time of the most recent sale.

Example: Assume the same facts as in the example illustrating the identified cost method. The shares in the long-term capital gain category would have an average basis of $15 [($10 + $10 + $20 + $20)/4]. The shares in the short-term capital gain category would have an average basis of $40 [($40 + $40)/2]. You specify that you want to sell three shares at $50—two from the short-term category, which would result in $20 in short-term capital gains, and one from the long-term category, which would result in $35 of long-term capital gains.

Single-Category Average Basis Method. Using this method, all shares are included in one category. The basis of each share is equal to the aggregate cost or other basis of all of the shares divided by the aggregate number of shares held.

You are restricted from using the single category method if it appears that the purpose of using this method is to convert long-term capital gains or losses to short-term capital gains or losses, or vice-versa.

Example: Assume the same facts as in the identified cost method example. The average cost of the shares is $23.33 [($10 + $10 + $20 + $20 + $40 + $40)/6]. Consequently, upon the sale of three shares for $50 each, you would recognize a long-term capital gain of $80.

9

Filing Status and How to Calculate Your Tax

INTRODUCTION

This chapter explains the basics of filing status issues and how to calculate your tax. The actual calculation you will have to make is straightforward:

If your allowable standard deduction exceeds your allowable itemized deductions, your taxable income is your adjusted gross income minus your standard deduction and personal and dependency exemptions.

If the sum of your allowable deductions exceeds your allowable standard deduction, you can itemize those deductions. Your taxable income will be your adjusted gross income, minus your itemized deductions and personal and dependency exemptions.

You can determine your income tax liability by using the tax tables supplied by the IRS with your tax return form booklet if your taxable income does not exceed $100,000. If your taxable income exceeds $100,000, use the tax rate schedules (reproduced in the Appendix of this book) to compute your tax.

This chapter also discusses special situations that could affect your tax liability, including investment income of children under age 14, the alternative minimum tax, and tax credits. Filing rules, estimated taxes, and withholding taxes are also explained.

WHO MUST FILE

In general, if you are a citizen or resident of the United States, you must file an income tax return by April 15 for the previous taxable year. For the taxable year 1996, income tax returns are due on April 15, 1997. You can gain additional time to file if you apply for an extension. (See discussion on page 137.) You must file a tax return if your gross income for the year is at least as much as the amounts shown in Table 9.1.

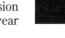

TABLE 9.1   1996 Filing Requirements

Filing Status*	Required to file return if Gross Income Equals or Exceeds**
Single	
Under age 65	$ 6,550
Age 65 or over	$ 7,550
Head of household	
Under age 65	$ 8,450
Age 65 or over	$ 9,450
Married filing jointly	
Both under 65	$11,800
One 65 or over	$12,600
Both 65 or over	$13,400
Surviving spouse***	
Under 65	$ 9,250
65 or over	$10,050
Married filing separately	$ 5,775

For details on determining your filing status, see discussion on page 139.
**These amounts are adjusted annually by a cost-of-living adjustment.*
***You must meet the "surviving spouse" requirements; otherwise you will be treated as single or head of household. (See pages 141–142.)*
Note: *The amounts in Table 9.1 do not include the additional standard deductions for blind individuals. Such individuals are entitled to an additional $750 standard deduction if married, and $950 if their filing status is single or head of household. These amounts are revised annually by a cost-of-living adjustment. (See page 32 for further discussion.)*

(See the discussion below for persons claimed by another taxpayer as a dependent.)

If married persons filing jointly do not live in the same household at the end of the taxable year, or if either of them can be claimed as a dependent by a third person, the limit for a married person filing separately usually applies.

The following persons must also file a return even if their income is less than the amounts shown above:

1. Persons claimed as dependents on another's return who have unearned income and whose total unearned and earned income exceeds $650. (See below for an exception applying to children under age 14.)
2. Persons with earnings from self-employment of $400 or more.
3. Persons receiving any advanced earned income credit payments.
4. Persons with a liability for the alternative minimum tax, recapture of investment tax credit, tax due on an early withdrawal from an individual retirement account (IRA), or Social Security tax on tip income.
5. Persons with wages of $108.28 or more from a church or qualified church-controlled organization that is exempt from employer FICA contributions.

6. Persons who owe any taxes.

Generally parents may elect (on IRS Form 8814) to include on their return the unearned income of a child who is under age 14 at the end of the tax year if that child's unearned gross income is between $500 and $5,000 and consists only of interest and dividends. If the parents make this election, the child will not be required to file a separate return. (See page 144 for a discussion of how children under 14 are taxed.)

To obtain a refund for tax that has been withheld, a return should also be filed even if it is not required.

Special rules for filing requirements applicable to nonresident aliens and other individuals with special status are not discussed in this book.

How to Get an Extension of Time to File

If you need more time to file your income tax return, you can easily apply for an automatic four-month extension. All you need to do is complete an application (IRS Form 4868, *Extension to File U.S. Individual Income Tax Return*) and send it in by the original due date of your income tax return. Additional extensions beyond the four-month period are granted only for good reason. Under normal circumstances, an extension of more than six months will not be granted unless you are outside of the United States. If an extension is granted, no penalty for late payment of tax will be imposed if at least 90% of the tax liability shown on the return is paid on or before the original due date.

An automatic extension of two months is also granted to U.S. citizens and U.S. residents whose tax home is outside the United States and Puerto Rico on the date the return is due. Unlike the automatic extension for other individuals (discussed above), no application is required for this particular automatic two-month extension and there is no minimum payment required to avoid a late payment penalty.

Even though the due date for filing a return is extended, any unpaid portion of the final tax will accrue interest from the original due date to the date paid.

Interest rates for underpayments are equal to the short-term federal rate plus three percentage points. (The short-term federal rate is announced by the Treasury Department in the Federal Register.) These interest rates are adjusted quarterly and become effective during the first calendar quarter following the adjustment. Interest is compounded daily.

Which Form You Should Use

All individual taxpayers resident in the United States are required to file their returns on Form 1040, Form 1040A, or Form 1040EZ. Most taxpayers who use this book will probably find that they are required to use Form 1040.

> ### *TaxOrganizer*
>
> *Although Form 1040EZ or Form 1040A may be easier to use, you should review your tax information before deciding which form to use. You may have deductions that can be itemized, which can be claimed only if you file Form 1040. You may therefore be overpaying your taxes if you use one of the easier forms that does not allow you to claim these deductions.*

> ### *TaxSaver*
>
> ***Electronic Filing.*** *If you are expecting a refund, you should consider filing your return electronically with the IRS instead of mailing in the paper forms. Electronic filing can shrink the time for receiving your refund down to three weeks. Remember, however, that most tax return preparers and other firms authorized to make electronic filings will charge a separate fee for the service—generally about $30 to $40. If you need the refund money right away, it may make sense to pay for filing electronically.*

Every individual (other than a nonresident alien) with net earnings of $400 or more from self-employment must file a report of self-employment income and compute the self-employment tax on Schedule SE (Form 1040), even if the filing of an income tax return is not otherwise required. The FICA tax calculation is composed of two parts. Part one, for old-age, survivors, and disability insurance (OASDI), is calculated at a rate of 6.2% applied to wages and 12.4% on net self-employment income up to $62,700 in 1996. Part two, for Medicare insurance, is assessed at a rate of 1.45% on wages and 2.9% on net self-employment income in 1996.

> ### *TaxAlert*
>
> *The dollar limit on wages and self-employment income subject to Medicare taxes for wages and other earned income received after 1993 has been eliminated. Thus, the 1.45% rate for employees (2.9% for self-employed individuals) applies to all wages and earned income.*

> ### *TaxOrganizer*
>
> *You should be aware that you are not excused from filing a return because the IRS did not send you the necessary forms. You can usually obtain the forms from your local IRS office, post office or bank, or* The Ernst & Young Tax Guide, *published annually. Copies of forms may be used.*

> ### *TaxOrganizer*
>
> *Even if you are not required to do so, you should still file a return if:*
> *(1) You had income tax withheld from your pay. Even if you are entitled to a refund, you cannot claim it unless a return is filed.*
> *(2) You qualify for the refundable earned income credit. (See page 150.)*

Accounting Periods and Methods

You must determine your taxable income for a fixed period of time for each tax year. This is defined as an "accounting period." Most individual income tax returns cover a calendar year based on a 12-month accounting period from January 1 through December 31, unless permission is granted in advance by the IRS to use a different 12-month period.

In addition, you must also account for your income and deductions in a consistent way that clearly reflects your taxable income. This is defined as an "accounting method." The two accounting methods most often used are the cash method and the accrual method. Individuals who do not own and operate their own business are required to use the cash method only. The cash method reports all items of income in the year in which you actually or "constructively" receive them. You have "constructively" received income when it is credited to your account or is set apart in any way that makes it available to you. You do not have to physically possess the funds. For example, interest credited to your bank account on December 31, 1996 is constructively received and taxable to you in 1996 if you could have withdrawn the funds in 1996—even if the amount is not entered in your passbook or actually withdrawn until 1997. On the other hand, you generally can deduct expenses only in the year you actually pay them.

If you are qualified to use the accrual method, you generally report income when you earn it, regardless of when you receive the money. You also generally deduct expenses as they are incurred and not when you pay them.

FILING STATUS

Your filing status will determine your filing requirements, standard deduction, eligibility to claim certain deductions and credits, and correct tax. Your filing status is determined by your status on the last day of the tax year, which for individuals is almost always December 31. So, if you were married on December 31, you are treated for tax purposes as being married for the entire tax year. Generally, the effective tax rate for single taxpayers is higher than for married taxpayers filing jointly or unmarried taxpayers filing as head of household. That is because the amount of taxable income that qualifies for the 15% tax rate is lower for single filers ($24,000) than for married taxpayers filing jointly and surviving spouses ($40,100), or heads of household ($32,150). (See tax table in Appendix.)

Single Taxpayers

Your filing status is *single* if (1) you are unmarried, or (2) you are legally separated from your spouse and you do not qualify to file as head of household or qualifying widow(er) with dependent child. (See pages 141–142.)

Children under age 14 whose unearned income (interest, dividends, capital gains, etc.) is $650 or over are taxed under special rules. (See page 144.)

Married Taxpayers

You and your spouse may agree to file either a joint return or separate returns. A joint return may be filed by a married couple even though only one person has gross income or deductions. A joint return, however, may not be filed if (1) the individuals have different taxable years, or (2) either spouse was a nonresident alien at any time during the taxable year unless an election to file a joint return is in effect. (The catch is that a joint return requires that the worldwide income of both spouses for the entire year be included in taxable income.)

TaxSaver

If you and your spouse each have income, you may want to calculate your tax two ways: filing jointly and filing separately. You can file your returns based on the method that yields the lower tax.

TaxAlert

Separate Filing Traps. *Certain aspects of filing separately are disadvantageous:*
- *The child care credit is not available.*
- *Social Security recipients also must watch out since all Social Security benefits of separate filers are subject to the "inclusion in income rules." The net effect is that separate filers who receive Social Security will have some portion of their benefits subject to tax. In contrast, joint filers are allowed a base amount of $32,000 of income before benefits are taxable ($44,000 before the 85% inclusion rules apply).*
- *Net capital losses of joint filers can offset up to $3,000 of other income, but the limit for separate filers is $1,500. If one spouse has more than $1,500 of net capital losses, separate filing could cost you.*

TaxOrganizer

Substantiation. *Careful record keeping is important to support allocations of income and deductions between spouses. Also, your ability to direct items to one spouse easily will be affected by whether you live in a common-law or community property state. In common-law states, income is traced based on earnings or ownership of property, and items to be deducted on one spouse's separate return must be paid out of that spouse's separate funds.*

Generally, income and deductions will be split 50/50 between spouses in community property states. States have different rules regarding whether income from separate property is treated as community or separate income, so it's important to check with your tax advisor in these states.

If one spouse dies, the survivor, if not remarried at year-end, may file a joint return for the year of death. A joint return is filed in the name of both spouses and includes the total income and deductions of the surviving spouse and the income and deductions up to the date of death of the other spouse. (See also Surviving Spouse, page 142.)

If a taxpayer and spouse file separate returns, the original election to file separately may normally be changed as long as an amended joint return is filed within three years of the original due date. However, if a joint return is filed, an amended separate return may not be filed for that particular taxable year after the due date, unless the executor of a deceased spouse's estate disaffirms the joint return.

TaxSaver

When to Get Married: If one of you has much less income than the other, consider getting married in December rather than January. You will generally be taxed less on the same income if you are married filing jointly than you would be if each of you filed single returns. If both of you have similar levels of income, choose January. Marriage partners who earn approximately the same income may pay more tax if they file a joint return or file separate married returns than they would if they could file two single returns. This is known as "the marriage tax penalty."

When to Get Divorced: If you both have similar levels of income, choose December since the marriage tax penalty may be avoided. If one has more income than the other and both want to save taxes, choose January.

Individuals legally separated under a decree of divorce or separate maintenance agreement are not considered married. Although there may be a tax incentive to do so, the IRS maintains that couples who divorce immediately before year-end and remarry immediately after the start of the new year are considered married at year-end for tax purposes.

Head of Household

A separate, lower tax rate schedule can be used if you are unmarried and can qualify as a head of household. In general, an unmarried taxpayer at the close of the tax year, other than a surviving spouse or a nonresident alien, qualifies as a head of household if the individual furnished over one half of the maintenance cost of:

1. His or her personal residence, which, except for temporary absences, is lived in during more than one half of the taxable year by a relative who qualifies as a dependent. You do not qualify as a head of household if you can only claim a relative (other than an unmarried child, grandchild, stepchild or adopted child; or a parent who does not live with you) as a dependent under a multiple support agreement. The residence can also be lived in by an unmarried son, daughter, grandchild, or stepchild even though not qualified for the dependency deduction, or

2. A household (even if separate) for a parent who qualifies as a dependent other than through a multiple support agreement.

In determining head-of-household status, a taxpayer whose spouse is a nonresident alien at any time during a taxable year is not considered married if an election to file jointly is not made. In addition, a married individual who otherwise qualifies for head-of-household status but for his or her marital status can file using head-of-household status if his or her spouse is not a member of the household for the last six months of the tax year.

> **TAXORGANIZER**
>
> *You should keep track of your support payments to establish your qualifications for head-of-household status.*

Surviving Spouse (Qualifying Widows and Widowers)

If your spouse died in 1996, you may use married filing jointly as your filing status for 1996 if you would otherwise qualify.

If your spouse died during either of the two years immediately preceding this current tax year and you meet all the following tests, you may be able to use *surviving spouse* as your filing status if:
1. During the current year, you furnished more than one half of the cost of maintaining your home which also constitutes the principal place of residence of your son, stepson, daughter, or stepdaughter;
2. You did not remarry before the end of the year; and
3. You were entitled to file a joint return with your spouse for the year your spouse died.

The return of a surviving spouse is accorded the same benefits as a joint return. This means that you are entitled to a lower tax rate schedule and a higher standard deduction amount if you do not itemize your deductions.

CITIZENS LIVING ABROAD

If you are a U.S. citizen or resident alien (a green-card holder) living overseas, you are subject to U.S. tax on your worldwide income regardless of where such income is earned, paid, or received. However, you can elect to exclude up to $70,000 of your foreign earned income and certain foreign housing costs, and you may also claim a credit against U.S. tax for foreign income taxes you paid.

To qualify for the exclusions, you must meet one of two tests: (1) the bona fide foreign residence test or (2) the physical presence test.

The Foreign Residence Test. The bona fide foreign residence test applies to U.S. citizens only. It requires you to be a resident in a foreign country (or countries) for an uninterrupted period that includes an entire taxable year.

The Physical Presence Test. The physical presence test applies to both U.S. citizens and resident aliens. It will be met if you are physically present in a foreign country (or countries) for 330 full days during any consecutive 12-month period.

Housing Costs. You may also elect to exclude from your U.S. taxable income the excess of reasonable overseas housing expenses over a base housing amount—which is $9,426 in 1996—multiplied by a fraction: the numerator of which is the number of qualifying days of residence or physical presence and the denominator of which is the number of days in the tax year. Interest and real estate taxes are excluded from housing costs for the purpose of calculating the foreign housing exclusion. The exclusion applies only to unreimbursed employer-provided housing costs.

If you are a self-employed individual, you can deduct your foreign housing costs in computing your adjusted gross income, but the deduction is limited to the excess of foreign earned income over the foreign earned income exclusion. Any nondeductible amounts can be carried forward to the following year to the extent that you receive foreign income in the succeeding year.

Expenses, including moving expenses (which are subject to special rules), and foreign tax credits that are attributable to excluded amounts cannot be deducted or credited against your U.S. tax bill.

TAXSAVER

If you are living in a foreign country with a higher tax rate than the United States' tax rate, you may be better off forgoing the foreign earned income and housing exclusions and claiming the foreign tax credits instead. Excess foreign tax credits may be carried back to prior tax years or carried forward.

The foreign earned income and housing exclusions are elected separately. The total of the earned income exclusion and the housing cost exclusion, however, cannot exceed your total foreign earned income. The exclusion amount of up to $70,000 is prorated on a daily basis based on the number of days in the taxable year that you meet either test. Once made, an exclusion election remains in effect for future years until revoked. If the election is revoked without the approval of the IRS, a new election may not be made until the sixth taxable year following the year of revocation.

Ordinarily, you are allowed a two-year replacement period when you sell your home, which enables you to defer paying tax on any gain from the sale. (See page 70.) However, this replacement period is suspended during the time you maintain a tax home outside the United States. The replacement period in such a case may not exceed four years from the date of the sale of your home.

Foreign Tax Credit

You may also elect to claim a credit for foreign income taxes paid or accrued during the tax year or you may claim the taxes paid as an itemized deduction.

As discussed above, if you elect to take either the foreign earned income exclusion or the foreign housing exclusion, or both, the amount of foreign taxes that you may receive credit for will be reduced accordingly. See page 152 for more about the foreign tax credit.

CHILDREN UNDER AGE 14

If your child was under 14 at the end of the taxable year and received more than $1,300 of unearned income, such as interest and dividends, your child's unearned income in excess of $1,300 will be taxed at your marginal tax rate.

Example: A child who does not itemize his or her deductions has $800 of earned income and $2,100 of unearned income. He or she would be taxed on $1,300 of unearned income at his or her rate. The remaining $800 would be taxed at his or her parents' marginal rate. The child's standard deduction is limited to $800 (based on the greater of $650 or the child's earned income, but not more than the regular standard deduction amount; see page 32).

TaxSaver

If your child is under age 14 and you are in the top income tax bracket, income-producing property that earns up to $650 should be transferred to your child because it will escape tax completely. The next $650 is taxed at only 15%. Because any amount over $1,300 is taxed at your tax rate, you may want to tailor the child's investment strategy so that any of the child's annual unearned income over $1,300 is generated from tax-exempt or from tax-deferred instruments, such as U.S. savings bonds that will mature after the child reaches age 14.

If you are divorced, your child's tax liability is determined by using the custodial parent's tax rate. If you are a married individual filing separately, your child's tax rate is the same as the tax rate of the parent with the greater amount of taxable income.

Any child who is subject to these rules must include the parents' Social Security numbers on his or her tax return.

Including Your Child's Income on Your Return. Parents may elect (on IRS Form 8814) to include the unearned income of any of their children under age 14 on their own return instead of filing separate returns for each child. This election may be made only if (1) your child's gross income consists solely of interest and dividends totaling more than $500 and less than $5,000, (2) your child makes no estimated tax payments for the year under his or her own name and Social Security number, and (3) your child is not subject to backup withholding and he or she did not have a 1995 overpayment applied toward a 1996 estimated tax.

TaxOrganizer

If you elect to include the unearned income of any of your children under age 14 on your return, you may save paperwork, but your family could end up paying more taxes. Including your child's unearned income on your return could increase the amount of state income taxes you pay if your state's tax is based on federal income and your child would not otherwise owe state tax. Your child would also forfeit the ability to claim itemized deductions and to deduct any penalty on the early withdrawal of savings.

TaxSaver

If your children are at least age 14, you should consider taking advantage of their 15% tax bracket, which applies to the extent their taxable income is below $24,000. Here are a few ideas to consider:
- *Convert EE bonds to HH bonds, which pay interest currently, or redeem the bonds and invest in something else, like CDs, which generally produce a greater return with little additional risk.*
- *Convert growth stocks to dividend-paying stocks and mutual funds.*

Tax Rates for Individuals

The 1996 tax schedule contains five rates for individuals—15%, 28%, 31%, 36% and 39.6%. The top tax rate on net capital gains—the excess of net long-term capital gains over net short-term capital losses—is capped at 28%.

Alternative Minimum Tax

The tax law gives special treatment to some kinds of income and allows special deductions and credits for certain expenses. Taxpayers who benefit from these laws have to pay at least a minimum amount through a special tax. This special tax is called the "alternative minimum tax."

Individuals, trusts, and estates must pay the alternative minimum tax (AMT) if it exceeds their regular tax liability for the year. The amount subject to the AMT will be determined by adding a number of preference items to your taxable income and making various adjustments to your regular taxable income. This amount is reduced by the exemption amounts, shown in Table 9.2, and the balance is subject to the AMT rate. Your tax advisor can help you with the calculation.

TABLE 9.2   Exemption Amount

Filing Status	Base Amount	Less 25% of the Amount by Which AMTI Exceeds
Single	$33,750	$112,500
Married filing jointly, surviving spouses	45,000	150,000
Married filing separately, estates and trusts	22,500	75,000

The AMT rate is 26% on alternative minimum tax income (AMTI) of $175,000 in excess of the exemption amount, and 28% on AMTI more than $175,000 above the exemption amount. For married taxpayers filing separately, the 28% AMT rate applies to the extent that AMTI is more than $87,500 above the exemption amount. Furthermore, the base exemption amounts are $33,750 for single individuals and heads of household, $45,000 for married taxpayers filing jointly, and $22,500 for married taxpayers filing separately, trusts, and estates.

Tax Preference Items

Tax preference items are income and expense items that receive special treatment under the tax laws. They must be added back to the taxable income shown on your return in figuring your alternative minimum taxable income. The AMT preference items are:

1. Allowable depletion, to the extent that it exceeds the adjusted basis of the property involved.
2. The amount by which excess intangible drilling costs exceed 65% of the net income from oil, gas, and geothermal properties for the taxable year.

TaxSaver

To avoid treating excess intangible drilling costs as a tax preference item, you may elect to capitalize and amortize these expenses over a 10-year period in your regular tax calculation.

3. Interest on specified tax-exempt private activity bonds issued after August 7, 1986, reduced by deductions that would be allowable if such income could be included in regular taxable income.
4. Accelerated depreciation on certain property bought and put into use before 1987. (Depreciation methods are described on pages 227–231.)
    (a) Allowable depreciation in excess of straight-line depreciation on real property and leased personal property that was placed in

service before 1981. (Straight-line depreciation is calculated by dividing the cost of the property by its useful life.)

(b) Accelerated cost recovery allowances in excess of the allowance that would be available on real property placed in service after 1980 and before 1987, using the straight-line method of depreciation over 15 years (18 years for most property placed in service after March 15, 1984, and 19 years for property placed in service after May 8, 1985). (*Note:* Straight-line depreciation is computed without considering salvage value); and

(c) Accelerated cost recovery allowances in excess of the allowance that would be available on leased personal property placed in service after 1980 and before 1987, using the straight-line method, no salvage value, the half-year convention, and an extended recovery period. The half-year convention discussed on pages 228–230 assumes the property was placed in service during the midpoint of the year for depreciation purposes.

5. The excess of the rapid amortization of pre-1987 certified pollution-control facilities over the depreciation that would be allowable.

6. One-half of the gain of qualified small business stock excluded from gross income will be treated as a tax preference item. See page 117 for a definition of a qualified small business stock.

Adjustments

Besides accounting for tax preference items, certain adjustments (increases or decreases) must be made to taxable income to arrive at alternative minimum taxable income. In general the adjustments are:

1. An alternative depreciation deduction (using less accelerated methods and longer depreciable lives) is substituted for the regular tax depreciation deduction for real and personal property and certified pollution-control facilities placed in service after 1986. Recomputations are done in the aggregate—that is, the amount of the adjustment is not determined on a property-by-property basis. *Note:* This adjustment does not apply if you have elected to apply the alternative depreciation system (ADS) for regular tax purposes. (See page 230 for details.)

2. Mining exploration and development costs must be amortized over 10 years using the straight-line method.

3. The percentage-of-completion method of accounting must be used for long-term contracts entered into on or after March 1, 1986. Certain small construction contracts entered into on or after June 21, 1988 must use new simplified procedures for cost allocations in the percentage-of-completion calculation.

4. An alternative tax net operating loss deduction replaces the regular net operating loss deduction.

5. The installment method of accounting is disallowed for certain installment sales occurring after March 1, 1986.

6. The treatment of itemized deductions is modified as follows:
   - Medical expenses are deductible only to the extent that they exceed 10% of the taxpayer's adjusted gross income.
   - State, local, and foreign real property and income taxes and state and local personal property taxes are deductible for alternative minimum tax (AMT) purposes only if they are deductible for regular tax purposes in computing adjusted gross income.
   Note: These are taxes related to business, rental property, and farming that are deducted on Schedules C, E, or F.
   - Investment interest is deductible to the extent of net investment income that is adjusted for amounts relating to tax-exempt interest earned on certain private activity bonds.
   - Home mortgage interest is allowed as a deduction for AMT purposes, but the definition of such interest is narrower than that of "qualified residence interest" for regular tax purposes. Refinanced home mortgage interest that is applicable to any mortgage in excess of the outstanding mortgage before refinancing is not deductible for AMT purposes. (See page 145 for further discussion.)
   - No deduction is allowed for miscellaneous itemized deductions which are subject to the 2% of adjusted gross income limit for the regular tax computation.
7. No deduction is allowed for personal exemptions and the standard deduction.
8. Circulation expenditures and research/experimental costs must be amortized over three- and ten-year periods, respectively.
9. Deductions for passive farm losses are denied except to the extent that the taxpayer is insolvent or the activity is disposed of during the year.
10. Rules limiting passive loss deductions also apply to the AMT, except that (a) otherwise disallowed losses are reduced by the amount by which the taxpayer is insolvent, and (b) all AMT adjustments and preferences are taken into consideration in computing income and/ or losses from passive activities.
11. For beneficiaries of estates and trusts, the difference between a distribution included in income for regular tax and the AMT income shown on Schedule K-1 must be taken into account.
12. For property disposed of during the year, the gain or loss is refigured to take into consideration the impact that AMT adjustments, such as depreciation, have on the taxpayer's basis in the property.
13. For partners in partnerships and shareholders in S corporations, the income or loss is refigured to take into account AMT adjustments.
14. If exercising an incentive stock option (ISO), the taxpayer needs to adjust for the difference between the option price and the fair market value at the time the option is exercised. (For corporate "insiders" who exercise an ISO within six months of when the option was granted, the adjustment between the option price and its fair market value is made six months after the option is granted.) In calculating

the AMT gain or loss on the subsequent sale of the ISO stock, the AMT basis in the stock is the sum of the option price paid and the AMT adjustment included in alternative minimum taxable income when the stock became substantially vested.

You will pay the alternative minimum tax only if it is higher than your regular tax. You may, however, offset your AMT liability by using any foreign tax credit, as computed under the AMT rules, that you are allowed to claim. Other nonrefundable credits cannot, under any circumstances, reduce your AMT liability. To the extent that no tax benefit is obtained for these nonrefundable credits for the year the AMT applies, such credits are generally carried back or forward to other taxable years.

AMT Credit.   The law provides a credit against the regular tax for all or a portion of the AMT you paid in previous years. The credit is equal to the AMT attributable to deferral, rather than exclusion, items. Deferral items, such as accelerated depreciation, are those that have the effect of reducing your regular taxable income relative to alternative minimum taxable income in early years but the situation reverses over time. When you pay AMT as a result of deferral preferences, the law gives you a credit that can be used to reduce your regular tax liability in the future. This credit helps you avoid double taxation on the same income. Exclusion preferences, such as certain tax-exempt interest income, reduce your regular taxable income permanently. Since these preferences never reverse in the future, no AMT credit is provided for exclusion preferences. The AMT credit is carried forward indefinitely from the year of payment and cannot be carried back.

TaxSaver

If you know you will be subject to exclusion-item-generated AMT in a given year, you should consider accelerating income into that year to be taxed at 26% or 28% rather than a possibly higher regular tax rate in the future. Likewise, consider deferring deductions, especially those that are not deductible for AMT purposes and will give you no benefit. For example, state income taxes are not deductible for AMT purposes. Therefore, you should not pre-pay your state income taxes in an AMT year. Many people ordinarily do pre-pay those taxes before year-end in order to claim that deduction for the current tax year. Another approach would be to elect to depreciate assets using the straight-line method of depreciation for regular tax purposes rather than an accelerated method.

CREDITS THAT REDUCE YOUR TAX

The credits discussed below may be used to offset your current income tax liability. For this purpose, income tax does not include certain other taxes, such as the alternative minimum tax and the additional taxes resulting from a premature distribution from certain retirement plans or an annuity contract.

Earned Income Credit

The earned income tax credit (EITC) is a refundable credit available to lower-income workers. For more information, see *The Ernst & Young Tax Guide 1997.*

Credit for Dependent Care Expenses

If you have dependent care expenses and your adjusted gross income is $10,000 or less, an income tax credit is available equal to 30% of certain employment-related expenses incurred for such care. The amount of the credit will decrease by 1% (but not below 20%) for each $2,000 (or part thereof) of your adjusted gross income in excess of $10,000. The maximum amount of employment-related expenses that can be taken into account for the credit is $2,400 for one qualifying individual and $4,800 for two or more qualifying individuals.

A qualifying individual is a dependent under the age of 13 for whom you are entitled to claim a dependency deduction, or a dependent or spouse who is physically or mentally incapable of caring for himself or herself.

For married taxpayers, expenses are limited to the lesser of the two earned incomes. However, the credit is available to married couples who file jointly when one spouse is physically or mentally incapable of caring for himself or herself or is a full-time student at an educational institution for five months during the year. Certain payments to relatives and to children over 19 who are not claimed as dependents will be considered qualified expenses. Married taxpayers must file a joint return in order to claim the credit.

Employment-related expenses are ordinarily expenses for household services and for the care of a qualifying individual that are incurred to enable you to be gainfully employed. Eligible expenses must be reduced by the amount excluded from your income for employer-provided dependent care assistance, including benefits received from cafeteria plans to which you have contributed. (See page 30.)

Credit for the Elderly and the Permanently and Totally Disabled

If you or your spouse is 65 years old or older, you may be entitled to a credit of as much as $1,125 against your tax. Furthermore, taxpayers under 65 years of age who are permanently and totally disabled may also be eligible for the credit. You are permanently and totally disabled if you cannot engage in any substantial gainful activity because of your physical or mental condition. A physician must certify that the condition has lasted or can be expected to last continuously for 12 months or more, or that the condition can be expected to result in death. Disabled veterans may file a VA Form 21-0172, "Certification of Permanent Total Disability," instead of the physician's statement.

In general, married persons who do not live apart must file a joint return to claim the credit. If both you and your spouse are 65 or older, you may qualify for the credit if your adjusted gross income is less than $25,000 and you received less than $7,500 of nontaxable Social Security or other nontaxable pensions. If you file as a single individual, you do not qualify for the tax credit if you are 65 years old or over and (1) you receive nontaxable Social Security or other nontaxable pensions of $5,000 or more, (2) your adjusted gross income is $17,500 or more, or (3) your tax is zero. Generally, the credit is not available to a nonresident alien.

Foreign Tax Credit

An individual may elect to claim a credit instead of a deduction for foreign income taxes. The foreign tax credit that may offset your U.S. tax liability is limited to the ratio of foreign-source taxable income to worldwide taxable income multiplied by the U.S. tax. To the extent that you use the foreign earned income exclusion (page 142), the foreign tax available for credit must be scaled down. To be able to use the credit in an earlier year, you must make a binding election to take the credit for foreign taxes on the accrual method.

Excess credits may be carried back two years and forward five years. The foreign tax credit must be recomputed to determine the foreign tax credit you are allowed to use against any alternative minimum tax liability.

TAXSAVER

Because $1 of tax credit reduces your tax liability by $1, whereas $1 of deduction will only reduce your federal tax liability by at most 39.6 cents, it is generally a good idea to elect to take a credit for foreign taxes paid rather than a deduction.

Other Credits

TAXALERT

Credit for Adoption Expenses. *After 1996, certain taxpayers who adopt a child will be entitled to claim a maximum non-refundable credit of $5,000 per child, for qualified adoption expenses. If you adopt a special needs child you would get an additional $1,000 credit. Qualified adoption expenses include adoption fees, court costs, attorney's fees and other expenses that are directly related to a legal adoption of an eligible child.*

The credit is phased out ratably for parents with adjusted gross income, as specially defined in the law for this purpose, above $75,000 and is fully phased out at $115,000.

Investment Tax Credit. The regular investment tax credit is generally no longer available for property placed in service after 1985, with certain exceptions.

Expenditures to rehabilitate certified historic structures and other qualified buildings that are to be used for nonresidential purposes are still eligible for the investment tax credit. For qualified buildings placed in service after 1986, the credit is equal to 10% of qualified expenditures for nonresidential buildings first placed in service prior to 1936 and 20% for certified historic structures. The 20% credit is available for both residential and nonresidential buildings. The regular investment tax credit and the business energy credit do not apply to any portion of the basis in the property that qualifies for the rehabilitation credit.

Transitional rules apply to property placed in service before 1994 and qualifying under additional transition rules.

General Business Credit. The investment credit is combined with the alcohol fuel credit (page 249), and the research credit (page 249) into one general business credit. This credit can be claimed against 100% of the first $25,000 of tax liability net of all other nonrefundable credits and 75% of the remaining tax liability. Excess credits can be carried back for 3 years or carried forward for a 15-year period. Excess credit carryovers generally are used on an earliest-year-first basis, followed by current-year credits and credit carrybacks.

If property on which the investment credit was previously taken is disposed of before the end of the period used in initially determining the credit, the credit must be recomputed, and the unearned portion may have to be recaptured as additional tax in the year of disposal. For ACRS property (see page 228), a portion (33% for three-year property, 20% for other property) of the credit amount is earned for each full year subsequent to being placed in service. If the property disposed of was subject to the limitation applied to used property, you may reselect used property on which no investment credit was taken in the year of acquisition to take the place of the property disposed.

Credit for Excise Taxes Paid on the Use of Gasoline and Special Fuels. A credit or refund is available for the federal excise tax paid on gasoline for nonhighway business use, qualified bus and taxicab use, and certain aviation use. A boat must be used as a commercial fishing vessel for the fuel use to qualify for the credit. A credit or refund is also available for special fuels used for certain nontaxable purposes or resold during the tax year. The credit claimed must be included in income if the cost of the product was deducted as a business expense according to your method of accounting.

ESTIMATED TAX PAYMENTS AND WITHHOLDING

The IRS requires that taxpayers pay their anticipated tax liability as it accrues through withholding and/or the payment of estimated taxes in quarterly installments.

Individuals are automatically exempt from estimated tax payments if they fall into one of two categories:

(1) Those whose tax for the current year, after credit for withheld taxes, Social Security tax refunds, and backup withholding is less than $500, and

(2) Those who had no tax liability for the preceding tax year and were U.S. citizens throughout such year. This rule does not apply if the preceding tax year consisted of less than 12 months or if a return was not filed for the preceding year.

Withholding Tax From Your Wages.   Income tax is generally withheld from your wages and salaries based on the amount you earned and the withholding information you have supplied your employer on Form W-4, *Employee's Withholding Allowance Certificate.* If you have significant income from other sources such as self-employment, alimony, interest, dividends, and rent, or the amount of tax withheld from your wages and salaries is not enough, you may have to make estimated tax payments.

Estimated Tax Payments.   Estimated tax may be paid in full when the taxpayer determines he or she is liable for such tax or in equal installments. Estimated tax payments for a calendar-year taxpayer are due on April 15, June 15, and September 15, and January 15 of the following year. If a filing or payment due date falls on a Saturday, Sunday, or legal holiday, the next working day is substituted. You can make your estimated payments either through crediting an overpayment from your prior year's return to the current year or by sending in your payment with a payment voucher, Form 1040-ES.

If conditions requiring estimated tax payments do not arise until after March 31, a calendar-year taxpayer must make payments on the due dates shown in Table 9.3.

TABLE 9.3   Estimated Tax Payment Deadlines

Date Requirement Met	Date Payments Due*
After March 31 and before June 1	June 15, and September 16, 1996, and January 15, 1997
After May 31 and before September 1	September 16, 1996 and January 15, 1997
After August 31	January 15, 1997

Corresponding dates apply to fiscal-year taxpayers for payments and returns.

The amount of estimated tax you pay may be amended on or before any subsequent installment date.

A complete return may be filed by January 31, with payment of the balance of tax due for the calendar year, in lieu of a January 15 payment of estimated tax.

TaxSaver

It is generally not a good idea to file your tax return by January 31 if you owe tax with the return. You will be better off keeping any additional tax you owe in an interest-generating bank account for two and a half months rather than paying your tax bill early.

The IRS does not issue reminder statements for installments due on estimated taxes. It is the taxpayer's responsibility to remit each installment on a timely basis. (See below for information on waiver of the underpayment penalty for certain taxpayers.)

Any unpaid tax is generally due by the original due date of the tax return, which is April 15, 1997, for a calendar-year 1996 taxpayer. If you have overpaid your tax, you may elect to have the overpayment refunded or applied against next year's tax liability.

TaxSaver

If it appears during the year that you will have underpaid your current year's taxes because previous estimated payments and/or withholding prove insufficient in meeting your actual tax liability, you can correct the situation by instructing your employer to withhold greater amounts from your wages for the rest of the year. Payments that are withheld are considered paid evenly throughout the year.

Underpayment Penalties. You may be penalized for not paying enough tax for a particular installment period. The amount subject to the penalty is the amount by which the required installment, defined as the lesser of items 1 or 2 below, exceeds the amount paid for the quarterly period:

1. 90% of the tax shown on the return (after certain adjustments), allocated evenly to each of the quarterly periods; or
2. 100% (or 110% for certain high-income taxpayers, see below) of the prior year's tax, allocated evenly to each of the quarterly periods (provided the prior year comprised 12 months and a return was filed for such year); if your previous year's adjusted gross income exceeds $150,000, you must pay 110% of last year's liability to be certain of avoiding any underpayment penalties.

   Example: Ms. Green's 1996 income tax liability is $55,000. Her adjusted gross income in 1995 was $175,000, while her 1995 tax liability was $40,000. Ms. Green will avoid an underpayment penalty in 1996 if the total amount of tax withheld and estimated tax payments exceeds

110% of her 1995 tax liability, or $44,000, because her 1995 adjusted gross income exceeded $150,000.

The underpayment penalty may also be avoided by using a special rule based on your annualized income. Under the special rule, no penalty is imposed for a quarter if the cumulative amount paid by the installment date equals or exceeds 90% of the cumulative estimated tax as computed on annualized income.

In general, the annualized method allows you to calculate your quarterly payment based on taxable income received up to the end of the latest quarter, annualized to a 12-month period. You can usually benefit from the annualized method if you do not receive your taxable income evenly throughout the year (for example, if you are the owner of a ski shop that receives most of its revenue during the winter months).

The use of the methods for determining the underpaid amount, described above, may vary from quarter to quarter to provide the minimum underpayment amount by quarter. Remember, however, that if you pay the annualized income installment, you must add the difference between the amount you pay and the required installment to the required installment for the next period if the annualized income method is not used for the next period.

The tax computed for purposes of determining the quarterly payments required to avoid the underpayment penalty includes the self-employment tax and all other taxes (including the alternative minimum tax), minus any allowable credits.

If the amount paid for a quarterly period is greater than the amount required to avoid penalty, the excess is applied first against underpayments in prior quarters, and then against subsequent underpayments. Any penalty is assessed from the installment due date to the date paid or the original due date of the return, whichever is earlier. The rate of the penalty is the same as the rate of interest for underpayments of tax. However, the penalty is not compounded daily, whereas the interest is.

Special requirements and exceptions are provided for farmers, fishermen, and nonresident aliens.

EMPLOYMENT TAXES ON SERVICES BY DOMESTIC EMPLOYEES

If you have a domestic helper who qualifies as your employee you and your employee may be subject to Social Security and Medicare taxes as well as federal and state unemployment taxes.

This may affect your 1996 Individual Income Tax Return (Form 1040) so it deserves your careful attention. This chart will give you the general rules for calendar year 1996. The application of this flowchart assumes that the household worker is properly classified as an "employee" rather than an "independent contractor" for payroll tax purposes. Although it has been called the "nanny-tax," you should know that it also applies to cooks, sitters, chauffeurs, yard workers, and so forth, who are employees. This chart will give you the highlights.

Did you:	If yes, then:
A. Pay to any household employee, age 18 or older, cash wages aggregating $1,000 or more in 1996? (Exclude wages paid to taxpayer's parents, spouse, or children under age 21.)	Employer and employee shares of Social Security and Medicare taxes are payable on the cash wages of each employee who received $1,000 or more in 1996.
B. Agree to withhold federal income tax on wages of any household employee in 1996?	Amounts withheld must be remitted to the IRS.
C. Pay total cash wages of $1,000 or more in any calendar quarter of 1995 or 1996 to household employees? (Exclude wages paid to taxpayer's parents, spouse, or children under age 21.)	Federal Unemployment Tax Act (FUTA) tax is payable on the first $7,000 paid to each employee in 1996.

and . . .
■ Amounts due are to be shown on Schedule H of Form 1040, which must be filed with your 1996 return. ■ You must have (or apply for) an employer identification number. ■ If either Question A or B is answered *yes* for a given employee, Form W-2 must be provided to that employee by 1/31/97 and transmitted with Form W-3 to the Social Security Administration by 2/28/97.

For more information, see Chapter 38, What to Do if You Employ Domestic Help, in the *Ernst & Young Tax Guide 1997*.

PENALTIES

The penalty imposed for late filing is 5% of the unpaid amount for each month or part of a month that it remains unpaid up to a maximum of 25% of the unpaid tax. If you fail to file for more than 60 days, the penalty may not be less than the smaller of either $100 or 100% of the tax required to be shown on the return. If the return is filed on time but is not accompanied by payment of the balance due as shown on the return, the penalty is one half of 1% of the balance due for each month or part of a month of delinquency (up to a maximum of 25% of the unpaid tax). The penalties apply unless the taxpayer can show reasonable cause for the delay. Additional penalties are also imposed on underpayments of tax due to negligence or fraud, and on substantial understatements of tax liability.

10

Year-End Planning for Individuals

INTRODUCTION

This chapter takes a look at the future direction of the tax law and suggests some strategies that you might adopt to better cope with change.

As this book went to press in late summer of 1996, a tax debate was simmering in Congress. In all likelihood, Congress will be kicking around new tax proposals in 1997 as well. You can reasonably assume that individual tax rates will not increase in 1996 and 1997.

What kind of tax strategies does that suggest? Generally, when tax rates are stable, you would be wise to defer as much income as possible from one year to a later year and to accelerate deductions so that you can postpone the payment of the tax. This strategy allows you the use of more money for a longer period of time. However, you need to take care to have enough cash on hand to pay the tax when it is due. On the other hand, if you expect to be in a higher tax bracket next year than you are this year, you might consider accelerating income into the current year and deferring deductions.

In theory, the strategy is simple: realize income when your tax rate is low and pay expenses when it is high. Marriage, divorce, promotions, retirement, illness, death, or sales of major assets can cause your taxable income to change from one year to another. All of these life-cycle events require special tax planning. The following discussion highlights several strategies that can help you save money on your taxes for 1996 and beyond.

The first step in your year-end planning will be for you to estimate your 1996 and 1997 taxable income. The worksheets provided on pages 170–172 will help you do this.

Shifting Income

There is a 24.6% spread between the highest (39.6%) and lowest (15%) marginal tax rates. Tax savings can potentially be realized by shifting income among family members, especially to children. Higher-income parents should consider transferring assets that generate ordinary income, such as dividends and interest, to children age 14 or older in order to take advantage of their lower tax bracket. For example, shifting $10,000 of investment income from a parent in the 39.6% tax bracket to a child over 14 who is in the 15% bracket (which currently applies to taxable income up to $24,000) can save the family $2,460 in taxes per year. Even greater tax savings may be achieved by spreading ordinary income among all of the taxpayer's children to take advantage of each child's lower tax bracket. Finally, since children under age 14 pay only $97.50 ($650 × 15%; see Chapter 9) in tax on the first $1,300 of unearned income they receive (unearned income above $1,300 is taxed at their parents' highest marginal tax bracket . . . the so-called "kiddie tax"), shifting income-producing property that earns up to $1,300 to a child under age 14 can save the family as much as $417.30 in taxes each year [$1,300 × 39.6% (parents' rate) − $97.50 (tax paid by the child)].

Accelerating deductions to the current year would be potentially beneficial if the deduction will not be lost or substantially diminished by the 3% of adjusted gross income floor on certain itemized deductions or other limitations on deducting itemized deductions. The 3% floor is explained on page 53.

Limits on Certain Itemized Deductions

Given the limits on certain itemized deductions and exemptions for certain high-income taxpayers (explained in Chapter 2), your best planning move, if possible, would be to exercise some control over the amount of your adjusted gross income. If you can keep your income below the level at which deductions become subject to certain limitations in one year, you would be able to deduct the full amount of personal exemptions and deductions. Obviously, you would want to take as many deductions as possible in such a year.

The Alternative Minimum Tax Rate

As discussed in Chapter 9, the Alternative Minimum Tax (AMT) is a tax system imposed on the regular tax system to prevent taxpayers from taking too great an advantage of special tax breaks such as accelerated depreciation, interest on certain tax-exempt bonds, and so on. Taxpayers who do not use these tax preferences to lower their regular income tax will not be subject to the AMT. Taxpayers who do avail themselves of tax preferences may still escape the AMT because their Alternative Minimum Taxable Income is reduced by exemptions:

Filing Status	Exemption Amount	Exemption Phased Out by 25% of Amount in Excess of	Exemption Fully Phased Out at
Married filing jointly	$45,000	$150,000	$330,000
Single	33,750	112,500	247,500
Married filing separately	22,500	75,000	165,000

High-income taxpayers who avail themselves of tax preferences may be subject to the tax if they do not plan carefully.

Taxpayers subject to the AMT will pay tax at the following rates:

Rate	Married Filing Separately	All Other Filers
26%	Up to $87,500 over exemption amount	Up to $175,000 over exemption amount
28%	Greater than $87,500 over exemption amount	Greater than $175,000 over exemption amount

Taxpayers subject to the alternative minimum tax may find that accelerating income and deferring deductions may be the most effective planning approach. For further discussion of the AMT, see Chapter 9.

FILING STATUS

In general, the effective tax rates on total family income for married taxpayers filing jointly and heads of households are lower than for a taxpayer who files individually (see Filing Status in Chapter 9 and the tax tables in the Appendix for more information.) Thus, if you are eligible to file a joint return for the year, you probably should. For a married person filing jointly for 1996, the 15% tax bracket applies to income ranging from $0 to $41,100. For an individual filing for 1996, the 15% tax bracket applies for taxable income ranging from $0 to $24,000. Not only can you save on your taxes, but for most people, it's simpler to file a joint return. Since a husband and wife are treated as one taxpayer, you won't have to sort out which deductions are his and which are hers.

Effects of Filing Status

There are circumstances where single individuals will find that their combined tax is higher after they marry. This is commonly known as the "marriage penalty."

Example 1: Bob Jones and Mary Smith each have taxable income of $50,000. As single individuals, they are each in the 28% bracket. But if they marry they will have a joint income of $100,000 and part of their income will be in the 31% bracket.

TaxSaver

If your filing status will change before the end of the year, you should decide whether to defer income and accelerate deductions or the opposite, depending on whether or not you will be subject to the marriage penalty. You also should consider whether you would be better off filing separate returns.

Example 2: Two people are married and one spouse has medical expenses of $10,000; the other has none. Both have adjusted gross income of $50,000. They are allowed a medical deduction for amounts in excess of 7.5% of AGI. If they file a joint return, the medical deduction would be $2,500 ($10,000 − [7.5% × $100,000]). If they file separate returns, all other things being equal, the medical deduction would be $6,250 ($10,000 − [7.5% × $50,000]).

TAX SAVER

You should figure your tax both jointly and separately to see which produces the best result.

Your filing status may also affect the new limitations on itemized deductions. All taxpayers, whether filing as individuals, heads of household, or jointly, have their itemized deductions reduced by an amount that is equal to 3% of the excess of their adjusted gross income over $117,950 ($58,975 for married persons filing separately). Certain expenses and losses, such as medical expenses, casualty and theft losses, and investment interest expense are not subject to this limitation but may be subject to other limitations. A working couple with a combined AGI over $137,950 is subject to a phaseout reduction of $600 (3% of $20,000). However, two single individuals each with AGI of $68,975 are both beneath the $117,950 limitation.

When to File as a Head of Household. If you are unmarried at the end of the year, you might save money by filing as a head of household, instead of a single return. To qualify, in addition to being unmarried, you must maintain a household that was the principal home for the year of a child, grandchild, or other relative who qualifies as your dependent.

If you are still married but have lived apart from your spouse for at least six months of the year, and you have custody of your child, you may be able to file as head of household instead of married filing separately. You will benefit from lower tax rates and you also may be able to claim the standard deduction even if your spouse itemizes deductions. If your income is high enough that some of your exemptions may be phased out, you should consider letting your spouse claim dependents.

If Your Spouse Died During the Year. If your spouse died during 1996, leaving you with one or more dependent children, you may continue to file jointly for the two years following your spouse's death and take advantage of the more favorable married filing jointly rates. You may claim an exemption for your deceased spouse in the year of death, but not in subsequent years.

INCOME

Compensation

High tax rates enhance the benefits of deferred compensation plans and other tax-deferral arrangements, if you anticipate being in a lower tax bracket when the income is eventually received. For example, 401(k) plans, individual retirement accounts, Keogh plans, other retirement plans, and life insurance policies that build up cash benefits over a period of years should most certainly be considered if you are in this situation.

Bonuses. Bonuses generally are income to you when you receive them, not when earned. But they are also deductible by your employer when paid. If you want to defer income, you may be able to arrange with your employer before the amount of the bonus is determined that you will not be paid your bonus until next year. Your employer may balk. Yes, he or she gets to keep the bonus money longer, thereby helping cash flow, but having the money in company coffers also increases the company's taxable income. So, if you want to defer your bonus payment, remember to ask early in the year. You can't wait until your employer is passing out the checks and say "I'd like mine next year."

Deferred Compensation. Another way to defer income from one year to the next is to use a deferred compensation plan. These plans are designed for executives who can afford to defer a portion of their income until a future date. Under these plans the executive makes an election to defer some portion of his or her income until a stated time and is taxed on the deferred income only when it is received.

Deferrals can be made from regular salary or from bonuses. To be effective, however, an election to defer income must be made before that income is earned. Further, the executive and the employer must enter into a *written* deferral agreement. Be aware, however, that the IRS may be suspicious of short-term deferrals, say, from December 1996 to January 1997. One problem with deferred compensation plans is that they must be subject to the claims of general creditors and may be subject to the whims of future management.

TAXSAVER

An acceptable way to fund deferred compensation—generally over a relatively long period—is to use a "rabbi trust." A rabbi trust is generally an irrevocable trust established by the employer to pay deferred compensation to the employee. Although the trust's assets must remain subject to claims of the employer's creditors, the trust arrangement protects the individual from the whims of the employer and from a change in control of the company. The employee is not protected if the employer becomes insolvent or goes into bankruptcy.

Even more secure than a "rabbi trust" is a "secular trust." Funds held in a secular trust are not accessible by an employer's creditors. However, the price for the added security is that you must pay tax currently on any amounts contributed to the trust. In turn, the company is allowed a current tax deduction when funds are transferred to the trust.

401(k) Plans. If your employer has a 401(k) plan, you can elect to defer into the plan a certain amount of your salary on a pretax basis. These amounts are withheld from your salary and are not reported as taxable income until withdrawn from the plan. Before the end of the tax year, it is usually a good idea to make sure you have made as large a contribution to your 401(k) plan as possible. You can elect to defer up to 20% of your wages up to a maximum of $9,500 in 1996. Also see the discussion of 401(k) plans in Chapter 5, IRAs, 401(k) Plans, and Other Retirement Plans.

Taxation of Social Security Benefits

The law taxes up to 85% of Social Security benefits received by higher income recipients. The added tax burden means that certain Social Security recipients would benefit from shifting some of their investments from income-producing assets to investments that favor capital appreciation. Or, you may stagger the recognition of income so that you create alternating years of high and low income. Under the right circumstances, you may be able to reduce the amount of Social Security benefits taxed in the *low-income* years without increasing the amount of benefits that otherwise would have been taxed in the *high-income* years.

Interest Income

Taxable Interest.   One way to defer interest income from now until next year is to purchase short-term (one year or less) certificates of deposit before the end of the year. Not just any CD will do: it must be the type on which interest is not made available, without substantial penalty, before the 1996 maturity date. The advantage is that you can postpone the accrual of interest income in 1995.

Treasury bills offer a similar opportunity. T-bills do not pay interest, but are sold at a discount and mature at their face value. The difference represents interest. It is not taxable to you until the T-bill matures if you hold it until that time. By buying a T-bill that matures next year, you can defer reporting interest from the date of purchase until the following year.

Example: Suppose you have $50,000 in a savings account that credits you with interest on the last day of each month. If, on November 1, 1996, you purchase a six-month CD or a three-month T-bill, you will be able to defer the November and December interest until next year.

Tax-Exempt Interest.   Tax-exempt bonds and bond funds should appeal to high tax bracket taxpayers, especially those in the 39.6% top marginal tax bracket. As tax rates rise, taxable securities must provide higher yields in order to match the yield offered by tax-exempt bonds of similar quality and time to maturity.

Example: If you are in the 31% tax bracket, a taxable bond yielding 8.69% is comparable to a municipal bond with a 6.0% tax-exempt yield. However, if you are in the 39.6% bracket, you would need almost a 10% yield on a taxable bond to match the municipal bond's 6.0% return. In addition, bear in mind that some states have income tax rates over 10%. Consequently, your combined federal and state marginal tax rate—factoring in the phase-out of deductions and exemptions for higher income taxpayers and other "back door" tax increases—can exceed 50%. An investor living in such a high tax state would need a 12% taxable bond to achieve the same after-tax return as a 6% municipal bond.

Here's a chart showing the equivalent taxable investment yields for tax-exempt yields ranging from 5%–10% at various individual tax rates.

Your Tax Bracket	*Tax-Exempt Equivalent Yields*					
	5%	6%	7%	8%	9%	10%
15%	5.88	7.06	8.24	9.41	10.58	11.76
28%	6.94	8.33	9.72	11.11	12.50	13.88
31%	7.25	8.70	10.14	11.59	13.04	14.49
36.0%	7.81	9.38	10.94	12.50	14.06	15.60
39.6%	8.28	9.93	11.59	13.25	14.90	16.55

For example, if you are in the 36% bracket, a 7% yield on a tax-exempt investment provides you with the equivalent after-tax return as a taxable investment yielding 10.94%.

Alimony

Alimony is treated as income to the recipient and a deduction for the payor. The tax law allows a great deal of discretion to both the payor and payee of the alimony about how to set up payments that will provide the maximum tax benefit to both parties. Therefore, there are a variety of year-end planning opportunities to consider.

Example: Individuals finalizing a divorce or separation agreement in the final months of 1996 can negotiate a disproportionately large deductible payment for 1996 as long as it does not exceed the average of the total payments for 1997 and 1998 plus $15,000.

This is a very complex area of the law. Therefore, you should consult with your tax advisor, and it is also important to keep your records in good order. See Chapter 2 for more details.

Business Expenses

Business Travel. The IRS allows employers to reimburse employees for business automobile travel at the rate of 31 cents per mile. However, actual expenses will frequently exceed the allowable reimbursement. In many cases you will be entitled to larger deduction for automobile expenses if you use your actual automobile expense figures rather than the IRS per-mile allowance.

Unreimbursed Business Expenses. Many self-employed taxpayers don't realize that they are entitled to deduct the cost of unreimbursed items such as business gifts up to $25 per recipient. These unreimbursed business expenses should be treated as trade or business expenses, not as miscellaneous itemized deductions subject to the 2% of adjusted gross income floor. An employed executive who buys an attaché case and is not reimbursed would treat the expense deduction as a miscellaneous itemized deduction, subject to the 2% floor. However, if a self-employed individual makes a similar purchase, it is a trade or business expense, fully deductible on Schedule C. For more information, see Chapter 3, Travel and Entertainment Expenses.

Vacation Homes

Review your personal use before the year ends to avoid the loss of your deduction for interest and taxes (see Chapter 4).

Capital Assets

Stock. You may wish to consider deferring the recognition of capital gains from 1996 to 1997. Several strategies can be used to defer the gain on the sale of stock until the following year (see the discussion of capital gains and losses in Chapter 7).

Passive Activity Losses. You can recognize suspended losses from a "passive activity" when you dispose of your entire interest in it. Year-end may be a particularly opportune time to recognize such losses. These passive activity losses can offset active or passive activity income or portfolio income. "Passive activities" are discussed on page 11. You should consult your tax advisor before recognizing passive activity losses.

E&Y FOCUS: Mutual Fund Strategies

As the year-end approaches, many funds will be realizing substantial amounts of their gains, which will flow through to you as capital gain distributions. You can ask your funds' distributors to estimate the expected distributions and their timing. This information is critical if you are trying to produce a net loss that will offset up to $3,000 of ordinary income.

Also, if you are contemplating a mutual fund purchase now, try to avoid "buying the distribution"—i.e., buying shares just before the fund's record date for the year-end distribution. Before you act, find out if the fund has significant realized gains. If it does, consider waiting until after the record date before making your purchase.

TAXSAVER

Specifying shares of stock, mutual funds and other investments is another tax-smart investment strategy. For instance, let's say you first purchased shares in a fund for $30, and over the years the share price rose to $50 as you continued to purchase additional shares. Now the price has dropped to $40 and you decide to sell a portion of your investment. Overall, you still have the potential to realize a large gain.

However, if you have adequate records, you can identify and sell the shares you paid $50 for, and sell them to realize a $10 loss that will offset any other gains you realized this year. See page 118 for additional details.

Business Property

Selling property at a loss this year can keep your adjusted gross income down. This not only reduces your taxable income but can also—if your adjusted gross income is above a certain level—actually increase the amount of your exemptions and itemized deductions.

The sale of certain business property qualifies for special tax treatment. If you sell it at a loss the loss is an ordinary income loss. If you sell it at a gain the gain is treated as long-term capital gain. It's one of the few win-win situations left in the tax law—sole proprietors should pay special attention.

Giving Business Property to Charity. If you are a self-employed individual and are thinking about giving business property to charity, make sure that you won't be better off from a tax standpoint selling the property and making an outright contribution to the charity from your personal funds.

ADJUSTMENTS AND DEDUCTIONS

These days, reducing your adjusted gross income (AGI) can be as important as reducing your taxable income. Your personal exemptions are phased out if your AGI is above a certain amount. Furthermore, your itemized deductions are limited if your AGI exceeds $117,950 ($58,975 if married filing separately).

Adjustments

You may be able to reduce your adjusted gross income through various adjustments:
- Your IRA deduction and your spouse's deduction, if applicable;
- One-half of self-employment tax;
- Health insurance for self-employed individuals;

- Keogh and Simplified Employee Pension (SEP);
- Alimony.
  All of these items, except alimony (see page 163), are discussed below.

Self-Employment Tax and Health Insurance for Self-Employed Individuals

If you pay self-employment tax, half of it is deductible. Since you are going to have to pay it anyway, you may want to consider paying it this year.

Self-employed individuals and employee-owners of 2% or more of the stock in an S corporation may deduct (as an adjustment to gross income) 30% of the premiums paid for health insurance coverage of the individual and his or her spouse and dependents. (The deduction for 1994 and earlier years was 25%.)

TAX*ALERT*

After 1996 the deduction for health insurance for self-employed individuals (and more-than-2% employee-shareholders of S corporations) will be 40% for 1997; 45% for 1998 through 2002; 50% for 2003; 60% for 2004; 70% for 2005; and 80% for 2006 and thereafter.

IRAs, Keoghs, and SEPs

IRAs. Contributions can be made up to the due date of your tax return, not including any extensions, and still be deductible on your previous year's tax return. Thus, you have until April 15, 1997 to make an IRA contribution and claim it on your 1996 return. By contributing pretax dollars to an IRA, you can accumulate savings while reducing your taxable income. For a further discussion of IRAs, see Chapter 5.

TAX*SAVER*

Although you can make a contribution to an IRA at any time up to the unextended filing date of the return in which the deduction is claimed, the earlier you make the contribution the greater the ultimate benefit. Here is an example:

Taxpayers A, B, and C contribute the maximum amount possible to their IRAs. Only the contribution pattern differs. A makes annual contributions of $2,000 beginning on Jan. 2; B contributes $166.66 January 31, and the end of each month thereafter; and C makes its initial contribution on April 15 of the following year. This table shows the effect over time of their contribution patterns assuming a constant 8% rate of return.

For example, assuming 10 years of contributions (i.e., $20,000), the balance of the account for taxpayer A would be $33,794 whereas taxpayer C would have $30,498.

| | Number of Years of Contribution | | |
Taxpayer	10 years	20 years	30 years
A contributes 1/1	$33,794	$106,754	$264,267
B contributes monthly	32,422	102,420	253,539
C contributes the next 4/15	30,498	96,342	238,494

Keogh Plans. Individuals with self-employment income may establish a retirement plan known as a Keogh plan, to which they may make tax deductible contributions. (For details, see Chapter 2.) Although a plan must be established by year-end, unlike an IRA, you have until the due date of your return, including extensions, to make the maximum allowable contributions. A Keogh plan is a qualified retirement plan. Participation in a Keogh plan limits IRA deductions. Consequently, before establishing one you should consult your tax advisor. A rule of thumb is that a start-up business should produce at least $15,000 in self-employment income before a Keogh plan becomes as cost effective as an IRA.

SEPs. A Simplified Employee Pension (SEP), like an IRA, can be established after the end of the taxable year for which the deduction is being claimed. The plan must be established prior to the due date of the *employer's* tax return including any extensions. For further details about SEPs, see Chapter 5.

ITEMIZED DEDUCTIONS

To receive the maximum tax benefit when itemizing your deductions, you should generally try to bunch your deductible payments in years in which they exceed the amount of your standard deduction and also exceed the floors based on adjusted gross income for medical expenses and miscellaneous deductions.

Your first decision is to choose between itemizing deductions or taking the standard deduction amount ($6,700 in 1996 for married taxpayers filing jointly and qualifying widow(ers); $4,000 in 1996 for single filers; $5,900 for heads of households; and $3,350 for married persons filing separately). You should choose whichever alternative yields the higher deduction. (See Chapter 2 for a further discussion of itemized deductions and the standard deduction.) If it is likely that you will opt to itemize your deductions, you'd be well advised before the end of the tax year to review them and see if there are ways you can slide some into whatever tax year might yield a more favorable result. Casualty and theft losses cannot be planned. It's also usually difficult to plan deductible moving expenses related to your job. So, for practical purposes, you should focus your review on the following four types of expenditures:

- Medical and dental expenses in excess of 7.5% of your adjusted gross income
- Certain state and local taxes
- Interest expenses
- Contributions to charity

Each of these types of expenses is discussed below.

Medical and Dental Expenses

Your medical expenses, including certain health insurance premiums, are deductible only to the extent that they exceed 7.5% of your adjusted gross income (AGI) (10% if you are subject to the alternative minimum tax, AMT). While you do not have control over medical emergencies, you do have control over elective medical procedures. These should be bunched in years when your AGI is lower. That way your medical expenses are more likely to exceed the 7.5% floor. You may be even better off if you participate in your employer's cafeteria plan (see page 30, Cafeteria Plans, for further explanation).

Taxes You Paid

State and local income and property taxes generally are itemized deductions. For the most part you will have paid your state income taxes, and in some instances your local income taxes, through withholding. However, before year-end you may wish to pay those taxes that you would normally pay early next year because your liability was not fully satisfied through withholding. Also, taxpayers with large state and local tax liabilities may be subject to the AMT, since these taxes are not deductible for AMT purposes.

Interest You Paid

Qualified Home Mortgage Interest. Typically, homeowners make monthly mortgage payments throughout the year. The mortgage interest on those payments generally is deductible subject to the rules and limits explained in Chapter 2.

Personal or Consumer Interest. Although personal or consumer interest is not deductible, interest on a home equity loan is deductible. Therefore, one way to increase your interest deduction is to consolidate your personal and consumer loans into a home equity loan. Many banks are now structuring what used to be personal and auto loans as home equity loans. (There is a further discussion of home-equity loans in Chapter 4.)

Contributions to Charity

Most taxpayers make many of their charitable contributions at the end of the tax year. The reason is simple: you can have use of the money for the entire year and, at the same time, you can take the tax deduction for that year. If you made your contribution in January, you would be entitled to the same tax deduction but would not have use of the money for the rest of the year. Charitable contributions are available only if you itemize your deductions. You'll find a comprehensive discussion of charitable contributions in Chapter 6.

TAX*SAVER*

A few points to consider, especially at year-end:
1. *If cash is not readily available, you can use a credit card to charge donations to charity. They will be deductible in 1996 even though you don't pay the charge until 1997.*
2. *If you are going to give publicly traded stock to a charity, check with your stock broker to ensure that you have readily transferable title to the property that you want to donate to charity.*
3. *Under a provision enacted in August 1996, a contribution of appreciated long-term capital gain stock to a private foundation will qualify for a full fair market value deduction.* **This applies only to gifts made during the period July 1, 1996 through May 31, 1997.**

Deferred Giving.   There are ways to make deferred contributions to a charity and also claim a deduction: (1) A charitable "remainder" trust lets a donor retain an interest in the property's current income stream and to claim a current charitable deduction for the present value of the remainder interest given to charity. (2) A charitable "lead" trust pays income to a charity for a term of years (the lead), at the end of which the principal of the trust reverts to the grantor or other noncharitable beneficiary. This technique can result in a current deduction equal to the present value of the income the trust will pay to the charity. You would include income on your return as the trust earns it. If the trust is funded with tax-free bonds, the interest you receive in future years is treated as tax free. If you want to establish a charitable remainder or lead trust, you should do so before year-end and with the assistance of a professional advisor. Also, see Chapter 2 for details.

Miscellaneous Deductions

Generally, only the amount of miscellaneous deductions that, considered as a group, exceed 2% of your adjusted gross income is deductible. Therefore, you should bunch these expenses as much as possible so that the total will exceed the 2% floor. If it appears that you will not exceed the floor this year, defer these expenses until next year if you can. Alternatively, accelerate expenses to this year if that will enable you to exceed the 2% floor.

TAXSAVER

Married persons who customarily file jointly should consider filing separately to maximize miscellaneous deductions. Note, however, that miscellaneous itemized deductions are not allowed for the calculation of the alternative minimum tax.

Exemptions

Review the amount of support you have provided so far this year to your dependents, children and parents, to ensure that you meet the support test that allows you to claim an exemption for them as dependents. Also be aware of the rules that phase out the tax benefits of exemptions if your adjusted gross income exceeds certain levels. See Chapter 2.

Paying Your Taxes

An important aspect of tax planning, particularly year-end tax planning, is how and when you pay your tax liability. This affects your cash flow and may result in real savings for you.

You should review not only your expected tax liability but also when that tax is paid. Significant overpayments are essentially interest-free loans to the government, but underpayments may result in a nondeductible penalty. See page 153.

TAXSAVER

If you have not paid enough up to this point, consider increasing your federal and state withholdings from salary or wages for the remainder of the year. Taxes withheld are considered paid evenly throughout the year. Therefore, increased withholdings at the end of the year could eliminate an underpayment in the beginning of the year. In addition, itemized deductions would increase as a result of the additional state taxes withheld. However, taxpayers claiming large state tax deductions may subject themselves to the AMT.

If you project a significant overpayment, reduce your tax payments for the balance of 1996 by at least the amount of your overpayment. This step should be done only when estimates are considered fairly accurate, or when you are certain not to have an underpayment penalty. Reducing current payments below your tax bill for the year will cause a larger amount to be due with your return. That balance due, unlike the return itself, generally cannot be extended beyond the original due date of the return (i.e., April 15, 1997, for 1996 calendar-year taxpayers).

Worksheet to Estimate 1996 and 1997 Federal Income Tax*

Gross income	*1995 (actual)*	*1996*	*1997*
Wages and salaries	$_____	$_____	$_____
Interest income	_____	_____	_____
Dividends	_____	_____	_____
Income or loss from trade or business	_____	_____	_____
Net capital gains or losses	_____	_____	_____
Rents and royalties	_____	_____	_____
Income or loss from partnerships, trusts, estates, and S corporations [1]	_____	_____	_____
Pensions and annuities	_____	_____	_____
Taxable Social Security benefits	_____	_____	_____
Other	_____	_____	_____
Less: Deductions for adjusted gross income (AGI)			
Alimony paid	(_____)	(_____)	(_____)
Payments to an IRA or Keogh plan [2]	(_____)	(_____)	(_____)
Other	(_____)	(_____)	(_____)
Equals: AGI	$_____	$_____	$_____

Itemized deductions

Medical and dental (in excess of 7.5% of AGI)	$_____	$_____	$_____
State and local income taxes, property taxes [3]	_____	_____	_____
Qualified residential interest	_____	_____	_____
Investment interest expense [4]	_____	_____	_____
Charitable contributions	_____	_____	_____
Casualty and theft loss (in excess of 10% of AGI)	_____	_____	_____
Moving expenses	_____	_____	_____
Other: Tax preparation fees, investment fees, and employee business expenses [5]	_____	_____	_____
Total itemized deductions	_____	_____	_____
Less: 3% of AGI adjustment [6]	(_____)	(_____)	(_____)
Adjusted itemized deductions	_____	_____	_____
Standard deduction	_____	_____	_____
AGI less the higher of adjusted itemized deduction or the standard deduction [7]	_____	_____	_____

Less: Number of exemptions × $2,500 (1995)[8] or $2,550 (1996)	(_____)	(_____)	(_____)
Equals: Taxable income	_____	_____	_____
Regular tax (from tax rate schedule, see page 267)[9]	_____	_____	_____

*Does not include the Alternative Minimum Tax (AMT) computation (see the discussion of the AMT on page 145).

1. Except for rental losses allowed up to certain AGI limits, passive activity losses in excess of passive activity income from each activity are disallowed.
2. If you or your spouse are participants in an employer-maintained retirement plan, your IRA deduction may be limited.
3. If you have unusually large deductions for state and local taxes and/or substantial tax preference items, page 146, you may be subject to the alternative minimum tax.
4. Investment interest expense deductions are limited to the amount of the taxpayer's net investment income.
5. Most miscellaneous itemized deductions are deductible only to the extent they exceed 2% of AGI. Employee business expenses in excess of reimbursement are miscellaneous itemized deductions.
6. See page 53 if your AGI is in excess of $117,950 ($58,975 if married filing separately).
7. See page 32 for more about 1996 standard deductions and page 33 for personal exemptions. To estimate your 1997 income, use 1996 amounts.
8. In 1997, the exemption amount will be adjusted for inflation. At this printing, the amount is not known. To estimate your income, assume it will be the 1996 amount of $2,550. These should be adjusted for the phase-out of exemptions as described on page 33.
9. If you have net capital gains the maximum rate is 28%.

II

How to Improve Your Financial Future

Everyone hopes for or dreams about a bright financial future. Yet, few Americans are doing much to secure it. Consider the fact, for example, that although Americans are richer per capita than individuals in most other countries, they save or invest a smaller percentage of their income than the Japanese, Swiss, Portuguese, Turks, Greeks, Italians, and Norwegians, to mention just a few. Now there are more and more reasons for Americans to be concerned. Many corporate pension plans are not as generous as they once were, and while many Americans are working well past age 65, they are living longer, too.

Taxes are not the only consideration in planning your financial future, but they are an important one. Savvy investors can defer taxes so that they have more of their money building their nest egg. At some point, depending on your age and need for income, you may want to consider investments that are tax-free. Now—not later—is when you need to plan how you are going to afford to retire. And, as unwelcome a task as it may be, you need to consider planning your estate and how you want to provide for your heirs. In fact, in some important respects, you can enhance the quality of your life by giving serious consideration to how you want your assets handled after your death.

11

Investment Planning

INTRODUCTION

The best way to achieve your financial goals and objectives is to plan. The planning process needs to take into account your personal investment biases and your tolerance for risk. Generally, the more risk you are willing to take, the higher the potential returns. But, are you comfortable trading stocks and bonds? Or would you feel better putting your money in fixed-income government securities? You also have to set realistic goals for the rate-of-return you expect to earn on your portfolio. The purpose of this chapter is *not* to suggest where you should and should not invest. That task is something you, and perhaps your investment advisor, have to tackle.

But tax-saving strategies enable you to keep more of your investment profits and improve your financial future. This chapter will provide you with brief descriptions of various popular investment products, their tax consequences, and tax strategies you should be aware of when establishing your financial plans and investment portfolio. Table 11.1 briefly describes various types of investments and the tax treatments of the income generated from them.

Where to Start. Investment planning can't take place in a vacuum. In coming up with your investment strategy, you need to take into account your current net worth and current and future cash needs.

GETTING STARTED

Before tackling the strategies and planning approaches discussed in this book, it will help if you focus on your individual financial position. Take a few moments completing these worksheets to get a grip not only on your net worth, but where your money comes from and where it goes.

Table 11.1   Tax Attributes of Various Investments

Security	Description	Tax Attributes
Cash, CDs, and Savings Accounts	Money in bank, government insured up to certain limits.	Annual interest taxed.
Treasury Bills	Short-term (up to 1 year) debt obligation of U.S. Treasury.	Interest earned taxed at maturity or earlier if bills are sold. Interest exempt from state and local taxes.
Treasury Notes	Medium-term (2 year to 10 year maturity) debt obligation of U.S. Treasury.	Annual interest taxed. Interest exempt from state and local taxes.
Treasury Bonds	Long-term (more than 10 years' maturity) debt obligation of U.S. Treasury.	Annual interest taxed. Interest exempt from state and local taxes.
Ginnie Mae—GNMA	A security representing a share in a pool of mortgages in which the timely payment of interest and principal is guaranteed by the Government National Mortgage Association.	Annual interest is subject to federal, state, and local tax. The principal, which can be paid off sooner or later than expected, is not taxable.
U.S. Savings Bonds	Debt obligation of U.S. Treasury. When held 5 years or longer, pays variable interest rate equivalent to 85% of average yield on Treasury securities with 5 years remaining to their maturity.	Interest exempt from state and local taxes. Federal tax is deferred on Series E and EE bonds. Can be exempt from federal tax if bonds are used to fund higher education, but income limits and other restrictions apply.

Table 11.1 Tax Attributes of Various Investments (continued)

Security	Description	Tax Attributes
Municipal Bonds	Debt obligations of states, cities, or towns or their agencies.	Interest exempt from federal tax and in state where issued. Interest on certain private activity bonds can be subject to AMT.
Corporate Bonds	Debt obligations of corporations.	Annual interest taxed. Special rules for bond premium and discount: the amount paid above or below a bond's face value.
Zero Coupon Bonds	Fixed rate debt obligations of U.S. Government, state or corporation. No annual interest paid. All earned interest paid at maturity.	U.S. Government and corporate interest taxable each year as though it had been received. State obligation interest is tax exempt.
Stock, Common and Preferred	Security denoting units of equity ownership in a corporation.	Dividends, when paid, generally taxable. Appreciation, if any, taxed when stock sold, generally at a favorable tax rate. Losses are deductible but subject to limitations.
Mutual Fund Shares	Shares in a company that invests money from many investors to buy stocks, or bonds, or both, in many corporations. Some funds invest in government bonds only.	The fund's earnings paid to shareholders are treated as dividends or capital gains. Dividends may be taxable or exempt depending upon their source.

Your Net Worth

AS OF _____

ASSETS
Cash Equivalents
  Checking/Savings Accounts $_____
  Money Market Accounts   _____
  Money Market Fund Accounts   _____
  Certificates of Deposit   _____
  U.S. Treasury Bills   _____
  Cash Value of Life Insurance   _____
    Total $_____
Investments
  Unexercised Stock Options
    (appreciation) $_____
  Mutual Fund Investments   _____
  Partnership Interests   _____
  Other Investments   _____
    Total $_____
Retirement Funds
  Pension (Present Lump Sum Value) $_____
  IRAs/Keogh Accounts   _____
  Employee Savings Plans, e.g., 401(k)   _____
    Total $_____
Personal Assets
  Residence(s) $_____
  Collectibles/Art/Antiques   _____
  Automobiles   _____
  Home Furnishings   _____
  Furs and Jewelry   _____
  Other Assets   _____
    Total $_____
TOTAL ASSETS $_____

LIABILITIES
  Charge Account Balances $_____
  Personal Loans   _____
  Investment Loans (margin, real estate,
    etc.)   _____
  Home Mortgages/Home Equity Loans   _____
  Life Insurance Policy Loans   _____
  Projected Income Tax Liability   _____
  Other Liabilities   _____
TOTAL LIABILITIES $(_____)

NET WORTH $========

Your Cash Flow

Annual
Amount

SOURCES OF CASH
Salary and Bonuses (net of deductions) $_____
Self-Employment Income   _____
Dividends   _____
Interest   _____
Net Rents and Royalties   _____
Social Security   _____
Pension Distributions from Trusts/
    Partnerships   _____
Other Income   _____
    Total Cash Available $_____

USES OF CASH

Home Mortgage (or apartment rent) $_____
Utility Payments   _____
Home Maintenance   _____
Property Taxes   _____
Car Payments   _____
Car/Commuting Expenses (including
    parking, subway, gas)   _____
Credit Card/Loan Payments   _____
Insurance Premiums (life, health, car,
    home, etc.)   _____
Income Taxes   _____
Employment Taxes   _____
Clothing   _____
Child Care   _____
Food   _____
Medical Expenses   _____
Education   _____
Vacations   _____
Entertainment   _____
Alimony   _____
Charitable Contributions   _____
Gifts   _____
Personal Items   _____
Other Payments   _____
Total Expenses $(_____)

Net Cash Inflow/(Outflow) $========

    You also need to think about saving money—and investing it prudently—for your retirement. You should also give some thought to estate planning. Will your estate be liquid enough to pay debts and estate administration expenses due after you die, or will assets have to be sold to cover these expenses? (See Chapter 13 for more information about estate planning.)

And, of course, there are taxes. An investment strategy, an estate plan, or almost anything else can't be developed properly without giving thought and consideration to tax consequences.

But we urge that you keep two important principles very much in mind:
1. You should adopt a systematic and disciplined saving program.
2. You should diversify your investment portfolio among different types of assets—cash and cash equivalents, fixed-income securities, equities, and real estate.

Diversification can ease the effects that market fluctuations can have on your portfolio. It does not eliminate risk or guarantee that you will meet your financial goals, but it is the most prudent way to reduce risk. Also, when purchasing specific stocks or mutual funds, you should consider "dollar cost averaging" i.e., the systematic purchase of a specific dollar amount at regular intervals regardless of the price level of the stock or the market in general. Dollar cost averaging is based on the assumption that the market rises in the long-term and fluctuates in the short-term. As a result of using this technique, you will purchase more shares when the market value of the investment has declined and fewer shares when the value has increased, resulting in a lower average cost per share than you might otherwise obtain. In addition, dollar cost averaging offers a regular and disciplined approach to investing in equities.

Capital Gains and Losses

The top tax rate on ordinary income in 1996 is 39.6% for taxpayers with taxable income over $263,750 ($131,875 for married persons filing separately), while the maximum tax rate on net long-term capital gain is 28%. The 11.6 percentage-point differential encourages high-income taxpayers to favor investments that offer capital appreciation, which are taxed at the lower capital gain rate when the investment is sold, over investments that generate current income and dividends, which can be taxed at a rate as high as 39.6%.

Gains on property you acquire will be treated as long-term only if the property is held for more than one year. Because ordinary income and capital gains are included in your adjusted gross income for purposes of figuring the limitation on itemized deductions and the phaseout of personal exemptions, the effective rates on ordinary income and capital gains actually exceed 39.6% or 28%, respectively. (For more information on how to figure a capital gain or loss, see Chapter 7.)

TAXSAVER

There are a number of planning techniques you can use to save or defer taxes if you sell securities or other capital assets. The advantage you have is that you generally control the timing of a transaction so you can recognize the capital gain or loss in the year of your choice. A cautionary note: Your decision to buy or sell should be based on sound economic and investment criteria and not solely on the tax effect of the transaction. Here's a list of some techniques you can use that can influence how and when you pay taxes:

Sell the Shares You Bought for the Highest Price First. If you bought shares in one company at different times, you may want to identify the specific shares you sell. This will enable you to sell the shares with the highest cost first and may produce, depending on the sales price, a loss or a lower capital gain. If you don't specify what shares you are selling, it will be assumed that the first-in were the first-out. See Chapter 8 (Mutual Funds) for a complete discussion of the Identified Cost Method.

Sell Now, Buy Back Later. If your objective is to generate a tax loss this year while preserving your investment position, you can sell the securities and repurchase them later. However, you cannot deduct any losses you sustain on the sale if you or your spouse repurchases (or enters into a contract or option to repurchase) substantially identical securities within 30 days before or after the sale. Such a repurchase would violate the wash sale rules, which are explained on page 119.

Purchasing Put Options. You can use a put to lock in your gain without paying tax in the current year. The use of put options is explained on page 118.

Selling Short Against the Box. This is another way to defer capital gains tax until a later year and at the same time lock in your gain. See pages 118–119 for further details.

Installment Sales. You can postpone the gain on the sale of assets such as real estate or stock of a closely held business—but not the stock of a publicly traded company—by using the installment sale method. As a seller, you may be able to report your gain only as you receive payments. For information on how to qualify a sale and report your gain under the installment sale method, see page 119. Installment sales can also be an effective year-end planning tool.

Charitable Remainder Trust. The use of a charitable remainder trust may provide (1) for the deferral or elimination of tax on capital gains, (2) a current income stream, and (3) a future gift to charity. Establishing such trusts requires careful analysis, involves additional costs, and should be done only after consulting with an experienced tax and financial planning consultant. See Chapter 6, Charitable Contributions, for further details.

Selling Your Home. Any gain on the sale of your home is taxable. However, if certain conditions are met the tax will be postponed. If you're over age 55 when you sell your principal residence, you may be entitled to elect a one-time exclusion of up to $125,000 of your profit. See page 71 for details.

TaxSaver

You can use capital losses to offset your capital gains, thus lowering your taxes. If you have capital losses greater than your capital gains in any year, you may use the net losses to offset up to $3,000 of ordinary income. For a further explanation, see Chapter 7.

Annuities

Annuities are arrangements in which an investor pays one or more premiums to an insurance company in exchange for the promise of distributions at some future date.

Annuities fall into two categories: fixed and variable. With a fixed annuity, the investor pays the premium to the insurance company and the company credits a specified rate of interest on the cash value of the annuity. That rate is generally guaranteed for a term of one or more years. With a variable annuity, the premium is allocated by the investor among one or more mutual fund-type accounts. The investor can typically choose among stock funds, bond funds, and money market funds. Premiums for an annuity can be paid annually or all at one time. The premium amount can be fixed or can vary, depending on the terms.

At some point, the investor can decide to withdraw the funds from the annuity. A variety of payment terms is available, including payments over the investor's lifetime or the joint lives of the investor and another person. The amount of the payments will depend upon a number of factors, including the amount of premiums paid and the earnings over the years.

Interest or gains earned from a tax-deferred annuity are not taxed until withdrawn. When distributed, they are taxed at ordinary income rates. In addition, the tax law provides that certain distributions that are not in the form of regular period payments, made before age 59½, are subject to a penalty of 10% of the taxable portion of the distribution.

E&Y FOCUS: Should You Buy An Annuity?

While taxes are of obvious concern to an investor considering a deferred annuity, the costs associated with using deferred annuities as tax-advantaged investments should also be considered.

Typically, the insurance company will allow the investor to withdraw, without charge, a certain percentage (e.g., 10%) of the cumulative premium paid or the actual value of the account each year. Amounts withdrawn in excess of stipulated percentages will be assessed a surrender charge. These charges vary among companies and products, but generally are between 5% and 10% of the amount withdrawn and generally decline over a period of five to ten years. Variable annuities may also be subject to additional annual charges that can total 0.5% to 2.25% of the value of the account. These charges lower the annual yield of your annuity.

As a general rule, to make the investment worthwhile, an investor should plan to let his or her money accumulate in the annuity for at least ten years, and not begin to withdraw funds until after age 59½.

An investor should also consider whether deferring tax is a worthwhile objective. Since the earnings and gains of the annuity will be taxed as ordinary income when distributed, the deferral might not be advantageous if ordinary income tax rates are higher at the time of withdrawal. Also, capital gains that might have been taxed at preferential capital gains rates are taxed when distributed at ordinary rates. On the other hand, the deferral will have allowed the money in the annuity to compound tax-free until withdrawal.

Here are some points to consider when selecting an annuity:

1. Since you could be "doing business" with the insurer for decades, it pays to buy from strong, quality insurers. However, you should note that variable annuities are *not* part of insurer's general account.
2. An investor who purchases a fixed annuity should examine whether the current interest rate is competitive and for how long a period the rate is guaranteed. You should ask for data on how the company determines the interest *after* the end of the period for which the rate is guaranteed.
3. An investor who buys a variable annuity should look at the breadth of investment choices within the annuity and the track record of *all* the funds.
4. For both fixed and variable annuities, consider the applicable surrender charges for withdrawals. Also, be sure you understand what the fees, expenses, and charges are and how they work.

Dividend Income

Most, but not all, dividends you receive are taxable, and that can make a world of difference when contemplating your investment options—and your taxes.

Ordinary dividends are taxable income and must be reported on your Form 1040. See pages 6–9 for details. The corporation making the distribution will inform you about whether the dividends are taxable or not.

Nontaxable corporate distributions include the following:

- Stock received in a stock split.
- Mutual fund dividends which represent tax-exempt interest.
- Return of capital.
- Dividends on insurance policies (unless they exceed net premiums).
- Dividends on veterans' insurance.
- Stock dividends or stock rights. If you receive a nontaxable distribution of stock or stock rights—in effect, a certificate entitling you to buy additional stock—your adjusted basis of the old stock must generally be apportioned between the old and the new stock, based on their proportionate market values. Tax is not paid until the stock is sold. See page 9.

Exceptions: If a corporation offers you a choice between a cash dividend or a stock dividend, can you choose between a taxable and nontaxable dividend? Unfortunately not. The previously nontaxable stock dividend will now be considered taxable income because you could receive taxable cash in its place. Therefore, is it better to take cash? Not necessarily. If you believe in the company's potential, you might choose the stock dividend with the hope that the price of the shares will rise. You must include in your taxable income the market value of the additional shares on the date the dividend is paid. The new shares will have their own basis, equal to the market value you include in your taxable income. Other instances in which stock dividends may be taxable include the following:

1. When preferred stock is issued to some shareholders and common stock to others;
2. When the dividends are on preferred stock;
3. When convertible preferred stock is issued and the same result in (4) occurs;
4. When there is an unequal distribution in which some shareholders receive cash and you receive a stock dividend that increases your percentage of ownership in the corporation; and
5. When there is an increase in a shareholder's proportionate interest in the company even if no shares are physically issued.

TAXSAVER

Should you participate in a dividend reinvestment plan? Many companies now offer dividend reinvestment plans, which let you use your dividend to buy more shares of stock rather than receive cash and with some companies purchase additional shares directly from the company. This can be an effective approach to saving money and buying additional shares at regular intervals without a brokerage commission. Of course, how good an idea this is depends on how the stock performs. It's not a way, however, to save or defer taxes.

You have to include your reinvested dividend in income. If the company allows you to buy stock at less than its fair market value under a reinvestment plan, you must report the difference between the fair market value of the stock and the amount you invest as taxable income. The fair market value of the stock is its price on the date the dividend is paid.

Individual Retirement Arrangements (IRAs)

IRAs represent an attractive investment vehicle for two reasons. First, earnings and appreciation on the funds you invest in your IRA accumulate "tax-free" until you begin withdrawals. Second, your contributions may also qualify for a deduction from your gross income. Pages 85–88 describe IRAs in general.

Interest Income

Investors are always looking for interest income at attractive yields. Interest you receive from U.S. Government obligations, bank accounts, corporate bonds, or loans you made to others, to name a few sources, is taxable at ordinary income tax rates. However, interest received from obligations of a state, U.S. territory or possession, or one of its political subdivisions, is excluded from gross income for federal income tax purposes; consequently, the interest paid is generally lower. The savvy investor should focus on the after-tax yield of an investment.

TaxSaver

Tax-free bonds, including tax-free zero coupon bonds, are one of the few remaining tax shelters available. But you should proceed with caution. Since the mid-1980s, municipal bond prices have been extremely volatile. Before purchasing a portfolio of municipal bonds, you may want to consult closely with an investment advisor. Also remember that the interest from certain municipal bonds is subject to the alternative minimum tax.

Series EE Bonds. Though subject to federal income tax, Series EE bonds offer an attractive "tax-sheltered investment." If you do not elect to pay taxes on interest each year, the interest on the bonds can be deferred and taxed when the bonds are either redeemed or reach final maturity, thereby allowing you to select the most desirable taxable year to recognize the income. If EE bonds are used for educational purposes, the interest, for many taxpayers, is not just deferred, it is tax-free. For more details, see page 7.

TaxSaver

Certain high-income taxpayers do not qualify for the tax break on Series EE bonds used for educational purposes. If this is the case, you might consider buying the bonds in your child's name. When the child reaches age 14, he or she may cash them in and will be taxed at his or her rate, rather than yours, which presumably is higher.

Investment Expenses

There are specific limits on what constitutes an investment expense and how much you can deduct. See page 51.

Investment Interest Expense

Investment interest expense is interest paid on indebtedness allocable to property held for investment. See page 42 for further details.

Rental Property

Rental income includes any payment you receive for the use of property. You may deduct expenditures that you incur in renting the property. Special rules apply to vacation homes that you rent out. See Rental Income and Expenses, page 10.

Tax Shelters

The 1986 Tax Reform Act eliminated most tax shelters, largely prohibiting investors from claiming what are now called "passive losses"—a loss from a business in which you do not materially participate (see page 11).

Municipal Bonds.   Municipal bonds are among the last, true tax shelters left. Interest income from "munis" can be tax-free—at the federal, state, and city level. A taxable investment would have to pay nearly 8% in order to throw off as much after-tax income as a municipal bond yielding 5.75% if, say, your marginal tax rate is 28 percent. For high-income taxpayers, municipal bonds are even more appealing. For example, residents of high-tax states like California or New York may find that the combination of federal, state, and local levies can push their overall marginal tax rate as high as 50 percent. That means that a taxable investment would have to produce an 11.5% return to equal the return of a 5.75% municipal bond exempt from municipal, state, and federal taxes.

Still, municipal bonds are not without risks. As noted in the TaxSaver on page 184, bond prices have fluctuated sharply over the last few years. Sharp drops in bond prices have occurred in response to reductions in the credit rating of a city or county. And now there is a new danger on the horizon. Just as home mortgages can be refinanced when interest rates fall, most long-term municipal bonds can be redeemed at the discretion of the issuer. January 1 and July 1 are the usual call dates.

Other Shelters to Consider.   "Working interests" in oil and gas partnerships still enjoy some tax breaks. While Congress has cracked down on real estate limited partnerships, investors in low-income housing and active landlords may still be entitled to claim some tax benefits. See discussion regarding business credits in Chapter 15 and active real estate participation in Chapter 1.

All tax shelters need to be evaluated carefully. Generally, you should make an investment when it satisfies your investment criteria, not because of the potential tax breaks you might receive.

TaxSaver

Many people haven't explored legitimate ways to shelter income—either by deferring taxes or earning tax-free income. Here's a list of questions you might ask yourself to see if there are any tax-saving opportunities you may have overlooked:

- *Am I maximizing my contribution to my 401(k) account?*
- *Do I have a Keogh plan or a Simplified Employee Pension in which I can make a contribution based on my self-employment income?*
- *Would my company set up a deferred compensation plan for me?*
- *Have I considered whether having more tax-exempt municipal bond interest is appropriate for my situation?*
- *Am I managing my investment income in a way that allows me to deduct all the interest I pay on my margin account?*
- *Should I make nondeductible IRA contributions?*
- *Will shifting income to a child who's in a lower tax bracket help reduce the family tax bill?*
- *Do I have appreciated stocks, art, or other assets to donate to charity?*
- *Have I looked into how trusts could fit into my estate plan?*
- *Have I considered a home-equity loan with deductible interest to replace nondeductible interest on car loans and credit cards?*

12

Retirement Planning

INTRODUCTION

A major concern for most middle-aged individuals is the accumulation of sufficient funds to ensure a secure retirement. However, retirement planning is probably one of the most neglected aspects of personal financial planning. This chapter offers ideas to help you develop your retirement strategies and objectives.

To formulate a sound retirement plan, you need to answer two questions: How much will I need? And where will it come from? Your retirement planning timetable depends on your personal circumstances and goals. But you'd be wise to follow a few general guidelines. First, it's never too soon to plan for retirement, and second, it's never too late. Late-in-life planning doesn't mean that you won't be able to retire on your timetable. Rather, it's simply more difficult to accumulate the necessary funds. The earlier you begin, the easier it will be to meet your goals.

PLANNING FOR RETIREMENT EXPENDITURES

As with any aspect of personal financial planning, the starting point is identifying your objectives. When considering how much money you will need to meet your retirement objectives, three factors predominate:

1. **Your Current Standard of Living and the Amount of Cash Flow Needed to Maintain this Standard.** A cash flow analysis for the current year should be prepared. This involves determining your annual cash receipts from all sources, including compensation and income from investments, and comparing that total to your annual expenditures including housing, food, transportation, and entertainment. From this analysis, you can develop a projection for your first year of retirement of how much income you will need on an annual basis. If possible, factor in the costs based on where you think you would like to live when you retire. There can be substantial differences between the cost of living in different parts of the country—Manhattan versus parts of Florida, for example. (See Chapter 2 for a discussion about domicile.)

2. **Medical Expenses and Insurance.** Because the medical expenses associated with a serious illness can destroy the best-made retirement plan, medical insurance coverage must be carefully evaluated.

3. **The Level of Discretionary Expenditures You Want (or Need).** A review of the discretionary expenditures you plan to make for items such as a new or second home or to assist children or grandchildren with educational costs will help determine how much in additional funds you will have to set aside to meet your objectives.

RETIREMENT CASH FLOW AND INFLATION

When planning for retirement expenditures, one especially important consideration is the effect of inflation. Because you probably don't plan to work during retirement—though more and more retirees do—your income will in large part be fixed. Inflation robs you of buying power and can erode the best retirement plan.

As a general rule, you should invest some of your money in assets that have historically been good inflation hedges, such as common stocks and quality real estate. The income streams from stocks and real estate tend to increase with inflation. Corporate earnings and rents rise. Note, however, that these types of investments increase your exposure to the risks of the market. If you invest in fixed income securities it is important not to invest all of your assets in securities of a single maturity. By purchasing fixed income investments of varying maturities, both short-term and long-term, you retain flexibility to deal with changing interest rates which usually rise as inflation rises.

SOURCES OF RETIREMENT INCOME

The three main sources of retirement income are company retirement plans, your own retirement savings, and Social Security. For many individuals, the absence of any one of these can cripple a secure retirement.

Company Retirement Plans

The most important aspect of any company retirement plan is understanding the benefits provided by the plan and the payment options available.

There are generally two basic choices on how plan benefits will be paid:

Joint and Survivor Annuities. In most instances, benefits will be paid in the form of an annuity, meaning that you (and your spouse, if you're married) will receive monthly payments for as long as you live. Most frequently, companies offer a joint and survivor annuity under which annual payments are made for the joint lives of the employee and spouse. If the employee dies before his or her spouse, a reduced amount (as elected by the spouse but usually equal to one-half of the initial payment amount) is paid for the remainder of the survivor's life.

Lump-Sum Payments. Some company plans may offer a "lump-sum" option, meaning that the entire retirement amount allocated to an employee is paid in a single sum. All pension plans and most other retirement plans require that *both* spouses waive the right to a joint and survivor annuity in order for a lump-sum distribution to be made.

Tax Treatment of Annuities and Lump-Sum Payments. In general, the entire amount of an annuity received each month will be taxable as ordinary income. If you contributed on an after-tax basis to your annuity retirement program, a special rule allows you to recover tax-free the amount of your contribution, spread out over the length of the annuity. This is accomplished through the use of an "exclusion ratio," which compares your contributions in the annuity to the total amount expected to be received.

While annuity payments are generally taxed as ordinary income, qualified lump-sum distributions may be entitled to special tax treatment. (See discussion under Pensions or Annuities, page 17 in Chapter 1.)

TAXSAVER

Which Plan To Choose. *If your employer's qualified retirement plans offer the choice, should you select annuity payments or a lump-sum?*

Your choice depends on various factors, including the amount of the distribution, your marginal tax bracket during retirement, the pretax yield that can be earned on investments, your expected distribution period, and the degree of control you want over your investments.

Since annuities generally provide for monthly payments over the lifetime of a retired employee and his or her spouse, recipients can expect a steady stream of payments each and every month no matter how long they live. A lump-sum fund, however, could be prematurely exhausted if a retired couple were to outlive their life expectancies.

On the other hand, if you choose annuity payments and you or your spouse dies prematurely, any unpaid portion of your account balance could be forfeited. With a lump-sum distribution, the retiree gets possession of the full amount of his or her account balance up front. Whatever is left over at the retiree's death is available to pass on to heirs.

Some retirees welcome the discipline imposed by receiving a monthly annuity check. It forces you to stick to a monthly budget, which may be similar to how you were used to managing money during your working years. Receiving a large lump sum up front may present too much of a temptation to overspend or may make it difficult to manage a budget.

However, being locked into monthly annuity payments prevents you from pulling out extra funds if needed for an emergency or taking advantage of an opportunity. Lump-sum recipients have full access to their account assets,

*as needed. Moreover, unless annuity payments are indexed or variable, infla-
tion will steadily erode your purchasing power. Lump-sum proceeds, on the
other hand, can be invested in assets that provide a hedge against inflation.*

*Recipients of a lump-sum distribution have complete flexibility to invest
and manage their account assets as they choose. Of course, they also face
the risk that poor investment results may leave them with insufficient retirement income. If you select an annuity, the promise of a predictable level of
monthly payments relieves you of any investment burden.*

*To figure out the best payment scheme for you, you need to consider both
the income tax ramifications of each type of distribution and your personal
objectives for the use of the funds. If you are comfortable about directly
managing your retirement funds, the investment flexibility and tax-planning
opportunities available with a lump-sum distribution normally are better
suited to your personal financial objectives.*

IRAs, Keogh Plans, and Simplified Employee Pensions (SEPs)

An important source of retirement savings can be an IRA, a Keogh plan,
or a Simplified Employee Pension (SEP). An individual retirement arrangement (IRA) is a personal retirement saving plan where the earnings
and appreciation on funds you invest compound "tax-free" until you begin
withdrawals. If you are self-employed and own your own business, you
may have a retirement plan commonly known as a Keogh plan. SEPs are
usually set up by employers to make contributions toward their own (if
self-employed) and their employees' retirement. All three plans, as well as
tax strategies related to each of them, are discussed in Chapter 5. Table
12.1 demonstrates the benefits of a consistent savings strategy.

Retirement Investment Strategy

There are many other ways to save for retirement; in some cases an investment can meet both your current lifetime objectives and your retirement objectives. For example, buying a vacation home *might* be appro-

TABLE 12.1 Compounding Table for Depositing $300/month

After-Tax Return	Year 5	Year 10	Year 15	Year 20	Year 25
4%	19,890	44,175	73,827	110,032	154,239
5%	20,402	46,585	80,187	123,310	178,653
6%	20,931	49,164	87,246	138,612	207,898
7%	21,478	51,925	95,089	156,278	243,022
8%	22,043	54,884	103,811	176,706	285,308
9%	22,627	58,054	113,522	200,366	336,337

priate both as a purchase you can enjoy currently and as an investment consistent with your retirement goals. You needn't be concerned about simply putting money away if your investment strategies are consistent with your long-range retirement goals. Nearly any investment can be used toward funding your retirement. However, as you near retirement a few changes in your investment strategies are frequently appropriate.

Investment Risk. The amount of investment risk assumed should probably be reduced—especially if you have already built up a retirement fund that meets your objectives. Should risky investments fail while retirement is decades away, you'll have time to recover. But if investments sour at, say, age 62, you may not have enough time to recoup the losses.

Liquid Assets. Your need for liquidity should be matched to your investments. A carefully planned strategy of converting illiquid assets (which served you well during your earning years) into more liquid assets that you can consume during retirement years should be pursued. The idea is to avoid forced sales of illiquid assets at inopportune times causing, among other things, unplanned tax liabilities.

Cash Flow. If you need current cash flow for living expenses, you should generally choose steady income over potential appreciation.

Diversification. Diversification—that is, not putting all your eggs in one basket—enables you to reduce the impact that an underperforming or failed investment could have over your entire portfolio. Diversification entails spreading your investment dollars across different asset categories, like stocks, bonds, and real estate, and among different investments within each category. Determining how much and in what assets and asset categories to invest depends upon your attitude toward risk and your financial objectives. However, even as you approach retirement and begin to shift your portfolio toward more conservative and liquid assets, it is important to keep your investments diversified.

Social Security

Social Security is an essential ingredient of personal retirement plans.

Figuring Your Benefit. The calculation of your probable monthly benefit is complicated. To save time and headaches, you can request an estimate of your tentative benefits by filing Form SSA-7004-PC, "Request for Earnings and Benefit Estimate Statement." The form is simple to complete and the information could be invaluable to your personal planning. Copies of the form can be obtained from your local Social Security office or by calling (800) 772-1213.

The maximum monthly benefit for a 65-year-old worker retiring in 1996 is $1,248.90. For each year short of the current normal retirement age of 65 that you retire, the maximum entitlement is reduced. The earliest age at which you're eligible to receive retirement checks is 62, with a 20% reduction in benefits. For those born after 1937, the normal retirement age is scheduled to increase gradually to age 67. Retirement benefits will still be available to these workers at age 62, but will be further reduced.

How to Lose Benefits. You can be penalized if you take Social Security benefits and continue to work. For 1996, retirees between ages 65 and 69 lose $1 in benefits for every $3 earned above $12,500. Recipients under 65 forfeit $1 of benefits for each $2 earned over $8,280. At age 70 or over, there are no limits on how much you may earn. Note that this rule is limited to *earned* income. So, for example, dividends and interest income don't jeopardize benefits, no matter what their amount.

Your spouse can receive either one-half your monthly benefit (scaled back if benefits begin before age 65) or his or her own individual entitlement based on personal earnings, if higher. As long as you were married for at least ten years, your former spouse remains entitled to a benefit equal to half your monthly benefit even after a divorce.

Working Beyond Age 65. Regardless of your age, if you work, your wages or self-employment income are subject to Social Security and Medicare taxes. On the other hand, there's a reward for working past normal retirement age. For each month you postpone collecting your Social Security benefits beyond age 65 (and before age 70) your retirement benefit is increased by what's called a "delayed retirement credit." The table below shows the monthly and maximum yearly delayed retirement credit for individuals who will reach age 65 by 2003.

Delayed Retirement Credit

Turn age 65 in	Monthly Credit	Maximum Yearly Credit*
1996 or 1997	5/12 of 1%	5.0%
1998 or 1999	11/24 of 1%	5.5%
2000 or 2001	1/2 of 1%	6.0%
2002 or 2003	13/24 of 1%	6.5%

*The maximum yearly credit increases by ½ of 1% every other year up to a ceiling of 8% for those turning age 65 in 2008 or beyond.

Income Tax on Benefits. Up to 85% of your Social Security benefits may be subject to federal (and perhaps state) income taxes. Whether 85%, 50%, or none of your Social Security benefits are subject to tax depends on how much of your "provisional income" exceeds certain thresholds. "Provisional income" for this purpose generally is made up of your federal adjusted gross income plus tax-exempt interest and one-half of your Social Security benefits. (For a detailed explanation see page 15.)

Early vs. Late Retirement. Generally, you'll come out ahead by withdrawing your Social Security benefits early—e.g., at age 62—rather than waiting to age 65, even though the monthly benefit may be 20% less. That's because you'll have received three additional years of benefits. Mathematically, it would take about 12 years—until age 77—for the higher benefits available based on retirement at age 65 to catch up. And this is calculated before taking into account earnings on the investment of the benefits during the intervening years. However, if you are going to continue to work after age 62, there is the possibility of your losing some of your benefits.

Taxes on Wages and Self-Employment Income. The Social Security program and the Medicare program are financed by a payroll tax on both the employee and the employer and by a self-employment tax. See the appendices for tax rate information.

13

Estate and Gift Planning

INTRODUCTION

Although it is not possible to take it with you, with careful thought and astute planning it is possible to provide your heirs, loved ones and friends with a significant portion of your wealth. This chapter discusses the estate tax, the gift tax, and the generation-skipping transfer tax. The chapter also contains some ideas and techniques in estate planning that may aid you in making your plans for the future.

Frequent tax law changes continue to have a significant impact on estate planning. This makes it more difficult to protect your assets from the ravages of time unless you plan effectively. As a result of these changes, and because your goals and expectations constantly change as you go through life, you should periodically review your estate and gift tax plan. A review will help you: (1) discover how your objectives may have changed; (2) assess whether your plan can still achieve your objectives; and (3) determine how recent legislative changes may affect existing plans and whether you can accomplish your goals more advantageously.

This chapter is intended as an introduction to estate planning. You should seek professional advice especially if your financial or family situation is complicated; if you own interests in closely held corporations or other illiquid assets; or if your spouse is not a U.S. citizen.

GETTING STARTED

A periodic review of your personal financial plan makes sense. Filing an annual income tax return forces most taxpayers to look over their situation. Yet many—perhaps most—individuals allow years to go by without adequately considering possible changes in property holdings or key provisions in wills and trusts. To be on the safe side, you should periodically examine the following six basic tax and financial considerations:
1. Have there been any changes in the tax laws or rulings that might adversely affect your present estate plan?

2. Does your estate have sufficient cash or other liquid assets to take care of debts, taxes, funeral expenses, and estate administration expenses?
3. Have there been any changes in your family's circumstances—births, adoptions, deaths, marriages, illness or disability, special schooling needs, etc.—that might call for revisions in your estate plan?
4. Should you initiate a plan to give away some of your assets as gifts to your children, to other family members, or to charitable institutions? If you have already been giving gifts, should you continue to do so? Which assets are most appropriate for such a gift program?
5. Is the current form of ownership of your family assets appropriate for saving taxes and expenses and providing you the flexibility you need to deal with unexpected situations?
6. Have you designated a beneficiary for, and decided on the form of payment of, distributions from qualified employee benefit programs?

Do You Need A Will?

A will is a legal document that specifies who receives what at your death and who will manage your estate. Even if you die without a will, you already have an estate plan of sorts. Generally, assets you own jointly with another person—a bank account, stock, personal residence, or business interest, or where you have designated a particular beneficiary as under an insurance policy—will be passed on to the joint tenant or designated beneficiary. But, assets you own in your name alone will be passed on in accordance with your state's laws.

If you die without a will—*intestate* is the legal term—state laws determine how your estate is divided up among your surviving spouse, children, and parents—and what happens when there is no surviving spouse. Only rarely, however, will state law conform with your wishes. Often, the biggest problem is not the distribution of the property, but rather the guardianship of minor children. If both parents die without a will that directs who will be guardian of a minor child, the court and the state social welfare department will make the decision. So, even if you do not have enough assets to have to pay federal estate tax, it's a good idea to draw up a will.

ESTATE TAX FUNDAMENTALS

Who Has to Pay Federal Estate Tax?

The law provides two major exemptions from federal estate tax:
1. For estates under $10 million, there is no federal tax on the first $600,000 of assets.
2. There is an unlimited marital deduction. Any amount given or left at death to a surviving spouse, whether given outright or in certain types

of trusts, is exempt from federal estate tax. For more information, see the discussion later in this chapter.

These exemptions certainly make planning easier for most Americans, but they shouldn't lull you into thinking that estate planning is unnecessary. For starters, you may be worth more than you think. Many middle-class families now own homes that are worth several times what they cost. Moreover, stock prices have tripled over the last 20 years, even though in constant dollar terms they have remained practically flat. If the future continues to mirror the past, inflationary trends will continue to inflate values. Even if your assets currently do not exceed $600,000, at the time of your death they might.

How to Value Your Estate

Assets Subject to Estate Tax. Federal estate tax is a levy on the transfer of property at death. Your gross estate will include the value of all property to the extent of your interest in it at the time of death. Following are types of property included in your gross estate by law:

Tangible Personal Property, Real Estate, and Other Assets. This category includes property you own that is transmitted at death according to provisions of a will or state intestacy laws. Such property is commonly referred to as the probate estate. Examples: real estate, stocks, bonds, furniture, personal effects, jewelry, works of art, an interest in a partnership, an interest in a sole proprietorship, a bank account, and a promissory note or other evidence of indebtedness you hold.

Jointly Owned Property. Only one-half of the value of property owned by a husband and wife jointly will be included in the estate of the first spouse to die. The unlimited marital deduction prevents the transfer of the property from the deceased to the surviving spouse from being subject to federal estate tax. Upon the survivor's death, however, the entire property will be subject to tax (assuming it is still held at the time of death).

If two people who are not married own property jointly, the entire value of the property is included in the gross estate of the first to die, unless the estate can prove that all or part of the payment for acquiring the property was actually furnished by the other joint owner. If you and another joint owner acquired property by gift or inheritance, only your fractional share of the property is included.

Life Insurance. Your gross estate will include life insurance proceeds that are received (1) by or for the benefit of your estate or (2) by other beneficiaries if you own all or part of the policies at the time of your death. "Ownership" includes the power to change the beneficiary of the policy, the right to cancel the policy and receive the cash value, the right to borrow against the policy, and the right to assign the policy, among other things.

TaxSaver

You can transfer a life insurance policy and ownership of the policy to your children or to a trust for your family's benefit and reap significant tax advantages. To be effective in keeping the proceeds out of your estate, the gift must be made more than three years before death. The three-year waiting period can be avoided for a newly purchased policy if proper steps are taken to have someone else (e.g., a trustee of an irrevocable trust) apply for the policy and own the policy from its inception. These types of irrevocable life insurance trusts can be structured so that you contribute money each year to the trust for paying premiums. Frequently, your payments can qualify for the annual gift tax exclusion (explained on page 203). Setting up such a trust can be an effective way to get insurance proceeds to your heirs without incurring gift or estate tax.

Employee Benefits. The value of payments from qualified pension plans and other retirement plans payable to surviving beneficiaries or the estate of an employee (or the owner, in the case of a Keogh/HR 10 plan) generally is included in your gross estate.

Certain Gifts and Gift Tax Paid Within Three Years of Death. Gifts of property made during your lifetime are generally not included in your gross estate, but must be figured in the estate tax calculation if they exceed the $10,000 annual gift tax exclusion (discussed later). However, life insurance proceeds are included in your estate if the policies or ownership of the policies were given away within three years of your death (see Tax Saver, above). Also included is any gift tax you have paid within three years of your death. Lifetime gifts that a decedent retains some interest in (e.g., a life income interest) or control over (e.g., voting rights in closely held stock given as a gift) will be included in the decedent's gross estate.

Allowable Deductions. Deductions are allowed for funeral and administration expenses of the estate, and debts, unpaid mortgages, and other indebtedness on property included in the gross estate. Also allowed are such special deductions as the marital deduction and the charitable deduction. (See later sections for more details on these special deductions.)

Funeral and Administration Expenses. Deductible funeral expenses include burial costs, costs for a burial lot, costs for future care of a gravesite, etc. Deductible administration costs include executor's commissions, attorney's fees, accounting fees, appraisal fees, and court costs.

Other Deductible Estate Expenses. To be deductible, debts must be enforceable personal obligations of the decedent, such as outstanding mortgages or personal bank loans, auto loans, credit card balances, utility bills, etc. The deductible amount also includes any interest accrued on such debt at the date of death. Transfers made under a marital property settlement because of a divorce may be treated as estate expenses. Taxes are also deductible debts if they are accrued and unpaid at date of death.

Deductible taxes include accrued property taxes, gift taxes unpaid at death, and income taxes.

Valuing Estate Property. Property is included in an estate at its "fair market value," which is the price at which property would change hands between a willing buyer and a willing seller. Property that trades on an established market may be valued easily. For example, publicly traded stocks and bonds are valued based on the average of the high and low selling price on the date of death (or, if elected, the date six months after death). However, interests in closely held businesses or partnerships must generally be appraised taking into account the business's assets, earning capacity, and other factors. An accountant can assist you in appraising business interests for estate or gift tax valuation purposes.

Your gross estate is valued as of the date of your death or six months later (also known as the alternative valuation date), whichever your personal representative elects. An election to value the estate six months after date of death will generally apply to all assets in the estate, but is available only if the election results in a decrease in your estate tax liability. The amount remaining after subtracting any allowable deductions is your taxable estate. The federal estate tax is computed on this amount. Gifts made after 1976 are also factored in, and can increase the marginal tax bracket of the estate.

Basis to Beneficiaries

Property acquired from a decedent generally gets a new basis. In most cases, the new basis is the fair market value at date of death or alternative valuation date, whichever is used for estate tax purposes.

How Your Estate is Taxed

Tax Rates. The federal estate tax is progressive, ranging from a marginal rate of 18% to 55%. The 55% top rate applies to estates larger than $3 million. (See the table of rates in the Appendix.) As noted previously, the first $600,000 of gifts and transfers at death are exempt from estate tax because of the unified credit (see below). A surcharge of 5% is imposed on taxable estates between $10 million and $21,040,000 to phase out the unified credit and the benefit of the graduated rates.

Credits. Your estate can claim certain credits before figuring the amount of federal estate tax owed. The credits include:

Unified Estate and Gift Tax Credit. Each individual is entitled to a so-called "unified credit" of $192,800. This is the amount of tax generated by a transfer of $600,000. In other words, no federal estate or gift taxes will be assessed on the first $600,000 of an individual's combined taxable gifts and transfers at death. To the extent that the credit has been used to offset gifts the decedent made during his or her lifetime, the credit against the estate tax is reduced.

If the amount you give away during your lifetime and in your estate exceeds $10 million, an additional 5% tax is imposed to effectively phase out the benefit of the unified credit and progressive estate tax rates. This phaseout means that a taxable estate of $21,040,000 or more pays tax at a rate of 55% on every dollar.

State Death Tax Credit. A credit is allowed for estate and/or inheritance taxes paid to any state or the District of Columbia. The tax must actually be paid on property included in the gross estate. The credit is limited to an amount computed under a graduated rate table based on the amount of the taxable estate, reduced by $60,000. (See the table in the Appendix.)

Foreign Death Tax Credit. A credit is allowed against the federal estate tax for any death taxes actually paid to a foreign country, Puerto Rico, or the Virgin Islands on property that is also subject to the federal estate tax. The credit is limited to the U.S. tax attributable to the property taxed by the foreign country.

Credit for Tax on Prior Transfers. Under certain circumstances a credit is allowed against the federal estate tax for part or all of any estate tax paid on property transferred to the present decedent.

State Tax Considerations. All states impose some kind of inheritance or estate tax. In many states, the estate tax is simply the amount of the federal credit for state death taxes. Consequently, in these states, if there is no federal tax, due to the unified credit, there is also no state tax. However, some states have estate or inheritance taxes which are not tied to the federal credit. Furthermore, some states do not allow an unlimited marital deduction, as the federal government does. In these states, state death tax considerations may influence how your estate plan should be structured.

The Marital Deduction. One of the most significant tax-saving provisions of the law is the marital deduction. As its name implies, it is a special deduction available only to married persons. An estate is allowed an unlimited deduction for the value of property transferred to the spouse of the deceased. Thus, in effect, the marital deduction permits a couple to postpone paying any estate tax until the surviving spouse dies.

TAXSAVER

Most married individuals will want to take advantage of both the unified credit and the unlimited marital deduction to reduce the federal estate tax to zero in the estate of the first spouse to die. (See the following examples about several ways this can be done.)

By placing property in a special trust, you can arrange for your spouse to receive a lifetime income interest in certain property. After your spouse dies, the property will be passed on to whomever you have stipulated in the trust document.

The marital deduction is unavailable for property transferred by gift or at death to a surviving spouse who is not a U.S. citizen at the time the transfer is made. Instead, the law provides that tax-free gifts to a non-U.S. citizen spouse can only total $100,000 per year. There is, however, no lifetime limit to the total value of gifts you can give tax-free to a spouse who is not a U.S. citizen.

Your will can be drafted so that your property is placed in a special type of trust that benefits a spouse who is not a U.S. citizen. The trust enables estate tax on the property to be postponed until the property is distributed out of the trust or the surviving spouse dies. This type of trust is called a Qualified Domestic Trust. It permits property to qualify for the marital deduction if certain requirements—which provide that the property will eventually be subject to estate tax—are met.

Examples: Here are three examples for computing the gross estate, the taxable estate, and the estate tax due for three different size estates of married individuals, each of whom was the first of the two spouses to die.

At his death, Tom had $3,000 in savings and checking accounts, 100 shares of marketable securities worth $70 each, and a residence worth $175,000. Tom's personal property consisted largely of a collection of rare coins valued at $80,000. The rest of his property included his car, clothing, and other personal effects. In addition, Tom accumulated $105,000 in his employer's deferred bonus and 401(k) plans, and his estate was the beneficiary of a whole-life insurance policy and an employer-maintained group-term policy.

Harriet's and Dick's gross estates were larger than Tom's. And there were other differences, as well. Harriet was the sole proprietor of a consulting business valued at $450,000 at the time of her death. Dick was a law firm partner whose interest in the firm was valued at $525,000 when he died. Dick also owned a beach house, which his father had willed to him outright.

Step 1: Computing the gross estate.

| | Computing the gross estate of | | |
	Tom	Harriet	Dick
Assets			
Cash	$3,000	$15,000	$60,000
Marketable securities	7,000	20,000	50,000

Business equity	0	450,000	525,000
Residence	175,000	235,000	185,000
Vacation residence	0	0	90,000
Personal property	95,000	25,000	40,000
Deferred compensation	105,000	25,000	75,000
Ordinary life insurance	10,000	80,000	570,000
Group-term insurance	50,000	50,000	75,000
Gross estate	$445,000	$900,000	$1,670,000

Step 2: Computing your taxable estate.

The executor of your estate will subtract from the total value of your gross estate all those deductions allowable under the tax law, including the marital deduction.

Tom's will provided that his wife was to receive his total estate after payment of debts, thereby reducing the taxable value of the estate to zero. Tom could do this because of the unlimited marital deduction (discussed above).

In Harriet's case, the size of her estate's marital deduction was the product of some planning. The deduction was designed to dovetail with the $600,000 unified credit in order to eliminate any estate tax liability.

Dick's estate planned to use less than the full amount of the marital deduction that could have been used. He and his wife, Elaine, decided that with his bequest and her separate assets, she would not require ownership of all of Dick's estate. Thus, because of their children's needs, a decision was made to give more than $600,000 of his assets to them, even though taxes would be paid by his estate. The plan could have been structured to pay no taxes at the time of Dick's death if he were to leave only $600,000 to the children with the rest going to Elaine. The children could have then received the additional assets from Elaine as gifts or from her estate, and depending on the size of her estate, the amount of taxes she would pay may be more or less than in their original plan.

	Tom	Harriet	Dick
Gross estate	$445,000	$900,000	$1,670,000
Deductions			
Funeral expenses	3,000	4,000	6,000
Estate administration expenses	2,000	15,000	44,000
Debts	2,000	1,000	2,000
Mortgages	38,000	28,000	48,000
Marital deduction	400,000	250,000	550,000
Charitable deductions	0	2,000	20,000
Total deduction	$445,000	$300,000	$ 670,000
Taxable estate	$ 0	$600,000	$1,000,000

Step 3: Computing the federal estate tax.

Computing federal estate tax is straightforward. A "tentative" tax is computed using the tax rate tables. Then, the unified credit ($192,800 maximum) and any allowable credit for state death taxes paid are applied as direct, dollar-for-dollar offsets against the tentative tax specified in the federal estate tax tables for your taxable estate. Estates over $10 million must add back the 5% surtax discussed previously.

	Tom	Harriet	Dick
Gross estate	$445,000	$900,000	$1,670,000
Deductions	445,000	300,000	670,000
Taxable estate	0	600,000	1,000,000
Tentative tax	0	192,800	345,800
Unified credit	0	192,800	192,800
State tax credit	0	0	33,200
Estate tax	$ 0	$ 0	$ 119,800

The Fundamentals of the Gift Tax

You might think that the government would make it easy to give money away to non-charitable recipients. In some respects it does. You can give up to $10,000 annually ($20,000 if you file a joint return and your spouse consents) to as many individuals as you want without paying any gift tax. But, above that amount, gift tax is imposed (see pages 199–200 regarding the unified credit). The reason is that without such a tax people could escape death taxes—assuming they were willing to give away a large portion of their property before death.

Any gift you give above the annual amount that is exempt from tax is, in effect, included in your estate when you die. The value of the gift is not the value at the date of your death but the value at the time you gave the gift. In addition, there are some special rules. A gift of life insurance, for example, made within three years of your death will be included in your gross estate at its full face value. Any gift tax you pay on gifts made within three years of your death is also added to the value of your taxable estate. Nevertheless, giving gifts can substantially reduce your overall gift and estate transfer taxes as well as fulfilling other desires. But gift-giving does require careful planning—and the commitment to make the gifts before it is too late.

Basis to the Recipient of a Gift

In general, the basis of appreciated property acquired by gift is the donor's basis for tax purposes. If a gift tax return was filed, the recipient—or donee—should examine it for information regarding the donor's basis, the holding period, and the amount of depreciation. The basis of gifts received after 1976 is increased by the amount of the federal gift tax attributable to the difference between the donor's basis and the gift's fair market value, if higher as of the date of gift.

How to Give Tax-Free Gifts

The Gift Tax Annual Exclusion. As noted above, you may give up to $10,000 each year to as many individuals as you want without incurring any gift tax. And, if your spouse joins in making the gift (by signing a consent on a gift tax return), you may give $20,000 to each person annually without paying any tax. But this annual gift tax exclusion applies only to gifts of "present interests"—items that can be used, possessed, and enjoyed presently. Examples of a gift of a present interest include gifts of money, holiday presents, and so forth.

Gifts of "future interests" do not qualify for the annual exclusion. Gifts of future interests include remainder interests, reversions, or any other interest that won't give the recipient the right to possess, enjoy, or profit from the gift until some future date or time. An exception: gifts in trust to minors are subject to special rules that may allow an otherwise future interest to qualify for the annual exclusion.

Gifts to Pay Medical or Educational Expenses. In addition to the annual exclusion, an unlimited gift tax exclusion is available to pay someone's medical or educational expenses. The beneficiary does not have to be your dependent or even related to you, although payment of a grandchild's expenses is perhaps the most common use of the exclusion.

TaxSaver

In order for a gift to be exempt from taxes, you must make the payment directly to the medical or educational institution providing the service. The beneficiary of the gift should not actually receive the payment. In addition, educational expenses include only tuition. Room and board, books, and other fees will not qualify for the unlimited exclusion, although they can, of course, qualify for the annual gift tax exclusion.

TaxSaver

You can reduce your taxable estate substantially through a planned annual program of $10,000 (or $20,000 if you are married) gifts. All gifts within the exclusion limits are exempt from federal estate taxes. In addition, outright gifts that qualify for the annual exclusion are also protected from generation-skipping transfer taxes (see page 209). Obviously, you cannot hope to significantly reduce the tax your estate will pay by making gifts in a single year. But, the estate tax savings can be substantial if you embark upon a carefully planned gift-giving program that extends for a number of years before your death.

TaxSaver

Another major tax advantage of making a gift is that future appreciation in the gift's value and after-tax income earned on the property are not included in your estate.

Example: Suppose you give stocks worth $50,000 to your children now. If you die in 10 years and the stock is worth $130,000, the $80,000 of appreciation will not be included in your estate. Nor will you (or your estate) include any dividends paid on the stock after the gift.

Gift Tax Charitable Contribution Deduction. An unlimited gift tax deduction is available for gifts to certain charitable organizations.

The Gift Tax Marital Deduction. The gift tax marital deduction allows you to transfer unlimited amounts of property during your lifetime to your spouse without gift tax. Property can be transferred outright or in trust. Also, a gift of a lifetime income interest in property to your spouse can qualify for the marital deduction, if it is structured properly. You should consult with your tax advisor.

**TAX*SAVER*

The gift tax marital deduction can help you lower the taxes on your estate. Consider: In order for one spouse to make full use of his or her unified credit, it may be desirable to make gifts to that spouse so that he or she will have an estate at least equal to $600,000 — the amount of assets required to make full use of the unified credit. Since the gift tax marital deduction allows you to make unlimited tax-free transfers to your spouse, you can build up his or her assets without worrying that your gifts will be taxable.

Some words of caution: The marital deduction is not allowed for gifts to a spouse who is not a U.S. citizen. (See section on the marital deduction under estate tax fundamentals earlier in this chapter.) Furthermore, the amount of the gift tax marital deduction for a particular state may differ from the federal amount. It is therefore vital to get professional advice before making any significant gifts.

Example: Giving Gifts Without Paying Gift Tax. This example illustrates how you can set up a substantial gift program and avoid paying any gift tax. Note, however, that part of the unified credit is being used. (The unified credit is discussed earlier in this chapter.)

During the course of one year, James made outright gifts of $100,000 to his wife Helen, and $40,000 to each of his three children, for a total of $220,000.

James incurred no gift tax on Helen's gift because of the unlimited marital deduction. James and Helen were entitled to a total of $60,000 in annual exclusions (based on $20,000 for each child) because they elected to treat one-half of those gifts as made by Helen. That still leaves, however, a taxable gift of $60,000 to the three children. By applying a portion of their unified credits, James and Helen can entirely eliminate paying gift tax. Assuming that this was their first gift using their unified credits, they will have reduced the remaining assets in their estates that will be considered tax-free from $600,000 to $570,000 respectively.

E&Y FOCUS: How Paying Gift Tax Can Reduce Your Overall Taxes

Most of us have a natural aversion to paying taxes, and gift taxes are no exception. However, if you have a sizable estate that is well in excess of what you need to live on, it might be worthwhile to consider how paying gift taxes *now* can save on estate taxes *later*. The end result is that more of your assets bypass the IRS and reach your heirs.

Example: Here's a simple example to show how paying gift tax can put more money in your heirs' hands. Assume Chris and Mimi have each survived their spouses and now have $2.5 million of liquid assets. Chris holds on to the full $2.5 million until death, while Mimi makes a gift of $1 million to her children (in addition to annual gifts that are excluded from tax). Assuming neither had previously made taxable gifts and Mimi lives for three years after the gift, this is how their taxes would compare:

Chris:	Taxable estate		$2,500,000
	Federal estate tax		833,000
	Net estate to heirs		$1,667,000
Mimi:	Pre-gift estate		$2,500,000
	Taxable gift	$1,000,000	
	Gift tax paid	153,000	
	Estate reduction		1,153,000
	Taxable estate		$1,347,000
	Federal estate tax		605,030
	Net estate to heirs		$ 741,970
	Plus gift		1,000,000
	Total to heirs		$1,741,970

By making the gift and paying gift taxes, the gift tax of $153,000 was removed from Mimi's estate. This resulted in $74,970 more of Mimi's estate actually getting to Mimi's children. That doesn't even take into account the benefit of keeping the post-gift appreciation and after-tax income on the $1 million out of Mimi's taxable estate. The one catch is that the gift must be made more than three years before death, or the gift taxes will be considered part of your estate. Of course, you must be comfortable with the non-tax consequences of making a large gift that will deplete your estate.

Giving Gifts to Minors

Before a parent or grandparent gives a gift to a minor child, certain legal and practical matters need to be considered. Because a child typically cannot manage his or her own affairs and because parents usually do not want to give young children unfettered control over gift property, some special arrangements need to be made. The tax law, too, poses some challenges since only gifts of "present interest"—property for the beneficiary's immediate enjoyment—qualify for the $10,000 annual gift tax exclusion. Furthermore, state laws frequently discourage outright gifts to minors. Many states commonly prohibit or discourage the registration of securities in the name of a minor and impose supervisory restrictions upon the sale of a minor's property. Consequently, gifts to minors can take different forms and have different tax consequences.

Outright Gifts. The $10,000 annual gift tax exclusion is available for these gifts unless the property being given as a gift is a "future interest." Income from the property is taxed to the minor, and the property is included in the minor's estate if he or she should die. However, because of the "kiddie tax," which requires that a child's income be taxed at the parent's rate until the child reaches age 14, your child may actually be taxed at your rates on any income he or she receives from the property.

Guardianship. A guardianship is an arrangement where property is under a guardian's legal control subject to formal (and possibly burdensome) accounting to a court. The gift, income, and estate tax consequences are the same as for outright gifts. Thus, such gifts also qualify for the $10,000 gift tax exclusion.

Custodial Arrangements. To overcome the legal disability minors have in owning property outright, all 50 states, the District of Columbia, and the Virgin Islands have adopted the Uniform Gifts (or Transfers) to Minors Act. Under this act, a custodian may hold both cash and securities for a minor until he or she reaches adulthood. Securities may be registered in the name of any bank, trust company, or adult as custodian for the minor. Custodial gifts to minors are considered completed gifts for gift tax purposes, and such gifts are eligible for the annual gift tax exclusion. The income from the gift property during the custodial period is taxable to the minor (subject to kiddie tax provisions). However, if you use the income for your minor child's maintenance and support, it is taxable to you because you are the person legally obligated to support the minor.

TaxSaver

Generally, you should not act as custodian of your own gifts to your minor child. If you do and if you die before your child becomes an adult, the value of your gift will be included in your estate. Instead, your spouse may be the custodian. If you and your spouse both make gifts to your minor child, in essence splitting your gifts to take advantage of the annual gift tax exclusion, you should consider making a third party the custodian for the child.

Present Interest Trust. Special rules enacted by Congress provide a method of making gifts to minors that qualify for the annual exclusion. A gift to a qualifying trust established for an individual under the age of 21 will be considered a gift of a present interest and qualify for the $10,000 annual gift tax exclusion. The trust instrument must provide that the gift property and its income:

- May be expended for the benefit of the beneficiary before reaching age 21, and
- To the extent not so expended, will pass to the beneficiary upon becoming age 21.

If the child dies before reaching age 21, the funds must be payable to the child's estate or as the child may designate under a general power of appointment. This rule applies to trusts for children under the age of 21, even if a state law has reduced the age of majority to age 19 or 18.

Crummey Trust. This is a different type of trust to which you can transfer property and have the gift qualify for the annual gift tax exclusion. The distinguishing characteristic of a Crummey trust (which takes its name from a court case) is that it gives the beneficiary the annual right to demand distributions from the trust equal to the lesser of the amount of the contributions to the trust during the year or some specified amount (e.g., $5,000 or 5% of the trust's value). The beneficiary (or legal guardian) must be notified of the power to withdraw the body of the trust, although the power is permitted to lapse or terminate after a short period of time, such as 30 days. If the beneficiary fails to make a demand during the window period, after being notified that a contribution was made, the right lapses for that year's contributions. To the extent the beneficiary (or guardian) has the right to demand distribution of the year's contribution, that contribution is considered a "present interest" and, therefore, qualifies for the annual gift tax exclusion.

In all other respects, the Crummey trust is very flexible. The trustee can be required to accumulate income until the child reaches a specified age above age 21. The trustee also can be restricted to using trust assets and income for specific purposes (e.g., college expenses). The trust is useful as a vehicle for permanently removing assets from the parents' gross estates.

Totten Trust. An "In Trust For" or so-called "Totten Trust" is created when a donor deposits his or her own money into a bank account for the benefit of a minor, and names himself or herself as trustee. Under the laws of certain states, this is an informal and revocable arrangement. Upon the donor-trustee's death, the funds avoid probate and pass directly to the minor. However, the trust is not considered a separate entity for tax purposes because the donor retains complete control over any property in the trust. Accordingly, the donor will be taxed on the income as if the trust were not in existence. Also, assets in the trust account will be included in the donor's estate.

Coping with the Generation-Skipping Tax

An additional tax may apply to gifts or bequests that skip a generation. For example, a gift of property directly from a grandparent to a grandchild (which effectively "skips" the intervening generation) would be subject to the generation-skipping transfer tax.

The reason for the tax is simple. It's designed to impose the equivalent of the gift or estate tax that would have been paid if the intervening generation had received the gift or bequest. So for a direct gift from a grandparent to a grandchild, the generation-skipping transfer tax represents the amount of tax that would have been paid if the property had first been transferred to the child, who then died leaving the property to the grandchild.

The Generation-Skipping Transfer Tax is Stiff. This tax is imposed at the maximum estate and gift tax rate of 55%. It is payable in addition to any estate or gift tax otherwise payable as a result of the transfer. Fortunately, most individuals will escape paying it. First, $10,000 ($20,000 if made with the consent of a spouse) outright gifts from a grandparent to grandchildren that qualify for the annual exclusion are exempt from this tax. Furthermore, each individual is entitled to an aggregate $1 million exemption from the tax for lifetime gifts and transfers at death. Since a married couple can "gift-split," they can make up to $2 million in generation-skipping transfers without incurring the tax. In addition, any subsequent appreciation on the transferred property after it is given will escape generation-skipping transfer tax.

TAX_SAVER_

A wealthy individual can maximize his or her opportunity to avoid the imposition of the generation-skipping tax on transfers to grandchildren and later generations by allocating the $1 million exemption for gifts during his or her lifetime.

If your living descendants are already well-provided for, you may want to consider establishing a "dynasty trust." As its name implies, the trust can benefit future descendants by sheltering assets from estate, gift, and generation-skipping transfer taxes for several generations.

How to Use Trusts

A trust is possibly the most useful personal financial planning tool available—aside from a written plan itself. A trust is an arrangement under which one person or institution holds legal title to real or personal property for the benefit of another person or persons, usually under the terms of a written document setting forth the rights and responsibilities of all parties. Its primary virtue is that it can hold property for the benefit of other persons, now or in the future, and often avoid some taxes that otherwise would have to be paid.

Irrevocable Trusts. An irrevocable trust may not be changed or revoked after its creation. It is usually created to remove property and its future income and appreciation from the estate of the creator of the trust. A present interest trust and a Crummey trust, both of which have just been discussed, are irrevocable trusts. You might also use an irrevocable trust if you want to make a gift to someone but want to prevent the assets from being spent too quickly. An irrevocable trust also can be used to protect assets you give from your beneficiary's creditors.

However, property placed in an irrevocable trust will not be removed from your estate if you retain certain interests or powers in the trust— such as an interest that entitles you to receive the income from the trust for the rest of your life or the power to determine which beneficiaries will receive distributions. In addition, any transfer to an irrevocable trust will be subject to gift tax to the extent you relinquish control over the property. If someone else will receive the current income from the trust, or if it is a present income trust, the $10,000 annual gift tax exclusion can shield at least part of the property transfer to the trust from gift tax.

Besides saving you estate tax, irrevocable trusts created for your children can cut your income taxes. The amount of income tax savings depends on how much other income your children already receive and whether the "kiddie tax" applies to them. Also, there are very strict rules which limit the amount of control you or your spouse may keep over the trust in order for you not to include the trust's income on your tax return. The income from the trust will be taxed to you if the trust is used to pay for an item that you are legally obligated to provide as support for the beneficiary.

Revocable Trusts. A revocable trust (also known as a "living trust") is created during your lifetime, and you may amend or revoke it at any time. The trust instrument stipulates how the assets held by the trust are to be managed during your lifetime. This type of trust can also act very much like a will; the trust instrument can include instructions about how the assets in the trust should be distributed after your death.

What distinguishes a revocable trust from other kinds of trust arrangements is that you keep the power to reclaim the trust assets or contribute additional property to the trust at any time and for any reason. Thus, in effect, if you set up a revocable trust you really have not committed yourself to anything—at least until you die and the trust becomes irrevocable. For all practical purposes, you continue to own the trust property; the trust merely gets legal title. Since you keep complete control over the trust and its assets, the property held in it will be included in your gross estate for estate tax purposes. Also, all income and deductions attributable to the property in the trust will be included on your income tax return. On the other hand, you will not be liable for any gift tax when you contribute assets to the trust. This is the case even though the trust names the beneficiaries who will inherit the property upon your death. However, a gift will occur if you give up your power to revoke or amend the trust; or if income or principal is actually paid to someone else.

Essentially, there are no tax advantages gained by establishing a revocable trust. But there can be some real financial and administrative advantages, including:

Avoiding Probate. Revocable trust assets pass to the beneficiaries you name in the trust document and are not controlled by your will. This cuts out the costs and delays arising from the probate process. And, unlike probate, the identity and instructions for distributing estate property are not part of the public record.

Avoiding Legal Guardianship. If you become incapacitated, the assets kept in your living trust would be managed by a trustee you named in the trust document. Otherwise, the determination of whether and to what extent you are disabled or incompetent and who is going to handle your affairs could be left to public, and potentially costly, guardianship proceedings. A durable power of attorney can also be an effective tool for prearranging the management of your affairs in the event you become incapacitated.

Relief from Financial Responsibility. If desired, an independent trustee can be used immediately to relieve you of the details of managing your property and investments, record-keeping chores, and the preparation and filing of income tax returns.

Living trusts have some drawbacks and are not suited for everyone:

- Expect to pay legal fees and other expenses, such as recording fees, to set up the trust and transfer property to it. You will also owe recurring trustee and administrative charges if you use a corporate trustee rather than managing the trust yourself.
- You will not necessarily save on other legal, accounting, and executor's fees paid to handle your estate. Whether you assets are held in a living trust or pass through probate, the same sort of work will generally be needed to value your assets, prepare federal and state tax returns, settle creditors' claims, and resolve disputes among beneficiaries.

TAX**S**AVER

Two reminders. If you establish a living trust, be sure that any property covered by the trust is legally titled in the trustee's name. This is a straightforward, but often overlooked, point. Also, after setting up a living trust, you must remember to conduct your personal business affairs through the trust. This is not difficult but can be a burden. Property held outside the trust at your death will be subject to probate—except for life insurance proceeds (payable to a beneficiary other than your estate) and property held jointly with right of survivorship, which by law would avoid probate.

How to Raise Cash to Pay Estate Taxes

In many instances, the estate of an owner of a closely held business—or for that matter, any estate—may not have sufficient cash to pay all the estate's obligations, including estate taxes. Without sufficient liquidity, the estate may be forced to sell a portion of the business to raise the necessary cash. But there are special rules for the estates of owners of closely held businesses. The techniques described below can help alleviate liquidity problems.

Stock Redemptions to Pay Death Taxes

A special provision (Section 303 of the Internal Revenue Code) allows certain redemptions or partial redemptions of closely held stock to be treated as a sale or exchange, not as a dividend. (Dividends would normally be treated as ordinary income and be taxed at a higher rate.) Since the estate's basis in the decedent's stock will be the stock's fair market value at the date of death, only post-death appreciation will be taxed upon the redemption and only up to the maximum capital gains tax rate of 28%. To qualify for what is called a Section 303 redemption, the value of all the stock of the corporation included in the decedent's gross estate must exceed 35% of the decedent's adjusted gross estate. The adjusted gross estate is the gross estate less the allowable deductions for funeral and administration expenses, debts, and certain losses (but before any charitable deduction or marital deduction). A qualifying redemption under Section 303 is limited in amount to the sum of the following items:

- Federal and state death taxes,
- Funeral expenses, and
- Estate administration expenses.

TaxSaver

An estate does not actually have to be illiquid in order to qualify for this special redemption. The estate may redeem stock up to the maximum amount referred to above, even if the estate otherwise has sufficient liquid assets to take care of its expenses and taxes. It is often desirable to redeem stock under this special provision because it can otherwise be difficult for the decedent's heirs to withdraw funds from the corporation without paying tax at ordinary income rates.

Installment Payment of Estate Tax. The estate taxes attributable to a decedent's closely held business can be paid over a 14-year period if certain conditions are met. This 14-year payout offers a favorable interest rate plus a five-year deferral on the first installment of estate taxes. The deferral provision only applies to an "interest in a closely held business." To qualify, the value of the closely held business must exceed 35% of the adjusted gross estate. The amount of estate tax that qualifies for a deferred payout is limited to the portion of the total tax that is attributable to the decedent's business interest. Thus, if the decedent's qualifying stock constitutes 62% of the adjusted gross estate, then 62% of the total estate tax liability may be deferred.

Even though none of the tax attributable to the closely held business interest is paid for five years, the interest on the tax for the first four years must be paid annually. Starting in the fifth year, the estate tax due plus interest may be paid in up to 10 yearly installments.

The interest rate charged on the deferred estate tax attributable to the first $1 million in value of the closely held business interest is 4%. The regular federal interest rate applies to the deferred estate tax in excess of that amount.

E&Y FOCUS: Estate Planning—Steps to Take Now

Here's a handy checklist of estate planning measures you need to consider:

- Review with your spouse your current financial situation and your entire personal financial plan (including plans for your retirement as well as plans for the years after one of you has died).
- If any adult member of your family does not have a will, or if any wills have not been reviewed within the last three years, contact your attorney. This is especially important because of the frequency of tax law changes.
- Compile a list documenting where all your important financial and legal papers are located. Inform all appropriate persons of your list. If you have not already done so, be sure your spouse or whomever you designate as your personal representative knows your attorney, accountant, trust officer, broker, insurance advisor, and other appropriate individuals.
- Compile information on the cost and approximate purchase date of all your assets, including your residence.
- To reduce federal estate taxes, consider assigning ownership rights of your group term life insurance to children, a trust, or other appropriate recipient.
- Review whom you have designated as a beneficiary for your employee retirement or Keogh plan and other employee benefits.
- Review how your assets will be passed on to your beneficiaries.
- Make sure that you have provided for the legal guardianship and personal custody of your minor children.
- Review your will or any trust you have set up with your attorney. In particular, you and your spouse should check the provisions in your wills that pertain to what would happen to your estates if both of you died at the same time. Have you, for example, properly divided your assets to take maximum advantage of the marital deduction and the unified estate and gift tax credit (discussed on pages 199–200)?
- If you and your spouse do not have durable powers of attorney, health care proxies, or living wills, consider having them drawn up soon. If the answer to any of the following questions is yes, you may need professional assistance to help you determine whether there are tax problems on the horizon. Remember: A 'yes' answer is a warning flag, but not necessarily a signal that there is a problem.

Are you:
- Making significant cash gifts to members of your family that are likely to continue indefinitely?

- Planning to make gifts to grandchildren within the next few years? In your will?
- Anticipating a significant inheritance? Is your spouse?

Do You:

- Hold assets jointly with your spouse, other than your residence and a working banking account?
- Have a simple will that leaves all property you own at the date of your death outright to your spouse?
- Own any real property in a state other than the state of your residence?
- Have a child or other relative with a serious medical problem that may require special consideration in your will or trust instrument?
- Have substantially more or less property than your spouse?

Have you:

- Moved your residence to a different state since you last executed your will?
- Named your estate as the beneficiary of your life insurance or your retirement plan benefits?

III

Tax Strategies for Businesses

One of the most important decisions you make in starting a new business is choosing how to organize your new concern—as a sole proprietorship, a partnership, an S corporation, or a regular corporation (otherwise known as a C corporation). There are, of course, advantages and disadvantages to each and the nature of your business to a considerable extent will determine the choice you make. Yet, you would be well advised to be familiar with each of the different options because the consequences of your choice will be far-reaching. Partnership treatment for tax purposes may also apply to the newer entities, such as a limited liability partnership (LLP) or a limited liability company (LLC).

A sole proprietorship is not a separate legal entity from its owner, and its income is simply included on the owner's individual income tax return. Partnerships and S corporations also are generally not subject to federal taxes at the entity level, whereas the income from a regular or C corporation is taxed at the entity level, and generally taxed again when it is distributed to shareholders. The rules of state taxation may differ and that cost at the entity level could be substantial.

This section of the book is far more than a primer on how different kinds of businesses are taxed. We've included tax-saving strategies that could benefit your company or partnership. There is also a special chapter on S corporations. Like income of a partnership or sole proprietorship, S corporation income, in general, escapes double taxation. But S corporation shareholders, like the shareholders of a regular corporation, are generally sheltered from the liabilities of the corporation.

14

Some Basic Planning Strategies for Businesses

Introduction

A business may generally be conducted as a sole proprietorship, a partnership, a limited liability company (LLC), or a corporation. This chapter offers some suggestions on how to choose the right structure for your business and what the tax consequences of that decision are likely to be. In addition, this chapter explains how to compute the income from your business that is subject to tax—either directly to you (for a proprietorship, partnership [including an LLC treated as a partnership for income tax purposes], or S corporation) or to the business itself (for a regular corporation). Finally, this chapter suggests some planning strategies that will help you minimize the amount of tax you owe.

Choosing the Proper Business Entity

In deciding the form in which you will do business, taxes are an important consideration *but* by no means the only one. In subsequent paragraphs we will discuss the various types of entities you can use in operating a business. Following are some items you need to consider in making that decision:

1. Are there any state laws governing your choice of a particular business entity? (For example, a state may require a business, such as a bank or an insurance company, to be incorporated or preclude certain professionals from limiting their personal liability.)
2. Do you need to protect your personal assets from the potential liabilities of the business?

3. Do you intend to pass on ownership interests in the business to your children or grandchildren or other relatives?

The answers to these questions can affect your choice of business entity.

You generally may incorporate, on a tax-free basis, an existing proprietorship or partnership, or even a new business. In addition, most property may be transferred to an existing corporation in exchange for the corporation's stock without recognizing any gain in the transferred property if, after the exchange, the existing corporation is controlled by those transferring the property.

How to Choose. The corporate form is frequently the form of choice for doing business because it offers flexibility in terms of the free transfer of shares, along with limited liability for its shareholders. However, under the current tax system, corporate income is generally subject to two levels of tax—at the corporate level when income is earned and at the shareholder level when dividends are paid. A qualifying corporation may elect to be an S corporation. By making an S election, the corporate level tax is generally eliminated and the corporation's income is only taxed at the individual level. However, because S corporation eligibility requirements limit a corporation's corporate structure, capital structure, and types and number of shareholders, many corporations are C corporations for tax purposes.

In any case, a taxpayer should carefully review the various business entity alternatives in order to make an informed decision regarding the structure of his or her business.

TYPES OF BUSINESSES

Sole Proprietorship

A sole proprietorship is simple to form, and does not require a separate transfer of assets. It is not a separate legal entity from its owner. Accordingly, a sole proprietor has unlimited personal liability for the debts of the business. In other words, a sole proprietor's liability is not limited to business assets; the proprietor's individual assets are also at risk.

A sole proprietorship is not treated as a separate taxable entity for federal income tax purposes. The income generated by the sole proprietorship is simply included on its owner's individual income tax return along with other items of income and deduction. Thus, the income of a sole proprietorship is taxed once, at its owner's individual income tax rate.

Gross profit or loss for the year from the sole proprietorship is reported on Form 1040, Schedule C (or Schedule C-EZ if certain tests are met. See page 240), and it becomes part of a sole proprietor's adjusted gross income. In addition to owing income tax on such income, the sole proprietor will usually be liable for self-employment tax (page 166) and will also be required to make payments of estimated taxes (page 153). A net loss from the business can generally be deducted by the owner in computing adjusted gross income.

Profit (or loss) is computed as income less allowable deductions. Income includes cash, property, and services received by the business from all sources unless specifically excluded under the tax code. Allowable deductions include all ordinary and necessary expenses incurred in connection with the business. For sole proprietorships in the business of selling goods or inventory, the primary expense will be the cost of goods sold. The cost of goods sold represents the cost of materials, labor, and overhead included in the inventory sold during the year. Other expenses that are deductible on Schedule C include salaries and wages, interest on loans used in the business, rent, depreciation, bad debts, travel and entertainment, insurance, and real estate taxes. (See the discussion on pages 241–242.)

A sole proprietor's business is easy to terminate. The business assets can be used by the sole proprietor for personal use, or in other businesses. Alternatively, a sole proprietor may sell the assets. Because a sole proprietorship is not a separate entity, a sale of the business will be treated as if each asset in the business had been sold separately. The gain or loss on such a sale is the total of the gains or losses as separately computed for each individual asset, and is taken into account on the sole proprietor's individual income tax return. For more information on computing the gain or loss from the sale of business assets, see page 165.

Partnership (Including LLCs treated as Partnerships)

In contrast to a sole proprietorship, a partnership is an entity that is separate and apart from the individual partners. A partnership is not a taxable entity; however, it must compute its income each year and file a partnership return (Form 1065) on or before the 15th day of the 4th month after the end of the partnership's tax year. Most decisions affecting the determination of partnership income are made by the partnership and are binding upon the partners. Partnerships are generally formed based on a written partnership agreement under applicable state partnership law, although oral agreements or the conduct and relationship of the parties may be sufficient for an entity to be treated as a partnership for federal income tax purposes. Generally, it is preferable to have a written partnership agreement in place which satisfies the requirements under the state partnership law. A limited liability company is formed under the applicable state's limited liability company statute.

As a partner or member in the case of an LLC, you are individually liable for tax on your share of partnership income, which is determined under the partnership agreement, even if such income is not distributed to you. You report your share of income or loss for the partnership year that ends with or within your own taxable year. This includes guaranteed payments of interest and salary paid to you as a partner in the partnership that are deducted in determining the partnership's income. These payments would normally be considered ordinary income to you on your personal return.

The items listed below are segregated by the partnership and included as separate items on each partner's individual return:

- Net income or losses from rental real estate activities
- Net income or losses from other rental activities
- Portfolio income or losses, including (a) interest, (b) dividends, and (c) royalties
- Gains and losses from the disposition of property used in a trade or business and certain involuntary conversions
- Charitable contributions
- Foreign income taxes
- Other items as required, such as contributions made on behalf of the partners to a qualified pension or profit-sharing plan and items subject to a special allocation under the partnership agreement that differ from the partnership allocation of profit and loss generally
- Any item that would result in a different tax liability to a partner if not taken into account separately (e.g., investment interest expense or percentage depletion)
- Allowable tax credits
- Deductions relating to the election to expense certain depreciable business assets

In addition, as a partner, you are required to account separately for your share of partnership items of income and deductions that are considered tax preference items. (See page 146.)

Generally, all partnerships must conform their tax years to that of their partners unless the partnership can establish, to the satisfaction of the IRS, a business purpose for having a different tax year. (Prior to 1986, partnerships had considerable leeway in selecting tax years.)

Deductions you claim for losses from the partnership may be limited by the at-risk rules and passive loss provisions. (See the discussion in Chapter 1.)

Partnership interests may be held by *general* partners or *limited* partners. The general partners in a partnership are jointly liable for the debts of the business. In addition, general partners are jointly and individually liable for wrongful acts committed by a general partner in the course of the partnership's trade or business. Like a sole proprietor, the personal assets of a general partner are subject to the claims of the partnership's creditors (although any partner required to pay a partnership liability may assert a right to be indemnified by the other partners). A limited partner, however, is usually subject to the claims of the business's creditors only to the extent of his or her capital contribution to the partnership or to the extent he or she is obligated to contribute in the future under the partnership agreement, this is also the case for an LLC member. If you are a limited partner rather than a general partner, you do not materially participate in the management of the partnership. A limited partnership (i.e., a partnership with limited partners) must have at least one general partner whose assets are subject to the claims of the business's creditors. An LLC, on the other hand, need not have a member whose assets are subject to the claims of creditors.

A partner may terminate his or her interest in a partnership by selling the partnership interest to another partner or to a third party. Alternatively, a partner may retire from the partnership and receive liquidating distributions. How the payments are characterized will determine how they are taxed. You should consult your tax advisor.

Many states have authorized the registration of a limited liability partnership (an LLP) as a new form of partnership. In an LLP the personal assets of a partner are not subject to partnership liabilities for the tortious conduct of other partners. LLPs may be treated like partnerships for federal income tax purposes.

Regular or C Corporation

A C corporation is recognized as a legal and tax entity separate from its owners. Stockholders are generally sheltered from any liabilities of the corporation. (Note: In closely held corporations, lenders often require stockholders to guarantee the payment of the corporation's debt, thus reducing the potential benefit of limited liability—one of the benefits of forming a corporation.) Ownership in a C corporation may be divided into any number of shares of various classes of stock with different rights as to voting and the receipt of dividends. A corporation can also issue debt or equity securities. Convertible bonds, stock rights, stock warrants, and stock options provide investors with alternative forms of investment.

A C corporation is taxed on its taxable income whether or not it is distributed to the stockholders. Earnings distributed to stockholders are taxable as ordinary dividends to the extent of the corporation's earnings and profits. As a result, corporate earnings are generally subject to "double tax"—first at the corporate level and again when distributed to stockholders.

TaxSaver

Paying higher salaries to stockholders of C corporations, if such remuneration is reasonable, can avoid the double taxation of the business income.

E&Y FOCUS: Executive Compensation

Closely held corporations contemplating an initial public offering (I.P.O.) should consider the impact an I.P.O. may have on executive compensation. A publicly held corporation is not allowed a deduction for compensation in excess of $1 million paid or accrued for the tax year to certain employees. The employees covered by the new rule, which was passed as part of the 1993 Tax Act, are the chief executive officer of the corporation (or an individual acting in that capacity) and the four highest compensated officers (other than the C.E.O.) whose compensation is required to be disclosed to shareholders under Securities and Exchange Commission (SEC) rules. Certain kinds of compensation, such as performance-based compensation, are excluded from the $1 million cap.

As a result, publicly held corporations faced with the $1 million cap on deductible compensation should consider restructuring their compensation packages for covered employees to ensure that as much compensation as possible is, for example, performance-based. In addition, incentive stock options, which do not generate a deduction for employers (where certain holding-period requirements are met), may become increasingly attractive for employers that are running up against the $1 million cap for covered employees.

To the extent that a corporation pays interest to a shareholder, double taxation of the business income is avoided because, although the interest is taxable to the shareholder, interest paid is generally deductible by the corporation. The IRS, however, carefully scrutinizes the characterization of debt from stockholders to be certain it is not disguised equity.

A "hybrid" entity known as the limited liability company (LLC) may be treated as a corporation for legal purposes but as a partnership for tax purposes. Several states have adopted LLC statutes. You should consult your tax advisor regarding the availability and tax treatment of LLCs.

S Corporation

Shareholders of an S corporation generally have the same advantage of limited liability as shareholders in a regular or C corporation. However, like a partnership, an S corporation is generally not subject to federal taxes at the corporate level. Its items of income, gain, loss, deduction, and credit pass through to its shareholders and are reported by them on their individual income tax returns.

If you expect your business to operate at a loss during its formative years, an S election may be beneficial. By electing S corporation status, the losses of the company will "flow through" and may be available, subject to limitations, to offset your personal income from other sources. If an S election is not made, the losses remain at the corporate level and can't be used until the corporation has income.

A corporation must formally elect to be taxed as an S corporation by filing Form 2553, "Election by a Small Business Corporation," with the IRS, as well as meeting certain other requirements. The election to be taxed as an S corporation and eligibility requirements are discussed in detail in Chapter 16.

ORGANIZATIONAL AND START-UP EXPENDITURES

Organizational and start-up expenditures incurred by a corporation are generally not deductible. An exception to this rule applies to companies that attach the appropriate election to their tax return for the year in which they begin business. These companies can amortize (write off ratably over a period of time) their organizational and start-up expenditures over a period of not less than 60 months.

Organizational expenditures are costs incident to the creation of the corporation that are capital in nature and that would be amortizable if incurred incident to the creation of a corporation having a limited life. Start-up expenditures are defined as amounts paid (or incurred): (a) that would have been deductible if incurred in connection with the operation of an existing business; and (b) in connection with (1) investigating the creation or acquisition of an active trade or business, (2) creating an active trade or business, or (3) engaging in a profit-making or income-producing activity that is converted into an active trade or business. In this last case (3), the expenses incurred prior to the day on which the active trade or business begins would be deductible. The term "start-up expenditure" does not include any amounts paid or incurred for interest, taxes, or research and experimental expenditures.

TAXSAVER

You can amortize certain expenses incurred in creating a business or, in the case of partnerships, in anticipation of an activity becoming a business. A partnership can only deduct its organizational expenses if, like a corporation, it makes an election (described above) to do so over a period of not less than 60 months. Start-up expenses that don't qualify as organizational expenditures can be amortized by an electing partnership in computing its income. Expenses involved in investigating the acquisition of a partnership interest may be deducted by the partner on his or her personal return.

ACCOUNTING PERIODS AND METHODS

Accounting Periods

Taxable income must be reported on the basis of the corporation's taxable year which, with few exceptions, will be an annual 12-month period. Generally, a C corporation may adopt a taxable year ending at the end of any month, assuming an annual accounting period is established. If an annual accounting period is not established, taxable income must be computed on a calendar-year basis.

As a general rule, S corporations and personal service corporations (i.e., corporations whose principal activity is the performance of certain personal services, primarily by the employee-owners) must use a calendar year. Partnerships must have the same taxable year as that of the partners who own a majority interest in profits and capital. However, these entities may use a different year if they can establish a business purpose for a fiscal year (e.g., the requested year is a natural business year). In addition, these entities generally may elect to have a fiscal year that does not defer more than three months of income for their owners. A partnership or S corporation that makes such an election must make a deposit with the IRS that is roughly equal to the taxes that are being deferred for the partners or shareholders.

Once an accounting period is chosen, permission from the IRS may be required to change to another year-end.

Accounting Methods

A corporation must compute taxable income in accordance with the method of accounting regularly employed in keeping its books. An "accounting method" includes not only the overall method of computing income, but also the accounting treatment of individual items. Federal tax law permits a variety of methods, including the cash method, the accrual method, the installment method (in limited situations), the special rules for long-term contracts (described below), or any combination of methods that clearly reflect income.

For tax purposes, the choice of the cash method of accounting is restricted to individuals, sole proprietorships, certain farming businesses, certain personal service corporations, S corporations, certain partnerships, and small businesses (i.e., corporations with average gross receipts for the preceding three years of $5 million or less). Corporations, large partnerships with corporate partners, and businesses that are considered "tax shelters" must use the accrual method of accounting. (For a further discussion of the cash and accrual methods, see pages 262–263.)

Unless otherwise required or permitted under the tax law, an accounting method may be changed only after securing permission from the IRS. The IRS may require a change in accounting method if the method used does not clearly reflect income.

Installment Sales. An installment sale occurs when property is sold and the buyer is permitted to pay for it over a period of time which extends beyond the tax year in which the sale occurs. The installment method of reporting such sales income generally allows businesses to defer the payment of taxes until the year in which a payment is received rather than the year in which the sale occurs. (See page 119.)

Generally, the installment method is mandatory for eligible sales. A taxpayer may elect not to use the installment method, however, by reporting the entire gain for the tax year in which the sale is made on a timely filed return.

TaxSaver

In certain cases, you may wish to "elect out" of the installment method and, instead, recognize the entire gain in the year of sale. This may be beneficial if you have capital losses or expiring net operating losses which may offset the recognized gain. Furthermore, if your tax rate is expected to increase in the year the cash is received, you may be better off recognizing the entire gain in the year of sale.

WHAT TO INCLUDE AND WHAT TO DEDUCT FROM INCOME

A corporation must generally report any income it receives unless such income is specifically excluded by a provision in the tax code. Reportable income may be cash, property, or services received and includes interest, dividends, rents, royalties, payments for services, gains from dealings in property, and income from the discharge of indebtedness. However, cash or property received by a corporation is, in certain circumstances, not taxable. For example, cash that is received in exchange for the issuance of stock or through debt financing is not subject to tax.

TaxSaver

The following may result in a deferral of income:
- *Delaying shipment on sales*
- *Making sales on consignment or approval*
- *Selling qualifying assets on an installment basis.*

Corporations are entitled to deduct ordinary and necessary business expenses paid or incurred during the taxable year, subject to various limitations. Deductible expenses may include:
- salaries and wages,
- rent,
- repairs,
- bad debts,
- interest—both actual payments and imputed interest,
- taxes,
- charitable contributions,
- casualty losses,
- depreciation and amortization,
- travel and entertainment,
- amortizable bond premium,
- depletion,

■ advertising, and
■ contributions to pension and profit-sharing plans.
    Special rules regarding some of these deductions are discussed in the following paragraphs.

Bad Debts

Taxpayers are allowed a deduction for specific debts owed to them that become wholly or partially worthless during the tax year.

Ordinary deductions are generally allowed for debts created or acquired in connection with a taxpayer's trade or business (e.g., trade receivables). Capital losses are allowed with respect to nonbusiness debts.

Certain businesses involved in the performance of services that use the accrual method of accounting may accelerate bad debt deductions by using a special accounting method which bases the bad debt deduction on the service provider's collection experience.

Charitable Contributions

A C corporation may deduct charitable contributions if such contributions do not exceed 10% of its taxable income computed before deducting such contributions, the dividend-received deduction (explained later), net operating loss carrybacks (also explained later), and capital loss carrybacks. Charitable deductions in excess of this 10% limitation can be carried over to the next five taxable years, subject to the same 10% limitation.

Deductions for property contributions are subject to the 10% limitation discussed above. However, no deduction is permitted for that portion of a contribution that would constitute ordinary income if the property contributed were sold at its fair market value (e.g., inventory). In effect, the deduction for contributions of inventory will be limited to tax basis.

Corporations (other than S corporations, personal holding companies, and service organizations) are entitled to claim a deduction for contributions of inventory and certain types of property to a charitable organization. When such property is transferred specifically for the care of the needy, the ill, or infants, the amount of the deduction for such contributions may exceed the corporation's tax basis in the contributed property, but is limited to the basis of the property plus one-half of the unrealized appreciation. Furthermore, the amount of the deduction may not exceed 200% of the basis of the contributed property.

Note: No charitable deduction is allowed in computing a partnership's taxable income, although each partner may claim a deduction for his or her share of the partnership's charitable contribution. An S corporation must separately state its charitable contributions. The S corporation's shareholders may deduct their share of the S corporation's contributions, subject to the limitations on contributions that apply at the shareholder level.

Example: During 1996, Fashion, Inc., a C corporation that manufactures women's coats, makes a contribution of women's coats to a shelter for the needy. The fair market value of the coats is $1,000 and the basis is $200. The corporation would be permitted to take a $400 deduction for the coats determined as follows: the deduction is limited to the corporation's basis in the property, $200, plus one-half of the unrealized appreciation, $400 [($1,000 − $200) ÷ 2]. Therefore, the deduction is limited to $600 ($200 + $400). However, because the amount exceeds 200% of basis, or $400, the second limitation is imposed, and the charitable contribution is limited to $400. The charitable deduction is also limited to 10% of the corporation's taxable income, as adjusted.

Corporations (other than S corporations, personal holding companies, and service organizations) are also entitled to claim a charitable deduction for contributions of research property. To be eligible for the deduction, the equipment must be constructed by the taxpayer and contributed to a qualifying educational institution such as a college, university, or a qualifying tax-exempt scientific research organization. The recipient must be the first to use the property. In addition, the contribution must be made within two years of substantial completion of construction and must be substantially used by the receiving institution for research purposes. The deduction for scientific contributions is limited to the donated property's basis plus one-half of the unrealized appreciation. However, the deduction may not exceed 200% of the basis.

An accrual-basis C corporation for which the board of directors authorizes a charitable contribution during the taxable year and then makes the contribution within two and a half months after year-end may elect to treat the deduction as if it were made in the year authorized.

See Chapter 6 for a detailed discussion of the documentation requirements for charitable contributions.

DEPRECIATION

Depreciation is the annual deduction allowed for recovering the cost of fixed assets. Generally, depreciation deductions can be claimed on property purchased for business use. These deductions are calculated using the "cost recovery" systems that are explained in this section. The amount of the tax deduction will depend on which "cost recovery" system is used.

Tangible Property. The depreciation allowance in the case of tangible property applies only to that part of the property which is subject to wear and tear, to decay or decline from natural causes, to exhaustion, or to obsolescence. The allowance does not apply to inventories or stock in trade, or to land apart from most improvements added to it. The allowance does not apply to natural resources which are subject to an allowance for depletion. No deduction for depreciation is allowed on personal assets, such as automobiles or other vehicles used solely for pleasure, a building used by the taxpayer solely as his or her residence, and furniture or furnishings therein.

Intangibles. Most acquired intangible assets—including goodwill and going-concern value—may be amortized on a straight-line basis over a uniform 15-year period. This includes the cost of franchises, trademarks or trade names, and other non-self-created intangibles. Generally, a business is not entitled to an amortization deduction for self-created intangible assets—i.e., assets created by the taxpayer as opposed to assets that have been obtained through a business acquisition.

The following is a list of some of the intangible assets that can be amortized over a 15-year period using the straight-line method if the assets were acquired after August 10, 1993.

- Goodwill;
- Going-concern value;
- Workforce in place;
- Information base, including business books and records;
- Know-how and similar items, including secret formulas, processes, designs, and patterns;
- Franchises, trademarks, and trade names; and
- Covenants not to compete and similar agreements entered into in connection with the direct or indirect acquisition of an interest in a trade or business (under prior law, these costs were generally amortized over the life of the covenant, typically three to five years).

Accelerated Cost Recovery System (ACRS). The cost of assets placed in service after December 31, 1980 and before January 1, 1987 must generally be recovered according to the accelerated cost recovery system (ACRS). To qualify for deductions under ACRS, capital expenditures must be for "recovery property," which is any depreciable, tangible property that is used in a business or held for the production of income.

Under ACRS, capital expenditures are generally recovered over periods of 3, 5, 10, 15, 18, or 19 years. The applicable recovery period depends on the type of property and the date it was placed in service.

Modified Accelerated Cost Recovery System (MACRS). The modified accelerated cost recovery system (MACRS) generally applies to tangible property placed in service after December 31, 1986.

Each item of property depreciated under MACRS is assigned to a property class. The property class establishes the period of time over which the cost basis of an item in the class is recovered. The class to which property is assigned is determined by its asset depreciation range (ADR) class life (a classification system established by the IRS). The ADR class life determines the property's recovery period and the method of depreciation that is used.

Under MACRS, tangible property falls into one of the following classes:

1. *3-year property.* This class includes property such as tractor units for over-the-road use, and certain horses.

2. *5-year property.* This class includes property such as automobiles, trucks, property used in connection with research and experimentation, computers and peripheral equipment, and office machinery (typewriters, calculators, copiers, etc.). It does not include office furniture and fixtures.

3. *7-year property.* This class includes property such as office furniture and fixtures (desks, files, etc.), and as designated, any single-purpose agricultural or horticultural structure. This class also includes any property that does not have a class life and that has not been designated by law as being in any other class.

4. *10-year property.* This class includes single-purpose agricultural or horticultural structures, any tree or vine bearing fruit or nuts, vessels, barges, tugs, and similar water transportation equipment.

5. *15-year property.* This class includes roads, shrubbery, municipal wastewater treatment plants, and certain telephone distribution plants.

6. *20-year property.* This class includes property such as farm buildings, and, as designated, any municipal sewers.

7. *Residential rental property.* This class includes any real property that is a rental building or structure (including mobile homes) for which 80% or more of the gross rental income for the tax year is rental income from dwelling units. If you live in any part of the building or structure, the gross rental income includes the fair rental value of the part you live in. A dwelling unit is a house or apartment used to provide living accommodations in a building or structure, but does not include hotels, motels, and inns in which more than half of the units are used on a transient basis. Residential rental property is depreciated over 27.5 years.

8. *Nonresidential real property.* This class includes any real property that is not residential rental property (defined above), and any real property that is Section 1250 property with a class life of 27.5 years or more. Section 1250 property includes all real property that is subject to an allowance for depreciation and that is not or has never been Section 1245 property (i.e., property subject to an allowance for depreciation that includes personal property and other tangible property used as an integral part of manufacturing, production, extraction, or the furnishing of transportation, communications, electrical energy, gas, water, or sewage disposal services). It also includes leased property (such as a building) to which the lessee has made improvements that are subject to an allowance for depreciation and the cost of acquiring a lease. This property is depreciated over 39 years.

TAXALERT

For MACRS property placed in service before May 13, 1993, the depreciation deduction for nonresidential real estate is determined by using a recovery period of 31.5 years.

The rate of recovery under MACRS is dependent upon three factors:
1. depreciation method,
2. recovery period, and
3. the applicable convention.

There are three simplifying conventions: half-year, mid-month, and mid-quarter. These designations refer to when the property is deemed to have been placed in service during the year. All property within an individual class placed in service in a given taxable year must be depreciated using the same recovery method, period, and convention. Real estate is an exception to this rule. The recovery method and period are determined on a property-by-property basis.

Alternative Depreciation System. The alternative depreciation system (ADS), which utilizes the straight-line depreciation method and longer recovery periods, must be used for property used predominantly outside the United States, tax-exempt use property, tax-exempt bond-financed property, imported property restricted by presidential executive order, and listed property (defined below) used 50% or less for business purposes. In addition, you may elect to apply ADS in lieu of post-1986 MACRS deductions to any other class of property. ADS is also used for the purpose of computing the depreciation adjustment for post-1986 assets in connection with the alternative minimum tax rules. See Chapter 15.

If you lease property, your depreciation deductions for any leasehold improvements you make are determined under MACRS without regard to the term of your lease. Thus, the costs of the improvements are depreciated over the applicable recovery period.

Short Tax Year. If property is placed in service during a short taxable year (i.e., a tax year of less than 12 months) or used in a new trade or business, the first-year deduction must be allocated by calculating the depreciation deduction using the applicable method for the number of months the property was used.

Recapture. For a discussion of recapture of depreciation on the sale of an asset, see page 237.

"Listed" Property. Any "listed" property placed in service after June 18, 1984, that is not used more than half the time in a qualified business use during any tax year does not qualify for MACRS depreciation, or for the asset expensing election (explained below). Instead, the property must be depreciated using the alternative depreciation system described above.

Listed property includes: (1) any passenger automobile; (2) any other property used as a means of transportation; (3) any property of a type generally used for entertainment, recreation, or amusement; (4) any computer and related peripheral equipment other than that used exclusively at a regular business establishment that is owned or leased by the person operating the establishment; (5) any cellular telephone or other similar telecommunications equipment; and (6) any other property specified by IRS regulations.

Miscellaneous. If you claim accelerated depreciation in excess of straight-line depreciation on certain pre-1987 leased real or personal property, the deduction will be considered a tax preference item for purposes of computing the alternative minimum tax. (See page 253.)

Sales or transfers of used property among related taxpayers for the purpose of receiving increased depreciation deductions are subject to certain restrictions, known as antichurning rules. The rules generally disqualify the property from being depreciated under a more rapid recovery method.

Expensing Assets Acquired (Section 179)

Instead of claiming a depreciation deduction, you may elect to expense (i.e., deduct currently) up to $17,500 per year of the cost of tangible personal property and other tangible property placed in service and used primarily in a trade or business.

TAX*ALERT*

The Small Business Job Protection Act of 1996 increases the allowable deduction for the equipment expensing election over an seven-year period, from $17,500 to $25,000. The increase is phased as follows: $17,500 for tax year 1996; $18,000 for tax year 1997; $18,500 for tax year 1998; $19,000 for tax year 1999; $20,000 for tax year 2000; $24,000 for tax years 2001–2002; and $25,000 for tax year 2003. A depreciation deduction provides a recovery over a period of years, while expensing provides for a more immediate recovery. A deduction is not available for real property or property held for investment.

TAX*SAVER*

If you have incurred a loss in the current year, the expense will not be allowed in the current year, but can be carried over. If you expect to have taxable income in the following year, it may be more advantageous to take the expense in the current year and obtain the full benefit of that expense in the following year, as opposed to depreciating the asset over five or seven years.

Certain Restrictions. The amount of the expense cannot be greater than the income derived from the active conduct of any trade or business (computed without regard to the property to be expensed). Costs disallowed under this income limitation are carried forward to the succeeding taxable year and added to the allowable amount of such year.

In addition, the maximum allowable amount of the expense is reduced (but not below zero) by $1 for each $1 of property placed in service in a tax year exceeding $200,000. For example, the $17,500 expense allowed for 1996 is not available for taxpayers who place more than $217,500 of qualifying property in service during 1996.

TAXSAVER

You should carefully consider the timing of your purchases of Section 179 property to maximize the tax deductions available.

In the case of a partnership or S corporation, the limitation applies to the partnership or corporation as well as to each partner or shareholder.

The dollar limitation on expensing must be apportioned among the component members of a controlled group. (See Chapter 15, page 239.)

TAXSAVER

An individual who is both a partner in a partnership and a sole proprietor should be careful to avoid a permanent disallowance that may result if the total election amount exceeds the limitations discussed above.

Inventories

If you are in a business in which the production, purchase, or sale of merchandise produces income, you must identify the particular goods in inventory so that the proper costs can be calculated. The cost of merchandise sold during the year is determined by taking into account your inventory at the beginning of the year, adding to that the cost of goods purchased or produced during the year, and by subtracting the inventory remaining on hand at the end of the year.

When goods are so intermingled that they cannot be identified with particular purchases, the goods sold or used in manufacture are deemed to be the goods purchased first and the goods that remain in the inventory are deemed to be the goods purchased last—the first-in, first-out (FIFO) method. A taxpayer may elect to compute his or her goods remaining on hand at the end of the year as being those purchased first—the last-in, first-out (LIFO) method. Under this method, the cost of goods sold during the year is deemed to be those purchased or used in manufacture last.

TAXSAVER

In periods of rising costs, a LIFO inventory method will generally reduce taxable income. In certain cases a company using LIFO can affect taxable income by timing the purchase of goods.

In times of decreasing prices, the FIFO method of accounting will generally provide a larger tax benefit than the LIFO method.

Taxpayers with inventories must use the accrual method of accounting for purchases and sales. In other words, a taxpayer may not deduct the purchase price of inventory when paid, but must wait until the inventory is sold. The inventory method used must conform to the best accounting practices in that particular trade or business and must clearly reflect income. Manufacturers are required to include both direct costs (such as material and labor) and indirect costs (such as those listed below) in inventory.

Uniform Inventory Capitalization Rules. Under the uniform inventory capitalization rules, certain indirect "period costs" must be capitalized into inventory. These indirect costs are generally associated with the cost of running a business over a specific time period, rather than costs associated with the production and sale of a product. To the extent the inventory remains unsold these indirect costs may not be deducted. Among these costs are:

- Costs related to purchasing and storing inventory
- Interest on debt either incurred or continued to finance the production of real property or certain tangible personal property
- Taxes (other than income taxes)
- Successful bidding expenses
- Depreciation
- Utilities related to equipment or facilities
- Engineering and design costs (other than research and experimentation)
- Compensation paid to officers attributable to production
- Insurance costs related to equipment or facilities
- Deductible contributions to pension, profit-sharing, stock bonus, or annuity plans for current service costs
- Past service pension costs incurred after December 31, 1987

These rules generally relate to either real or tangible personal property you produce, or property acquired for resale. There are some exceptions, including: (1) property you produce for use other than in a trade or business; (2) self-constructed assets if substantial construction began before March 1, 1986; (3) property produced under a long-term contract; (4) certain development and other costs of oil and gas wells or other mineral property; (5) certain farming activities; and (6) property acquired by a small business (less than $10 million in gross receipts) and held for resale to customers. The uniform inventory capitalization rules generally apply to all types of taxpayers (i.e., individuals, corporations, and partnerships), although special capitalization rules apply to farmers.

Imputed Interest

When a debt instrument is issued for nonpublicly traded property and the interest rate is not stated or is insufficient, a portion of each payment will be characterized as interest rather than principal. The recharacterized amount is recognized as interest income to the seller, and an interest expense to the borrower. The imputed interest rules apply to payments due more than six months after a sale or exchange of property where some or all of the payments are due more than one year after the date of sale, and where such payments exceed $3,000, but are no greater than

$250,000. (Payments in excess of $250,000 are subject to the original issue discount rules, discussed below.)

Computing Unstated Interest. As a general rule, unstated interest is computed by taking the sum of the installment payments and discounting them using the applicable federal rate (AFR). The AFR, which is published monthly by the U.S. Treasury Department, is based on the average yield on marketable U.S. obligations during the preceding month. The AFR is limited to 9%, compounded semiannually, for certain debt instruments that have a principal amount under $3,622,500 and this amount is adjusted annually for inflation based upon the consumer price index. Special rules apply for sales of land between family members, sales of farms by individuals and small businesses, and sales of principal residences.

Accrual-method taxpayers must report interest income (expense) as it accrues, while cash-method taxpayers must recognize interest income (expense) as payments are made. (The accrual and cash methods of accounting are explained on page 224.)

Original Issue Discount (OID)

In general, a debt instrument has original issue discount (OID) if the stated redemption price at maturity (all payments due under a debt instrument except interest that is unconditionally payable at a fixed rate at least once a year during the entire term) exceeds the issue price of the debt. The issue price depends on whether the debt is issued for money or property. The OID rules apply to long-term (more than one year) debt intruments, such as bonds or notes, that (1) are issued at a true discount, i.e., for less than the face amount of the debt; (2) require accelerated or deferred interest payments, e.g., the debt instrument has a stepped interest rate, payable at 6% for the first three years and 10% for the last five years, or the interest is not paid currently; (3) are issued with another property right, e.g., warrants, in exchange for cash or property traded on an established market; and/or (4) do not provide for "adequate stated interest," and are exchanged for property, where there is no public trading (see discussion of Imputed Interest, above). The OID is recognized as an interest expense by the issuing party, and as interest income by the debt holder, as it accrues, without regard to their method of accounting (cash or accrual).

Special rules, enacted in response to the explosive growth of so-called "junk bonds," apply to debt instruments issued after July 10, 1989, that have a term of more than five years, significant OID, and a yield that is more than five points over the AFR. A regular corporation that issues such an instrument may not deduct any portion of the OID on the instrument until interest is actually paid in property other than stock or obligations of the issuing corporation. Further, to the extent that the debt instrument's yield is more than six points over the AFR, no deduction is allowed for that portion of the OID, even when paid in cash.

Dividends-Received Deduction

In order to reduce the multiple taxation of corporate dividends, the law allows, with certain exceptions, a *C corporation* receiving a dividend from a domestic corporation to deduct 70% of the dividend. In the case of any dividend from a domestic corporation owned 20% or more by another corporation, 80% may be deducted. This deduction is limited to 70% (80% if a 20%-or-more owned corporation is involved) of taxable income computed without regard to certain adjustments, including the dividends-received deduction itself.

An affiliated group—generally one or more corporations connected through stock ownership with a common parent corporation—may elect a 100% dividends-received deduction on intragroup dividends that are paid out of earnings. This applies as long as the distributing corporation and the recipient corporation were members of the group on each day of the taxable year.

Qualified Pension, Profit-Sharing, and Stock Bonus Plans

Payments made by an employer to qualified employee retirement plans are deductible as long as the plans satisfy the qualification requirements established by the tax laws and IRS regulations. Investment earnings and gains attributable to contributions made under a qualified plan are not taxable to the employer or to the trust that holds the investment. In addition, accumulated amounts are not taxable to the employee until such amounts are distributed.

Research and Experimental Expenses

If you incur research and experimental expenditures in connection with a trade or business, you may elect to treat these expenditures as either (1) deductions in the year the expenses are paid or incurred or (2) deferred expenses that will be amortized over a period of not less than 60 months, beginning with the month you first realize benefits from the expenditures. The election will apply to all research and experimental expenditures you pay or incur, or, if so limited by the election, to all expenditures for a particular project.

TaxSaver

Once made, the election applies to all such expenditures you incur unless a different method is authorized by the IRS. If you fail to make an election, your research and experimental expenditures must be capitalized. Expenditures for acquiring or improving land or depreciable or depletable property for use in connection with research and experimentation are not considered qualifying research and experimental expenditures. Depreciation (cost recov-

*ery) and depletion expenses attributable to such property, however, do qualify
as research expenditures.*

Qualified research expenditures may also be eligible for a tax credit.
(See page 249 for additional information.)

Leasing Expenditures

Leasing expenses are deductible as incurred. Consequently, the IRS reviews leasing transactions carefully to ensure that they are not sales-financing arrangements set up to produce a lease expense deduction. Typically, a leasing transaction does not transfer the benefits and burdens of ownership to the lessee. This is different than in a financing arrangement where the parties contemplate a transfer as an indication of ownership. Court decisions on leasing expenditures have generally focused on the intentions of the parties, the substance, rather than the form of the transaction, and whether and under what terms there is an option to purchase at the end of the lease term. The courts have looked unfavorably at arrangements that permit the lessee to purchase the leased asset at the end of the lease term for a nominal or "bargain" amount.

LOBBYING EXPENSE DEDUCTION

No deduction is allowed for amounts paid or incurred for participation or intervention in a political campaign on behalf of a candidate for public office (campaign expenses) or for attempts to influence the general public, or segments thereof, with respect to legislative matters, elections, or referenda (grass roots lobbying expenses). In addition, no deduction is allowed for lobbying of foreign governments.

Furthermore, no deduction is allowed for the costs of any attempt to influence state or federal legislation and any communications with a *covered executive branch official* in an attempt to influence official actions or positions of that official. However, special rules apply to taxpayers in the business of lobbying.

TAXSAVER

A number of contacts with the government should not be considered lobbying contacts, including (but not limited to) those compelled by subpoena, statute, regulation, etc.; those made in response to public notices soliciting communications to the public; those made to a federal official with regard to judicial proceedings, criminal or civil law enforcement inquiries, investigations, or proceedings. Congress has expressed an intent that such contacts should not be considered lobbying. Thus, expenses incurred in dealing with the IRS and Treasury Department on matters involving private letter rulings, technical advice memoranda, and regulation commentary would remain deductible.

BUSINESS CAPITAL GAINS AND LOSSES

Two requirements must be met for the capital gain or loss provisions to apply: (1) there must be a sale or exchange, and (2) the property sold or exchanged must be treated by the Internal Revenue Code as a capital asset.

A sale or exchange is defined for this purpose in generally the same manner as it is for ordinary business transactions. A sale is a transfer of property for money or for a mortgage, note, or other promise to pay money. An exchange is a transfer of property for other property or for services.

The rules for figuring a taxable gain or a deductible loss apply to both sales and exchanges. Capital assets are all assets other than the following: (1) inventory, (2) depreciable property, (3) real estate used in a business, (4) notes and accounts receivable acquired in the ordinary course of a business for services rendered or from the sale of inventory, or (5) in certain cases, copyrights or literary, musical, or other artistic compositions. Letters and memorandums prepared by or for you are also not classified as capital assets.

Net capital gains on sales or exchanges of business assets are taxed at a corporation's ordinary income tax rate. Net capital losses, on the other hand, may not be deducted from ordinary income. They may, however, generally be carried back three years and any excess losses may be carried forward and applied against net capital gains recognized during the following five years. The loss carryovers are treated as short-term capital losses and are offset against any net capital gains in the carryback and carryforward years. Special limitations on the carryover of net capital losses apply following certain corporate acquisitions and changes in ownership. (See page 251.)

TAXSAVER

Corporations should review their tax positions before year end and consider additional sales of capital assets to coordinate the timing of gains and losses and prevent the expiration of unused losses.

Depreciation Recapture

Any gain realized on sales and certain other dispositions of depreciable personal or other tangible business property (except buildings and their structural components that are "real property") is treated as ordinary income to the extent of depreciation deductions taken prior to the sale.

Expensing certain assets in the year the property was placed in service is treated as depreciation for purposes of these rules. (See page 230.)

Gains realized on the disposal of depreciable real property, such as a building, must be recaptured under rules that are both more complicated and more beneficial than the rules for depreciable personal property. The rules also differ depending on when the property was acquired and how much depreciation has been claimed. In general, any gain equal to the excess depreciation over straight line depreciation is ordinary income and any remaining gain on the disposition is a capital gain. One important exception to this rule is nonresidential real property acquired from 1981 through 1986 under the Accelerated Cost Recovery System (ACRS). Depreciation on this ACRS property is recaptured up to the lesser of either the gain or the total depreciation taken on the property. However, there is no recapture on this type of property if the straight line ACRS method was elected.

NET OPERATING LOSS DEDUCTION

If the corporation's deductions for the year exceed its income for the year, the resulting amount is a net operating loss. Net operating losses generally may be carried back 3 years and forward 15 years and may be used to reduce taxable income incurred in those years. You may elect to forgo the 3-year carryback period and carry forward the entire loss.

TAXSAVER

The election to forgo a net operating loss (NOL) carryback is irrevocable. Therefore, when deciding whether to forgo a net operating loss carryback consider:
1. *The marginal tax brackets in the carryback years versus the tax brackets in the carryforward years.*
2. *The time value of money (what will you be able to earn with the refund money).*
3. *The effect on tax credits.*

In general, a 10-year carryback period is available for the portion of the loss that is attributable to the costs of investigating, defending, or settling product liability claims and certain other statutory or tort liabilities. In lieu of the 10-year carryback, the corporation may either elect a 3-year carryback or forgo the carryback period altogether, as mentioned above. Special limitations apply to the carryover of a net operating loss of a corporation that is a party to an acquisition or that experiences a change in ownership. (See page 251.)

A corporation generally may not carry back the portion of a net operating loss created by interest deductions arising from a major stock acquisition or a significant distribution or redemption (referred to as a corporate equity reduction transaction, or CERT).

15

Determining Income, Deductions, and Taxes for Your Business

INTRODUCTION

Once the taxable income of your business has been determined, you must next calculate the tax on such income. This chapter tells you how to determine the tax for all business entities: sole proprietorships, partnerships, and corporations. While regular or C corporations are tax-paying entities, your share of the income from a sole proprietorship, a partnership, or an S corporation is included and taxed on your individual return.

This chapter explains which federal tax forms each business entity is required to file, and suggests strategies to consider while completing the forms that could help you reduce your taxes.

SOLE PROPRIETORSHIP INCOME

You must report your business income for the year from a sole proprietorship on Form 1040, Schedule C (or Schedule C-EZ for a limited number of users). In addition to owing income tax, you as the sole proprietor may also be liable for self-employment tax (see page 166). You may also be required to estimate your tax liability in advance and make payments during the year, instead of waiting until April 15 of the following year (see page 152). A net loss from the business can generally be deducted in computing your adjusted gross income. (Also see the discussion of sole proprietorships in Chapter 14.)

Who Has to File Schedule C? You have to file Schedule C if you are the sole owner of an unincorporated business or are a self-employed professional. This includes a wide variety of activities, such as owning a store; being a self-employed lawyer, doctor, accountant, or other professional; working as a freelance writer or independent consultant; or owning a manufacturing operation. Schedule C must be filed whether you pursue this activity full- or part-time and whether or not you also have another job. Farmers use a special schedule, Schedule F. Schedule C cannot be filed if your business, trade, or professional practice is in the form of a corporation, partnership, or joint venture.

If you operate your own business while you are also employed by another one, you have to separate your deductions relating to each business.

Example: A freelance writer who is also employed as a reporter needs to separate deductible expenses relating to the freelance writing activity from the reimbursable expenses relating to being a reporter.

If you operate more than one sole proprietorship, you must file a separate Schedule C for each trade or business.

Example: During the day, Dave operates a store that sells party favors. At night, he operates a security service. The businesses are separate and distinct and a separate Schedule C should be filed for each one.

Who Doesn't Have to File Schedule C? Not every income-producing activity is considered a trade or business. For example, investing in stocks and other securities for you own account (rather than for clients) is not considered a trade or business. It doesn't matter if you pursue this activity full-time or whether you generate substantial profits. Your income from these activities will be considered dividends, interest, or capital gains, as appropriate. Your deductions, if any, will be treated as miscellaneous itemized deductions and will only be deductible to the extent that they exceed 2% of your adjusted gross income.

An activity that you pursue as a hobby—even if you make money at it—will not be classified as a business by the IRS, and you do not need to file Schedule C; of course, your hobby income is reported as "other income" on your return. Expenses of a hobby, however, may be deductible to the extent of income that the activity produces. To determine whether an activity is a trade or business or a hobby, the IRS is likely to consider several factors. If, for example, you do not keep careful records of your income and expenses, do not maintain a separate bank account, and spend little time on the activity, the IRS may not consider the activity to be a trade or business. All the facts in regard to the activity are taken into account. No one factor alone is decisive. Here are a few:

Whether your losses from the activity are due to circumstances beyond your control (or are normal in the start-up phase of your type of business).

Whether you change your methods of operation in an attempt to improve the profitability of the activity.

Whether the activity makes a profit in some years, and how much profit it makes.

Whether you can expect to make a future profit from the appreciation of the assets used in the activity.

Example: John is a successful doctor. He is also an avid fox hunter. He raises horses which he uses in fox hunting but he also sells them to his hunting friends. Over the years the expenses of raising and selling the horses have exceeded his income from this source. The IRS will probably view the horse-raising operation as a hobby.

How to Complete Schedule C. Schedule C contains four basic sections. A line-by-line discussion of how to fill out the form is beyond the scope of this book but is provided in *The Ernst & Young Tax Guide*, published annually. What follows are some suggestions to consider when completing the form:

Business Address. You should use your home address if you use part of your home as your principal place of business. If you don't, you may have a difficult time claiming a home office deduction (see page 50). If you plan to claim a deduction for home office expenses, you must also complete Form 8829, *Expenses for Business Use of Your Home.* Although filing a Form 8829 will not automatically result in an audit, the return may be more closely scrutinized.

Accounting Method. Most small businesses use the cash method of accounting, i.e., reporting income when it is actually received and expenses when they are actually paid. Remember that you are also required under the cash method to report income when it is "constructively" received. For example, if interest is credited to your business money market account on December 31, 1996, it must be reported as income in 1996, even though you don't get your bank statement until 1997. Or, if you receive checks from customers in 1996, you must generally report income, even though you don't deposit the checks in your business account until 1997. If your business involves inventory, then you must ordinarily use the accrual method of accounting for purchases and sales (see page 224). In some cases, you may use a combination of the cash and accrual methods. You should consult with your tax advisor.

Income. If your business provides only services, you will have no cost of goods sold. Your gross receipts will equal your gross profit.

What Can be Deducted. For an expense to be deducted, it (1) must be paid (or incurred, if you use the accrual method) by you within the taxable year in carrying on your trade or business, (2) must not be a capital investment, and (3) must be ordinary and necessary. Extravagant expenses run the risk of being disallowed. While certain costs in manufacturing or producing property must be capitalized, this provision does not apply to writers, artists, and photographers. The IRS is on the alert for taxpayers who try to claim deductions on Schedule C that would otherwise be subject to the 2% floor on miscellaneous itemized deductions.

Advertising. You do not have to prove that the advertising immediately led to increased sales in order to claim a deduction.

Bad Debts. You cannot deduct losses from bad debts for receivables that you have not yet reported as income if you are a cash-method taxpayer. Accrual-method taxpayers include items in income where they have done everything required of them. If a customer subsequently refuses to pay them, a bad debt deduction can eventually be claimed, in effect reversing the original inclusion in income.

Car and Truck Expenses. You cannot deduct expenses for the personal use of a car or truck but can deduct those expenses incurred during the course of business.

Depreciation. A discussion of depreciation is provided in Chapter 14. Remember that, under certain circumstances, in the first year you acquire tangible personal property, you can expense (deduct) a portion of the cost. For 1996 up to $17,500 may be expensed. (The Small Business Job Protection Act of 1996 incrementally increases the maximum amount allowed as an expense until it reaches $25,000 in tax year 2003.)

Employee Benefit Programs. In most instances as a sole proprietor, you may not deduct the amount you pay for your own benefits. If your spouse or children work for you, the cost of their benefits is deductible, as are payments for benefits of your other employees. However, you are allowed a deduction for your health insurance premiums for you and your family, but the deduction cannot exceed your net earnings from the business. The percentages allowed as a deduction are as follows: 30% for 1996; and (as authorized by the Health Insurance Portability and Accountability Act of 1996) 40% for 1997, 45% for 1998 through 2002, 50% for 2003, 60% for 2004, 70% for 2005, and 80% for 2006 and thereafter.

TAX*ALERT*

Medical Savings Accounts. *Beginning in 1997 and continuing for four years, the Health Insurance Portability and Accountability Act of 1996 authorizes self-employed individuals covered under a high-deductible health plan and employees of "small employers" (on average no more than 50 employees during either of the two preceding calendar years) covered under an employer-sponsored high-deductible plan to deduct contributions to Medical Savings Accounts (MSAs), exclude employer contributions from income, earn income tax-free in their MSAs, and receive tax-free distributions from their MSAs to pay medical expenses. The number of eligible individuals who can set up MSAs is capped at a national level of 750,000. Deductions are generally limited to 65% of the annual deductible for individual coverage (the deductible amount must be at least $1,500 and no more than $2,250) and 75% of the annual deductible for family coverage (the deductible amount must be at least $3,000 and no more than $4,500). The maximum out-of-pocket expense for covered expenses cannot exceed $3,000 for individual coverage and $5,000 for family coverage.*

In general, an eligible individual cannot be covered under any other health plan. However, health plan coverage in addition to a high-deductible plan is permissible if the additional coverage is certain "permitted insurance" or is coverage for accidents, disability, dental care, vision care, or long-term care.

Insurance.　Generally, business-related insurance premiums—for fire, theft, malpractice and liability insurance, etc.—are deductible. Insurance premiums prepaid for a year are deductible when paid, even though the coverage carries over to the succeeding year. Premiums paid for more than a 12-month period must be deducted *pro rata*.

Interest.　Interest on business loans is deductible; however, if you prepay interest, it may only be deducted in the tax year to which it relates. Special rules apply if you borrow to construct or manufacture assets. You should consult with your tax advisor.

Legal and Professional Services.　You can deduct most fees for professional services (legal, accounting, etc.) incurred in your trade or business. However, fees paid in connection with the acquisition of a capital asset (title insurance, for example) should be added to the cost of that asset. Fees for advice on personal matters are generally not deductible.

Pension and Profit-Sharing Plans.　Contributions for your employees to qualified plans are deductible. Remember, in order to obtain a 1996 deduction for your contributions, your plan must be in existence by December 31, 1996. For more information about deductions for pension and profit-sharing, Keogh, and SEP plans, see Chapter 2.

Rent or Lease.　You may deduct amounts paid as rent for business premises. The IRS says that prepaid rent is only immediately deductible to the extent that it relates to the year in which it is paid. The balance is deductible over the period to which the payment relates.

Taxes and Licenses.　Federal income taxes can never be deducted, but certain other taxes—including real property, payroll, and your contribution as an employer to FICA (Social Security)—are deductible.

Depositing Payroll Taxes.　Payroll taxes, withheld income taxes, and Social Security taxes are paid to the government—either directly to the IRS or to a depository bank. Electronic filing requirements may also be applicable.

TaxAlert

Effective July 1, 1997, employers who deposited more than $50,000 in payroll taxes in 1995 must file electronically. The payee and frequency of deposits depend on the total amount of payroll taxes withheld each pay period. You should check with your tax advisor for how these rules apply to your situation.

TAXSAVER

In general, the larger the deposit, the more frequent such deposits must be made. Thus, growing companies with increasing payrolls should become extremely familiar with these rules to avoid late payment penalties.

Travel, Meals, and Entertainment.   Business-related expenses of this nature can generally be deducted, subject to a 50% ceiling. Note that most dues paid for memberships in clubs are not deductible as business expenses. See Chapter 3 for more about travel and entertainment expenses and the limited deduction for club dues.

Utilities and Telephones.   Utility and telephone bills are generally deductible. You cannot claim a deduction for the basic monthly charge you pay for local telephone service for the first telephone line in your home, even if it is partly (or solely) used for business. Charges for extra services—such as call-forwarding, three-way calling, call-waiting—are deductible to the extent they relate to business use. A cellular phone installed for business purposes may be depreciated under the MACRS method of depreciation (see Chapter 14 for an explanation) to the extent that business use of the telephone exceeds 50%. If your business use is less, you must use the straight-line method of depreciation over 5 years. If your business usage of the phone does not exceed 50% for any one year, you must add back to your income part of the depreciation you've claimed in prior years.

Wages.   You can deduct wages, salaries, and other compensation—including amounts paid to your relatives—as long as the amounts are reasonable for the services provided. You cannot deduct any amount paid by your sole proprietorship to yourself.

Other Expenses.   There are a variety of business expenses not specifically listed on Schedule C that can be claimed. Some of the more common expenses include: (1) union dues and dues for professional associations; (2) subscriptions to business-related publications; (3) bank service charges on business accounts; (4) security and refuse removal fees; and (5) laundry and dry-cleaning fees for uniforms you are required to wear on the job, as long as the clothes are not suitable for off-the-job use.

PARTNERSHIP INCOME

Even though a partnership is not a tax-paying entity (see discussion in Chapter 14), it must compute its income each year and file a partnership return (Form 1065). Form 1065 is due on the 15th day of the fourth month following the close of the partnership's taxable year (April 15 for calendar-year partnerships; if the due date for filing a return falls on a Saturday, Sunday or legal holiday, the return will be due on the next business day). Extensions of time are available. The partnership also may have to file state and local returns in each jurisdiction in which it does business and where its partners reside. Failure to do so may subject the partnership (and each partner) to significant penalties.

Schedule K-1. A Schedule K-1 shows each partner's distributive share of the partnership's income or loss, deductions, and credits. A Schedule K-1 for each partner should accompany the partnership return sent to the IRS, and each partner should receive a copy of his or her own Schedule K-1. Each partner's distributive share is generally determined by the partnership agreement. Each partner needs to enter the information provided on Schedule K-1 in the appropriate place on his or her personal tax return.

A partner is considered to be self-employed, rather than an employee of the partnership. Therefore, if you are a general partner, your share of partnership income will be subject to self-employment tax. In addition, you cannot exclude from your income the value of certain fringe benefits—health insurance, for example—that the partnership provides for you and your family.

Limitation on Deduction of Partnership Loss. A partner may not deduct losses in excess of his or her adjusted basis for his or her partnership interest. Generally, one's basis in a partnership is the original capital contribution. This basis is adjusted over time to take into consideration any additional capital contributions, an allocable share of partnership liabilities, and previously reported items of partnership income, gain, loss, deduction, and distributions.

Special Allocation of Losses and Other Items. Under certain circumstances, the partnership agreement can provide for tax benefits to flow disproportionately to one or more of the partners. This special allocation of partnership items must be equalized at some point in the future, and should be reviewed by your tax advisor to ensure that you are in complete compliance with these complex rules.

S CORPORATION INCOME

Corporations electing S corporation status are generally not subject to corporate income taxes. (S corporations are discussed in Chapter 14 and in greater detail in Chapter 16.) However, an S corporation must file an annual tax return on Form 1120S for its taxable year. Form 1120S is generally due on the 15th day of the third month following the close of the taxable year (March 15 for calendar-year S Corporations; if the due date for filing a return falls on a Saturday, Sunday or legal holiday, the return will be due on the next business day). Extensions of time are available. Attached to the return is a Schedule K-1 for each shareholder, which reports his or her share of the S corporation's income, loss, deductions, and credits. The S corporation must also send each shareholder a copy of his or her Schedule K-1.

REGULAR OR C CORPORATIONS

Filing Requirements

A corporation's federal income tax return (Form 1120) is due on or before the 15th day of the third month following the end of its taxable year (e.g., March 17, 1997, for the calendar year 1996; March 15, 1997 falls on a Saturday and if the due date for filing a return falls on a Saturday, Sunday or legal holiday, the return will be due on the next business day). An automatic extension of time to file of up to six months may be granted if an extension request (Form 7004) is properly filed. An extension of time to file, however, does not extend the time to pay the tax due. A corporation must pay the balance of tax due as shown on its tax return on or before the original due date of the return. Penalties are imposed for failure to pay corporate income taxes when due under circumstances similar to individuals. (See page 156.)

Tax Rates

Current corporate tax rates are in the appendices at the back of this book.

Estimated Tax Requirements

A C corporation is required to make estimated tax payments if it expects to have a year-end tax bill of $500 or more. Form 1120-W is available from the IRS to assist you in estimating your company's tax and in determining the deposits to be made. Payments are due on the 15th day of the 4th, 6th, 9th, and 12th months of the corporation's taxable year. If the due date for filing a return falls on a Saturday, Sunday or legal holiday, the return will be due on the next business day. (See Tax Payments below.)

Computing Quarterly Installments. Corporations may be penalized for not paying enough tax for an installment period. In general, the required quarterly installment is the lesser of:
1. One-fourth of the tax shown on the return for the current year, or
2. One-fourth of the tax shown on the return for the preceding year.

In order to calculate the required quarterly installment based on the prior year's tax, the following conditions must be met:
1. The prior year's return must have covered a 12-month period;
2. A tax liability of $1 or more must have been shown on the prior year's return; and
3. The corporation cannot be a "large" corporation, although a large corporation may use this method for the first installment for the year. A "large" corporation is a corporation with taxable income of at least $1 million in at least one of the three preceding tax years. (See page 248.)

The required quarterly installment may also be based on either annualized or seasonal income for the current year. If it is based on the company's annualized income, the required quarterly installment is equal to 100% of the tax, allocated evenly and cumulatively to each of the quarterly periods. To calculate its annualized income, the company must place its taxable income for the corresponding portion of the tax year on an annualized basis (i.e., multiply taxable income for the corresponding portion of the tax year by 12 and divide by the number of months in the period), compute the tax, and, after deducting prior installments for the year, pay the tax according to cumulative percentages.

Only certain corporations with a seasonal pattern in income can base their required quarterly installments on seasonal income. If it is based on seasonal income, the required quarterly installment is computed by annualizing income, assuming that income earned in the current year is earned in the same seasonal pattern as in the three preceding tax years. One hundred percent of the tax, allocated evenly and cumulatively to each quarterly period, and computed by using annualized seasonal income, must be paid under this method.

If estimated payment installments are determined by using either the annualized method or the seasonal income method, and some other method is used for a subsequent installment (i.e., 100% of the current year liability or 100% of the prior year liability), you may need to adjust subsequent payments. IRS rules require that 100% of the reduction in estimated taxes resulting from using the annualized or seasonal income methods for previous installments must be paid with the subsequent installment to avoid an underpayment penalty. The tax computed under each exception includes all taxes such as the alternative minimum tax (AMT), minus any allowable credits.

Underpayment Penalties. Corporations will be penalized for paying less than the required quarterly installment. The penalty is equal to the amount of the underpayment multiplied by the applicable federal rate (AFR). (See page 233 for more about the AFR.) The penalty is assessed from the installment due date to the earlier of the date on which a subsequent installment is paid or the original due date of the return.

A payment of estimated tax is applied against underpayments of required installments in the order in which the installments are required to be paid, regardless of the installment to which the payment relates. Thus, if an underpayment exists for a corporation's first quarter, any second quarter payment will first be applied to the underpayment for the first quarter. An overpayment of a required installment may be applied to subsequent underpayments, unless the overpayment is already allocated to an earlier underpayment. No penalty is imposed for an underpayment of estimated tax if the tax shown on the return is less than $500.

Special Rules for "Large" Corporations. Large corporations may not use the prior year's tax exception, except to determine the amount of the first installment for the tax year.

Quick Refund of Overpaid Estimated Tax

If a corporation overpays its total tax liability by making estimated tax payments that are higher than necessary, it may apply for a quick refund on Form 4466. The refund request must be made within two-and-a-half months after the close of the corporation's taxable year and before the date on which the corporation files its tax return. In addition, the overpayment must be equal to at least 10% of the corporation's expected tax liability and, in any case, must not be less than $500.

Tax Credits

Certain nonrefundable credits are available to businesses. They are presented below in the order in which they are applied against the tax. Any corporation claiming a credit should consult with its tax advisor.

Foreign Tax Credit. The U.S. income tax system generally taxes the worldwide income of taxpayers. Most foreign jurisdictions also tax the same income in their jurisdiction, thereby creating a double tax on such income. To minimize this impact, at the option of the corporation, foreign income taxes imposed on foreign source income may either be deducted in computing taxable income or taken as a credit against U.S. taxes. In addition, foreign income taxes paid by certain foreign corporations from which dividends are received or deemed to be received will be considered "paid" by the corporate shareholder and may be included in computing its foreign tax credit.

TaxSaver

In general, it will be preferable for a corporation to elect the credit against U.S. taxes rather than to claim a deduction for foreign taxes paid. A credit offsets tax liability on a dollar-for-dollar basis. A deduction will bring a benefit of only 35 cents on the dollar at the top marginal tax rate.

A foreign tax may be allowed as a credit against a corporation's U.S. tax only if it is treated as an *income* tax under U.S. tax law. The same is true if it is an income tax substitute for an income tax imposed on the general population of a foreign country. Under U.S. tax law, a "creditable" tax is any foreign tax that attempts to tax net realized gains. Examples of creditable taxes include: income-withholding taxes; flat or progressive taxes on gross income less reasonable deductions; and gross-receipt taxes that are "in lieu" of an income tax. Noncreditable foreign taxes are capital, stamps, sales, VAT, or other consumption taxes. Foreign taxes that are not creditable taxes are still allowed as a deduction from income.

Nonconventional Fuel Credit. Subject to certain limitations, taxpayers producing fuel from nonconventional sources (shale oil, tar sands, etc.)

are generally allowed a credit of $3 per barrel for the fuel produced that is equivalent to a barrel of oil.

General Business Credit. Each of the five credits discussed below (investment, targeted jobs, alcohol fuel, credit for increased research, and low-income housing) is calculated separately and then combined for purposes of applying an overall limitation. Unused general business credits may be carried back 3 years and forward 15 years. Transition rules are provided for pre-1984 credit carryforwards under prior law. General business credits are deemed to be used in the order listed below:

Investment Credit. The investment credit is made up of the following three components: (1) the rehabilitation credit; (2) the energy credit; and (3) the reforestation credit. See page 52.

Alcohol Fuel Credit. A credit is allowed for certain sales and use of alcohol as a fuel.

Credit for Increased Research. A nonrefundable credit equal to 20% of the excess of the qualified research expenses (paid or incurred before July 1, 1995) for the taxable year over a base amount is allowed.

> **TAXALERT**
>
> *The Small Business Job Protection Act of 1996 extends this credit to qualified research expenses paid or incurred during the period from July 1, 1996 to May 31, 1997. The base amount is generally calculated using historical research and development expenses, and gross receipts. The costs eligible for the credit are limited to those expenses that represent an increase over the prior years' expenditures. The base amount cannot be less than 50% of the costs for the current year.*
>
> *The 1996 Act also permits taxpayers to elect an alternative research credit (with lower fixed-base percentages and credits) that may only be made for a taxpayer's first taxable year beginning after June 30, 1996. Thereafter, the election must remain in effect unless revoked with Treasury Department approval.*

The term "qualified research" refers to experimental and laboratory research and development. The deduction allowed for research and development expenditures must be reduced by the research credit claimed. However, you may elect not to claim the full amount of the credit to avoid the reduction of the deduction.

In addition, certain corporations are allowed an additional 20% credit for basic research payments. In general, basic research payments are payments in cash to certain qualified organizations for basic research.

There are special rules regarding the determination of the base percentage for start-up companies. A start-up company is assigned a base percentage of .03 for each of its first five tax years after 1993 in which it incurs qualified research expenses. For subsequent tax years, the base percentage is computed based on actual levels of research spending.

Disabled Access Credit. Certain small businesses are allowed a 50% credit against their income tax for "eligible access expenditures" that are at least $250 but no more than $10,250. Eligible expenditures are those paid to enable small businesses to comply with the Americans with Disabilities Act of 1990. Allowable expenditures include amounts paid to remove architectural barriers which affect a disabled person's access to a business or costs for special services and equipment for the disabled. Businesses with gross receipts under $1 million or 30 or fewer full-time employees during the preceding tax year are eligible for the credit.

Companies that spend more than $15,000 to eliminate architectural barriers or are too large to qualify for the credit may deduct expenditures up to $15,000 each year.

Special Rules and Taxes for Corporations

This section is intended to familiarize a business executive with some of the special rules and taxes that can apply to corporations. In all cases, the rules and taxes only apply in a limited number of situations. In addition, you should consult with a professional tax advisor if any of the items discussed are applicable to your company or personal situation. Whenever possible, we have tried to point out tax strategies that you and your tax advisor may want to discuss. Taxpayers who are involved with closely held corporations should pay particular attention to the special rules discussed below.

SPECIAL RULES

Controlled Groups of Corporations

Controlled groups are corporations that are related by common ownership. To prevent abuses that could result from the establishment of multiple corporations, restrictions are placed on certain tax benefits available to controlled groups of corporations.

A controlled group can only benefit from lower tax rate brackets to the extent that it would if it were taxed as a single corporation. In addition, the benefit of the graduated tax rate structure must be divided equally among the group of controlled corporations, unless the corporations consent to a different allocation. The income of a controlled group must be aggregated for purposes of computing the 5% surtax on income between $100,000 and $335,000, and the 3% surtax on income between $15 million and $18,333,333.

Members of a controlled group are also limited to one $40,000 exemption for purposes of calculating the alternative minimum tax. (See page 253.) Controlled corporations are also subject to the following additional limitations:

1. one $250,000 accumulated earnings credit;

2. one $2 million exemption for purposes of computing the environment tax;
3. one $17,500 limitation for the expensing of fixed asset additions (page 231); and
4. one $1 million base amount for the large corporation test related to the calculation of estimated taxes (page 246).

S corporations are generally excluded from a controlled group for purposes of the above restrictions.

Consolidated Returns

Corporations that make up an "affiliated group" (which uses a different qualification test than a controlled group) may elect to report their income and deductions on a consolidated income tax return. The primary benefits of filing a consolidated return are: the ability to offset income of profitable group members with losses of unprofitable group members; the ability to postpone reporting gains on intercompany sales; and the ability to offset capital gains with capital losses between members. In general terms, an affiliated group is one or more chains of corporations connected through stock ownership with a common parent corporation. To be considered connected through stock ownership, the parent corporation must directly own 80% of at least one other corporation. Direct stock ownership of at least 80% in the aggregate is also required for all other members of the group. The ownership is computed in terms of voting power and value of stock. For this purpose, certain preferred stock is not counted in calculating the 80% threshold. An election to file a consolidated return is generally binding on the affiliated group for all future years.

The Treasury Department has established extensive regulations governing the filing of consolidated tax returns. These regulations set forth rules for using net operating loss carryovers, computing intercompany profits and losses where the group has sales among its members, establishing accounting periods and methods, determining earnings and profits of group members, and numerous other matters.

Tax-Free Changes in Corporate Ownership

Corporations can in certain cases reorganize, liquidate, or acquire other corporations without the corporation or its shareholders recognizing gain or loss. The recognition of the gain or loss is deferred because the corporation's or the shareholder's original basis is carried over to the new entity. Income taxes are not payable until some future date when a taxable sale, exchange, or termination occurs.

Certain Carryovers. A successor corporation in a tax-free reorganization, liquidation, or acquisition can generally carry over unused net operating losses, general business credits, job credits, foreign tax credits, and capital losses from the predecessor corporation. This transfer of tax attributes is limited if there has been a substantial change in stock ownership or, in some cases, if there has been a change in the corporation's business. In addition, if the principal purpose of an acquisition is to obtain tax benefits that would not otherwise be available, those benefits may be disallowed by the IRS.

TaxSaver

If you are seeking to acquire a corporation with net operating losses or other carryforward items, you should plan carefully to avoid the limitations that apply when a substantial percentage of the corporation's stock changes hands.

Likewise, corporations seeking outside equity investors need to exercise care in planning transactions. If the change in corporate ownership exceeds certain limits, the ability to use the loss and credit carryovers may be limited or denied.

SPECIAL TAXES

Accumulated Earnings and Personal Holding Company Taxes

Certain corporations that do not distribute their earnings for a taxable year may be subject to either a tax on an excess accumulation of earnings or a tax on undistributed personal holding company income. In computing these taxes, the amount of earnings is determined in accordance with specific provisions of the Internal Revenue Code. Consideration is given to dividends paid and certain other adjustments. Documentation of a corporation's reasonable business needs is often critical in defending against assessment of the accumulated earnings tax. Such reasonable needs may include business expansion or acquisition, or potential liabilities that are contingent upon the outcome of litigation.

TaxSaver

Throughout the year, corporations should monitor their accumulation of earnings and the types of income they receive in order to detect potential exposure to these taxes. If a corporation determines that one of these taxes may apply, there are methods available to reduce or eliminate any resulting tax liability.

For example, if a corporation is vulnerable to the accumulated earnings tax, the use of "consent" dividends may be appropriate. "Consent" dividends are hypothetical (in that they are not actually paid) distributions to a shareholder who consents to treat some or all of the corporation's income as a dividend even though no cash is received. Since special rules apply to consent dividends, you should consult a professional tax advisor.

Corporate Alternative Minimum Tax

The Alternative Minimum Tax (AMT) is based on a corporation's regular taxable income increased by tax preference items and increased or decreased by adjustments to arrive at an amount upon which the corporate AMT rate of 20% is applied. In general, it is a "separate" tax system that attempts to prevent a corporation from realizing too much benefit from certain favorable tax provisions. The AMT is available as a credit to offset a future year's regular tax liability for years in which the regular tax exceeds its AMT liability.

It is beyond the scope of this book to explain in detail how the AMT is calculated. In any case, you will need to get professional tax advice.

TaxSaver

A company should be aware that planning techniques used to reduce its regular tax might not provide a current tax benefit if the company is subject to the alternative minimum tax. Moreover, in certain cases, regular tax planning techniques can even subject the company to the AMT. For example, the use of Modified Accelerated Cost Recovery System depreciation could result in an AMT liability.

While traditional regular tax planning techniques (e.g., accelerating deductions and deferring income) can result in an AMT liability, the company may, nevertheless, want to make sure that such techniques are employed because the minimum tax credit can be used to offset a future year's regular tax liability.

TaxSaver

Since the AMT is, in effect, an independent income tax system apart from the regular income tax, a company needs to keep separate records for items such as depreciation on assets acquired after 1986, AMT net operating loss carryovers, and AMT foreign tax credit carryovers. Specifically, since different amounts of depreciation are allowed under the two tax systems, separate basis amounts must be tracked for purposes of computing gain or loss upon a sale of such assets.

While many companies have recognized the need to maintain a separate set of records for AMT purposes (since the AMT system has been with us since 1986), it may not be as widely known that a third set of records is required for adjusted current earnings (ACE) purposes.

TaxSaver

In certain cases, a corporation can reduce its AMT exposure by leasing equipment rather than purchasing it. Regular tax depreciation deductions could be partially disallowed for AMT purposes, but lease payments should be fully deductible for both regular tax and AMT purposes.

16

S Corporations

INTRODUCTION

Income earned by C corporations is taxed at the corporate level when earned and taxed again at the shareholder level when distributed as dividends. An S corporation election permits a corporation to avoid this "double taxation." S corporation income generally is only taxed at the shareholder level. This in itself can be a tremendous tax-saving opportunity.

Yet, for legal purposes, an S corporation is indistinguishable from any other corporation. S corporation shareholders have limited liability and other rights and protections similiar to shareholders of regular corporations. If your corporation meets the requirements to qualify for S corporation status, you should seriously consider making an S election.

This chapter discusses how to elect S corporation status, the advantages of being an S corporation, and other considerations associated with operating as an S corporation.

Electing S Corporation Status

A corporation must meet certain requirements in order to be an S corporation. Specifically, a corporation can elect S corporation status only if the following conditions are met:

- The corporation is a domestic corporation.
- The corporation has only one class of stock (but the voting rights within the class can differ).
- The corporation has no more than 35 shareholders.

TaxAlert

The Small Business Job Protection Act of 1996 permits S corporations to have as many as 75 shareholders for taxable years beginning after December 31, 1996. (A husband and wife are treated as one shareholder for this purpose.)

- The corporation is not a member of an affiliated group of corporations (i.e., the corporation does not directly own 80% or more of another corporation).

TAX ALERT

The 1996 Act also eliminates this requirement for taxable years beginning after December 31, 1996. S corporations will be able to own 80% or more of the stock of a C corporation. However, an S corporation will not be permitted to join in the filing of a consolidated return with affiliated C corporations. In addition, the Act permits an S corporation to elect to treat a wholly-owned domestic subsidiary as a "qualified subchapter S subsidiary" (QSSS). A QSSS is not treated as a separate entity for tax purposes. Instead, its items of income, gain, loss, and deduction are treated as income by the parent S corporation and the parent S corporation is considered to own the QSSS's assets and liabilities.

- The corporation's shareholders are individuals, estates, and certain qualifying trusts including certain small business trusts, which have multiple beneficiaries and accumulated income, tax-exempt organizations, and, in limited situations, other S corporations (for taxable years beginning after 1996).
- The corporation's shareholders are citizens or residents of the United States.
- The corporation is not a Domestic International Sales Corporation (DISC) or former DISC, or an insurance company. Corporations claiming a possession tax credit and financial institutions have historically been ineligible to be shareholders of S corporations. However, 1996 Act repeals the possession tax credit (beginning tax year 1996) and permits financial institutions which do not use a reserve method of accounting for bad debts to elect S corporation status (for taxable years beginning after 1996).

In order to elect S corporation status, the corporation must meet all of the above requirements on the day the S election is filed and on every day of each year for which the election is to be effective.

To be effective for the current year, an S election must be made during the preceding year, or within the first two-and-a-half months of the current tax year. All persons who are shareholders on the day the election is made must consent to the election. In addition, if the election is filed within the first two-and-a-half months of the year in which it is to be effective, all persons who held stock prior to the filing of the election must consent, even if they don't own stock on the day the S election is filed. An S election is made on a Form 2553, *Election by a Small Business Corporation.*

Advantages of Being an S Corporation

Income earned by a regular corporation is taxed at the corporate level when earned, and is generally taxed again at the shareholder level when distributed as dividends. Thus, the income of a regular corporation is subject to "double taxation." An S corporation's income or loss is reported directly on the shareholders' returns, generally escaping tax at the corporate level. The income is taxable to the shareholders even if it is not distributed, but generally it is not taxed again when distributed. The income increases the shareholder's stock basis, potentially reducing gain or increasing loss when the stock is sold. Additionally, the shareholders may be able to shelter the income with losses from other sources. If a corporation is profitable, electing S status can be especially advantageous because the double taxation of its income may be eliminated.

Example: Assume Corporation A earns $500,000 during its 1996 tax year and distributes its after-tax earnings to its shareholders. If Corporation A operates as a regular corporation, the total amount of tax the corporation and its shareholders will pay is $300,680 ($170,000 + $130,680), and only $199,320 of the earnings are available to the shareholders, computed as follows:

Corporation A taxable income	$500,000
Corporate level tax at 34%	170,000
Income distributed and taxed to shareholders	$330,000
Shareholder level tax at 39.6%	130,680
Remaining income available	$199,320

On the other hand, if Corporation A operates as an S corporation, the total amount of tax incurred by the corporation and its shareholders is only $198,000, leaving $302,000 available for the shareholders—a savings of $102,680. This is computed as follows:

Corporation A taxable income	$500,000
Corporate level tax at 34%	N/A
Income distributed and taxed to shareholders	$500,000
Shareholder level tax at 39.6%	198,000
Remaining income available	$302,000

To the extent the income is not distributed to an S corporation shareholder, the income will increase the shareholder's basis in the corporation stock. Upon disposition of the stock, therefore, the shareholder's gain is reduced.

Note that the highest individual tax rate (39.6%) currently exceeds the highest corporate tax rate (35%). If the corporation anticipates retaining all of its earnings for a significant period of time, this rate differential may make C corporation status more favorable.

If the corporation is incurring losses, an S election may also be advantageous. Like S corporation income, S corporation losses are reported directly on the shareholders' individual returns. The losses may offset income from other sources. However, a shareholder's currently deductible share of the corporation's losses is limited to his or her basis in the corporation's stock and debt of the corporation owed to the shareholder. For taxable years beginning after December 31, 1996, the 1996 Act requires that adjustments for distributions be taken into account before losses and deductions when computing the change in basis for loss years. Thus, distributions absorb available basis prior to losses. The losses may be subject to other limitations as well. See the discussion of the at-risk and passive activity loss rules in Chapter 1.

TaxSaver

Shareholders of S corporations that incur losses often find themselves unable to claim deductions if the losses exceed the shareholder's basis in the corporation's stock. An S corporation shareholder generally can obtain basis in S corporation debt only by actually loaning money to the corporation. If an S corporation borrows money from a bank, the loan does not provide the shareholders with basis against which a loss could be claimed, even if the shareholders guarantee such loans. Consult your tax advisor about restructuring these loans so that the shareholders can utilize the losses being passed through by the company.

TaxSaver

If your corporation can qualify as an S corporation, you should consider making the election if:
1. *The shareholders expect their individual tax rates to be lower than the applicable regular corporate tax rate in the future, or they want to avoid the double taxation on income;*
2. *The corporation anticipates having losses from operations that can be used by the shareholders to greater advantage than being carried back or forward by a regular corporation;*
3. *Most of the income to be earned by the corporation will be distributed to the shareholders; or*
4. *Your regular corporation might be either subject to the accumulated earnings tax or the executive compensation paid to shareholders might be considered unreasonably high. (See page 252 for details.)*

Factors that may weigh against an S election include:
1. *You anticipate that losses will result in greater benefits if the corporation is a regular corporation. This might be the case when the losses can be carried back or forward to offset income of the regular corporation in other years and the use of the losses by the individual shareholders to offset other income is limited.*
2. *You expect to retain the net income in the business and the corporate tax rate will be lower than the individual rate of the S corporation's shareholders. Currently, the highest individual tax rate (39.6%) exceeds the highest corporate tax rate (35%). Keep in mind, however, that C corporation income will, generally, be ultimately double taxed.*
3. *The corporation has a significant LIFO reserve that would be recaptured or anticipates selling assets that would result in a significant built-in gains tax liability.*

State Tax Considerations

While S corporation income generally is exempt from corporate tax at the federal level, not all states exempt S corporations from state taxes at the corporate level. This can result in double state taxation on corporate earnings or dividend distributions.

Most states recognize S corporation status. However, several states tax S corporations in the same way they tax C corporations.

Some states require a separate S election at the state level while others base their acceptance on the federal election. In addition, a number of states require an S corporation to withhold state income tax on income that is distributable to its shareholders as a means of ensuring that nonresident shareholders comply with state tax laws. Penalties are frequently assessed on taxpayers who do not comply. Lastly, many states allow an S corporation to file one composite tax return on behalf of its nonresident shareholders to reduce the administrative burden on multi-state S corporations with several shareholders. Because corporations engaged in multistate commerce are subject to the tax rules of many states, state corporate tax can be *very* complicated. Please consult your tax advisor.

Operating as an S Corporation

Pass-Through of Income and Losses. S corporation income is taxable directly to the corporation's shareholders based on their respective ownership percentages. A loss for the corporation's taxable year is deductible on a *pro rata* basis, but may be limited to the shareholder's basis, amount at risk, or passive activity income. In cases where a shareholder either joins or leaves the S corporation during the year, income or loss for that shareholder is usually allocated in proportion to the number of days that the shareholder held the stock during the taxable year. In certain cases, however, the corporation may elect or be required to "close the books," and treat its tax year as two separate years for purposes of allocating income or loss.

An S corporation is required to separately identify items that would be subject to special treatment on the shareholders' individual returns. These items include interest, dividend, and royalty income; capital gains and losses; gains and losses on business property; investment interest expense; and charitable contributions. Items not subject to any special limitations are passed through in aggregate. Tax credits also generally pass through directly to the shareholders.

Health insurance premiums paid by an S corporation for the benefit of shareholder-employees owning more than 2% of its stock are deductible by the S corporation and includable in the shareholder's income as additional compensation. The percentages allowed as a deduction are as follows: 30% for 1996; and (as authorized by the Health Insurance Portability and Accountability Act of 1996) 40% for 1997, 45% for 1998 through 2002, 50% for 2003, 60% for 2004, 70% for 2005, and 80% for 2006 and thereafter.

Taxable and nontaxable income that flows from the S corporation to the individual shareholder increases the shareholder's basis in his or her stock. According to the IRS, however, an S corporation's nontaxable cancellation of indebtedness ("COD") income does not increase any shareholder's stock basis. Likewise, deductible and nondeductible expenses decrease a shareholder's basis in his or her stock. Distributions from an S corporation are generally tax-free to the extent of a shareholder's basis (however, such distributions reduce basis). If the S corporation was a regular corporation prior to electing S status, a distribution in excess of the earnings accumulated since electing S corporation status may be taxed as a dividend to the shareholder.

Corporate Level Taxes. S corporations generally are not subject to corporate tax, but if an S election is made for a corporation that operated as a regular corporation for a period of time, certain taxes may apply. A brief discussion of these taxes follows:

LIFO Recapture Tax. If a regular corporation using the LIFO (last-in first-out) method of accounting for inventory elects S corporation status, the corporation must include its LIFO reserve in income for its last taxable year as a regular corporation. The LIFO reserve amount that must be included in income is the excess of the inventory value computed under the FIFO (first-in first-out) inventory method over the value computed under the LIFO method. The increase in tax attributable to including the reserve in income is payable over four tax years, with the first payment due on the due date (without extensions) of the last regular corporate return.

Built-In Gains Tax. S corporations that were formerly regular corporations, and that elected S corporation status after December 31, 1986 may be subject to a special "built-in gains" tax. The tax is paid at the corporate level. It generally applies to income or gain accrued in the corporation's assets *before* it elected S status, to the extent that the income or gain is recognized during the corporation's first 10 years as an S corporation.

The tax does not apply to the appreciation of assets occurring after the date the corporation makes its S election.

The tax, if applicable, will be imposed using the highest regular corporate rate, currently 35%.

The corporate level tax reduces the amount of the gain from the disposition of an asset that passes through to S corporation shareholders.

In addition, there is a "net income limitation" to the amount of the built-in gains subject to this tax. The taxable built-in gains are limited to the current year's taxable income, determined as if the corporation was a regular corporation. If the S corporation election was made on or after March 31, 1988, any recognized built-in gain not subject to tax because of this taxable income limitation must be carried over to the subsequent tax year and is subject to that year's taxable income limitation. If the taxable income limitation prevents the recognition of built-in gain income beyond the 10-year period, these gains will escape tax at the corporate level.

Unexpired net operating losses, capital losses, business credit carry-forwards and alternative minimum tax credit carryforwards may be used to offset the built-in gains tax.

Passive Investment Income Tax. An S corporation with regular corporation earnings and profits and passive investment income (for example, interest, dividends, and rents) exceeding 25% of its gross receipts may have to pay a special tax. If those conditions exist for three consecutive tax years, the corporation's S election terminates.

Investment Tax Credit Recapture. Any investment tax credit recapture on assets placed in service during any period as a regular corporation must generally be paid by the S corporation.

TaxSaver

Any new corporation that can qualify for S corporation status can reap a huge tax benefit on the subsequent sale of corporate assets. A regular corporation would have to pay tax at the corporate level on any gain from the sale of assets; an S corporation would not. That can amount to an enormous tax benefit for an S corporation. But, as explained above, an existing corporation that has been a regular corporation and did not elect to become an S corporation by December 31, 1986 cannot simply elect S status and hope to avoid the corporate tax on gains from the sale of assets it held at that time unless the corporation waits at least 10 years before selling the assets. Note, however, that any appreciation occurring after becoming an S corporation will escape double taxation.

Taxable Year. Generally, an S corporation is required to report on a calendar year basis unless it can demonstrate to the satisfaction of the IRS a valid business purpose for a fiscal year-end. However, a newly formed S corporation can elect a year-end (ending not earlier than September 30) by making a "required payment" to the IRS, which is intended to eliminate the tax benefit from the deferral. A C corporation electing S status may also make this election, but it can only elect a year ending not earlier than its current year end or September 30.

TaxSaver

In most cases, an S corporation or partnership would have to demonstrate to the IRS that the different fiscal year is its "natural business year."

The use of a year other than a calendar year can result in a deferral of taxes, and with a natural business year the corporation does not have to make a "required payment" to offset the benefit of the deferral.

Terminating S Corporation Status. Once an S election is made, it is generally effective for all subsequent tax years. However, a corporation's S election will terminate if the corporation violates any of the eligibility requirements explained earlier in this chapter. In addition, an S election will terminate if the corporation has regular corporation earnings and profits and more than 25% of its gross receipts is from passive investment income for three consecutive years. Shareholders of an S corporation who hold more than one-half of the number of issued and outstanding shares may also revoke the corporation's S election.

TAXSAVER

A company should take steps to safeguard against unwanted transfers of stock that would terminate its S election. For example, a minority shareholder not otherwise able to individually revoke the company's S election could nevertheless do so by transferring stock to a shareholder not qualified to hold S corporation stock. One way of protecting against unwanted transfers is to execute agreements limiting the shareholder's ability to transfer stock.

TAXSAVER

When To Consider Terminating S Corporation Status. *The following factors should be taken into account when evaluating whether you should terminate an S election:*

- *Since the passage of the 1993 Tax Act, the top corporate tax rate (35%) is now lower than the top individual tax rate (39.6%). In addition, the alternative minimum tax rate for C corporations can be lower than the applicable individual rate for S corporation shareholders. Before the 1993 Act, the top individual rate was lower than the top corporate rate.*
- *Because a C corporation is not subject to the rules limiting the number and kind of shareholders discussed earlier, it has much more flexibility and more financing alternatives and opportunities.*
- *Preferred stock is prohibited in an S corporation and not in a C corporation. S corporations cannot have more than one class of stock. Unlike C corporations, all outstanding shares of an S corporation generally must have the same rights to distributions and liquidation proceeds.*
- *Certain dividend income eligible for a 70% dividend received deduction is available to C corporations but not S corporations.*
- *A C corporation has more favorable exclusions for certain employee benefits (e.g., exclusion of health insurance benefits).*
- *S corporation eligibility requirements can limit the international tax planning opportunities that are available.*

Once a corporation's S election has terminated, the corporation generally cannot elect S status again for five years. However, under certain limited conditions, the IRS may permit the corporation to re-elect S status before five years have passed. In addition, if the event that caused the S election to terminate was inadvertent, the IRS may grant a waiver of the inadvertent termination and allow the corporation to continue to be treated as an S corporation.

TAXALERT

A provision in the Small Business Job Protection Act of 1996 waives the requirement that IRS permission be obtained to re-elect S status for terminations occuring in taxable years beginning before January 1, 1997.

17

Year-End Tax Planning for Businesses

INTRODUCTION

The political climate will undoubtedly dictate whether business taxes are changed. If they are, Congress will probably continue its efforts to raise revenue from businesses by technical changes in the tax code. These changes might include further restrictions on accounting methods that permit businesses to defer payment of taxes. In addition, businesses with foreign operations are likely to face continued scrutiny.

Timing of Income and Deductions

A business's overall accounting method can substantially affect tax planning. Most individuals and many owners of service businesses use the cash method of accounting for tax purposes. However, most other businesses must use the accrual method of accounting.

Under the cash method, items of income are reported when actually or "constructively" received (that is, when unrestricted use of the funds is available). Items of expense are reported when actually paid. Under the accrual method, the right to receive an income item and the liability to pay an expense item generally determine when those items are reported. For tax purposes, however, an accrual method taxpayer usually may not deduct a liability until goods or services are provided.

The typical business will want to defer income and accelerate expenses (although this strategy would need to be reevaluated if it appeared likely that tax rates were going to rise substantially). Consider the following potential suggestions for accomplishing this goal:

- Delay deliveries on sales (but consider the potential property tax).
- Make sales on consignment or approval (delaying billing and payment).
- Make the maximum deductible charitable contributions.

- Contribute the maximum deductible amount to tax-qualified retirement plans.
- In certain cases, corporations on the LIFO (last-in, first-out) inventory method can affect taxable income by timing the purchase of inventory.

TAXALERT

Remember to consider the impact of the alternative minimum tax (AMT). With the relatively small differences between the AMT rate and the regular corporate tax rate, more corporations are subject to AMT than ever before. However, because the corporate AMT tax can be fully credited against future corporate income tax, its effect may not be very severe.

Depreciation

The date new property is placed in service can significantly affect the amount of your 1996 depreciation deduction. In general, personal property is treated as if it was placed in service at the midpoint of a tax year (July 1 for calendar-year taxpayers) no matter when it was actually purchased and placed in service. However, it's not always that simple. If more than 40% of the personal property purchased during the tax year is placed in service during the last three months of the year, different procedures apply. Under these circumstances, all personal property purchased and placed in service throughout the year will be treated as being placed in service in the middle of the quarter in which it was placed in service. This will usually result in a lower first-year depreciation deduction than if the property were treated as having been placed in service at the midpoint of the tax year.

In certain situations, however, having depreciable property subject to the more-than-40% rule is advantageous. Thus, you should review your fourth-quarter acquisition plans to determine whether you want the more-than-40% rule to be activated.

In general, real property is treated as placed in service in the middle of the month in which it is actually placed in service.

For tax purposes, depreciation is calculated using the modified accelerated cost recovery system (MACRS). An alternative depreciation system must be used when determining if the AMT applies. The difference between depreciation calculated under MACRS and the alternative depreciation system is an adjustment item used in computing the AMT. If you wish to avoid the AMT you should consider leasing instead of purchasing depreciable assets.

Taxpayers may expense up to a certain amount of capital purchases for tangible personal property in the year acquired, provided such expenses do not exceed the taxable income derived from the business. The Small Business Job Protection Act of 1996 increases the maximum amount allowed as an expense over a seven-year period, from $17,500 to $25,000. The increase is phased in as follows: $17,500 for tax year 1996; $18,000 for tax year 1997; $18,500 for tax year 1998; $19,000 for tax year 1999; $20,000 for tax year 2000; $24,000 for tax years 2001–2002; and $25,000 for tax year 2003. To limit this write-off for larger businesses, the maximum amount is reduced dollar-for-dollar by the cost of eligible property in excess of $200,000.

Other Business Expenses.   If you employ your children in your unincorporated business, their earned income will be taxed at their tax rates, and you will get a deduction for their salaries. Also, for children under age 18, neither you (as employer) nor they will be subject to FICA tax on wages you pay to them.

Capital Asset Transactions

Corporations generally compute capital gains and losses in the same manner as individuals. For capital losses, however, corporations may only offset such losses against capital gains and not against any portion of ordinary income as is true with individuals. Excess capital losses can be carried back three years and forward five years to offset capital gains. Unused capital losses expire and are lost forever. Corporations should review their tax positions before year end. Additional sales or exchanges of capital assets should be considered to coordinate the timing of gains and losses and prevent expiration of unused losses.

Charitable Giving

Your corporation may be able to reap special benefits from its charitable contributions. As a means of accelerating the maximum deduction (generally 10% of taxable income) into the current tax year, a corporation that uses the accrual method of accounting may deduct contributions made within 2½ months after the close of the tax year, provided the contributions have been authorized by the board of directors by year end. The IRS requires that a statement regarding the board's action be attached to the return. For a corporation whose tax year coincides with the calendar year, contributions must be made by March 17, 1997. In addition, gifts of *current* inventory may not be subject to the 10% limitation (see Chapter 14).

Executive Compensation

In general a taxpayer may claim a business deduction for a reasonable allowance for salaries or other compensation for personal services rendered. However, a publicly held corporation is precluded, subject to some exceptions, from taking a deduction for compensation in excess of $1 million paid to its chief executive officer and the four other most highly compensated officers. This rule does not apply to (1) payments to a tax-qualified plan, (2) fringe benefits that are excludable from gross income, and (3) qualified performance-based compensation, including stock options or other stock appreciation rights, provided it meets certain independent director and shareholder approval requirements.

TaxSaver

There are a number of strategies companies and top executives can consider to minimize the effect of the $1 million annual cap on compensation deductions.

One strategy is to use nonqualified deferred compensation arrangements to minimize or completely avoid the new $1 million limitation with respect to base salary. These arrangements could be elective, nonelective, or a combination of both. The goal would be to defer base salary to a point in time when it is deductible.

There are two basic structures that can be used. First, base salary could be deferred under an agreement which provides that it will be paid when the employee is no longer a covered employee. Alternatively, the deferral agreement could provide that the deferred base salary will be paid at the first point in time that it is deductible. This approach could create problems in administration, however, since deductibility will depend on the other components of the employee's compensation package, e.g., bonuses and stock option exercises.

Highly paid employees and employers should also consider converting their bonus plans to arrangements that meet the requirements for performance-based compensation.

Companies should also consider granting stock options and stock appreciation rights (SARs) at fair market value. If the options or rights are granted at fair market value and the other requirements for performance-based compensation are met, the income from the exercise of the stock options or SARs will not be counted as part of the $1 million limitation.

TaxAlert

Compensation that is tied to pre-established performance goals is exempted from the $1 million deductibility limitation. However, in order for 1997 incentive plans to receive an exemption, performance goals must be established and approved by the compensation committee no later than December 31, 1996.

Dividends-Received Deduction

The law permits a corporation to deduct 70% (or, in some cases, 80% or 100%) of qualifying dividend income that it receives from taxable domestic corporations. A special provision limits this to 70% of the recipient corporation's taxable income, computed without regard to certain adjustments, including the dividends-received deduction itself.

Dividends-received deductions that are limited as a result of the net income limitation are lost forever. However, this rule does not apply if the recipient corporation would have a net operating loss (NOL) after taking into account the dividends-received deduction. In such a case, the dividends-received deduction is allowable and increases the NOL carryover.

A corporation with qualifying dividend income should plan carefully to ensure that this deduction is not lost because of these rules.

Estimated Tax Filing Requirements

Businesses should conserve cash by making payments only when taxes are owed and only in the required amounts. Overpayments are essentially interest-free loans to the government, while underpayments may result in a nondeductible penalty.

A lower estimated installment amount may be paid if it is shown that use of an annualized income method or, for corporations with seasonal incomes, an adjusted seasonal method would result in a lower required installment. See Chapter 15.

State Tax Considerations

In your year-end business tax planning, you should consider the substantial role state taxes play in a business's overall tax liability.

Taking Advantage of Net Operating Losses. A company may be able to utilize losses generated by an affiliated company in states in which the companies are required to file separate returns. To do so, income-generating assets may have to be transferred to the company with the loss, certain other intercompany transactions may have to occur, or the companies may have to merge. You will need to consult your tax advisor to plan how to maximize your tax benefits.

Distributions and Transactions Between Different Companies. Intercompany transactions that are not subject to federal taxes under the federal consolidated return rules may be subject to direct or indirect state taxes. Some states tax a portion of dividends paid by one company to another. On the other hand, some sales of tangible property between companies and some management fees that one company pays another may be exempt from state taxes. You should consult your tax advisor to determine whether state taxes could be reduced or eliminated by restructuring certain distributions and other transactions between companies.

Appendices

1996 Income Tax Rates

The tables for 1996 reflect the rate brackets indexed for inflation.

Single Individuals*

If 1996 taxable income is:		The tax is:	Of excess
Over—	But not over—		over—
$ 0	$ 24,000	$ 0 + 15%	$ 0
24,000	58,150	3,600.00 + 28%	24,000
58,150	121,300	13,162.00 + 31%	58,150
121,300	263,750	32,738.50 + 36%	121,300
263,750	—	84,020.50 + 39.6%	263,750

Heads of Households*

If 1996 taxable income is:		The tax is:	Of excess
Over—	But not over—		over—
$ 0	$ 32,150	$ 0 + 15%	$ 0
32,150	83,050	4,822.50 + 28%	32,150
83,050	134,500	19,074.50 + 31%	83,050
134,500	263,750	35,024.00 + 36%	134,500
263,750	—	81,554.00 + 39.6%	263,750

Married Individuals Filing Joint Returns and Certain Widows and Widowers*

If 1996 taxable income is:		The tax is:	Of excess
Over—	But not over—		over—
$ 0	$ 40,100	$ 0 + 15%	$ 0
40,100	96,900	6,015.00 + 28%	40,100
96,900	147,700	21,919.00 + 31%	96,900
147,700	263,750	37,667.00 + 36%	147,700
263,750	—	79,445.00 + 39.6%	263,750

*Does not take into account the alternative minimum tax; net capital gain taxed at maximum of 28%.

1996 Income Tax Rates

Married Individuals Filing Separate Returns*

If 1996 taxable income is:		The tax is:	Of excess
Over—	But not over—		over—
$ 0	$ 20,050	$ 0 + 15%	$ 0
20,050	48,450	3,007.50 + 28%	20,050
48,450	73,850	10,959.50 + 31%	48,450
73,850	131,875	18,833.50 + 36%	73,850
131,875	—	39,722.50 + 39.6%	131,875

Estates and Nongrantor Trusts*

If 1996 taxable income is:		The tax is:	Of excess
Over—	But not over—		over—
$ 0	$ 1,600	$ 0 + 15%	$ 0
1,600	3,800	240.00 + 28%	1,600
3,800	5,800	856.00 + 31%	3,800
5,800	7,900	1,476.00 + 36%	5,800
7,900	—	2,232.00 + 39.6%	7,900

*Does not take into account the alternative minimum tax; net capital gain taxed at maximum of 28%.

Note: The 1997 tax rate schedules for individual taxpayers and estates and trusts have not yet been compiled. The rate brackets are indexed each year to account for inflation. In December, 1996 the Internal Revenue Service will prescribe the appropriate indexed 1997 tax rate tables.

1996/1997 Corporate Income Tax Rates**

If 1996 taxable income is:		The tax is:	Of excess
Over—	But not over—		over—
$ 0	$ 50,000	$ 0 + 15%	$ 0
50,000	75,000	7,500 + 25%	50,000
75,000	100,000	13,750 + 34%	75,000
100,000	335,000	22,250 + 39%	100,000
335,000	10,000,000	113,900 + 34%	335,000
10,000,000	15,000,000	3,400,000 + 35%	10,000,000
15,000,000	18,333,333	5,150,000 + 38%	15,000,000
18,333,333	—	6,416,667 + 35%	18,333,333

**Does not take into account the corporate alternative minimum tax; net capital gain taxed at maximum of 28%.

Social Security Taxes

Old-Age Benefit Tax on Employers and Employees

Social Security rate on the first $62,700[a] of wages	6.20%
Medicare rate on the wages for 1996	1.45%
Maximum Social Security Tax for Calendar Year 1996:	$3,887.40

Self-Employment Tax[b]

Social Security rate on the first $62,700[a] of self-employment income	12.4%
Medicare rate on self-employment income for 1996	2.9%
Maximum Social Security Tax for Calendar Year 1996:	$7,774.80

[a]The wage base can increase based on a statutory formula. Any change is published in the *Federal Register* no later than November 1 each year. There is no wage base for Medicare taxes.
[b]A self-employed individual may deduct one-half of his or her self-employment tax for the year as a business expense in arriving at adjusted gross income.

Unified Estate and Gift Tax Rates

Taxable transfers over (1)	But not over (2)	Tentative tax on amount in col. (1) (3)	Rate of tax on excess over amount in col. (1) (4)
$0	$10,000	$0	18%
10,000	20,000	1,800	20%
20,000	40,000	3,800	22%
40,000	60,000	8,200	24%
60,000	80,000	13,000	26%
80,000	100,000	18,200	28%
100,000	150,000	23,800	30%
150,000	250,000	38,800	32%
250,000	500,000	70,800	34%
500,000	750,000	155,800	37%
750,000	1,000,000	248,300	39%
1,000,000	1,250,000	345,800	41%
1,250,000	1,500,000	448,300	43%
1,500,000	2,000,000	555,800	45%
2,000,000	2,500,000	780,800	49%
2,500,000	3,000,000	1,025,800	53%
3,000,000	—	1,290,800*	55%

Plus 5% of the cumulative transfers in excess of $10,000,000 but not exceeding $21,040,000.

Unified Estate and Gift Tax Credit

The unified estate and gift tax credit is $192,800. This has the effect of exempting estates of $600,000 or less from estate taxes.

Computation of Maximum Federal Estate Tax Credit for State Death Taxes

Adjusted taxable estate* more than— (1)	But not more than (2)	Maximum credit amount in col. (1) (3)	Rate of credit on excess over amount in col. (1) (4)
$0	$40,000	$0	None
40,000	90,000	0	.8%
90,000	140,000	400	1.6%
140,000	240,000	1,200	2.4%
240,000	440,000	3,600	3.2%
440,000	640,000	10,000	4.0%
640,000	840,000	18,000	4.8%
840,000	1,040,000	27,600	5.6%
1,040,000	1,540,000	38,800	6.4%
1,540,000	2,040,000	70,800	7.2%
2,040,000	2,540,000	106,800	8.0%
2,540,000	3,040,000	146,800	8.8%
3,040,000	3,540,000	190,800	9.6%
3,540,000	4,040,000	238,800	10.4%
4,040,000	5,040,000	290,800	11.2%
5,040,000	6,040,000	402,800	12.0%
6,040,000	7,040,000	522,800	12.8%
7,040,000	8,040,000	650,800	13.6%
8,040,000	9,040,000	786,800	14.4%
9,040,000	10,040,000	930,800	15.2%
10,040,000	—	1,082,800	16.0%

*The taxable estate less $60,000.

Tax Calendar

Your 1996 individual income tax return is due on April 15, 1997, if you are a calendar-year taxpayer. You shouldn't wait until then to get your tax affairs in order, however. The calendar that follows, although not intended to be comprehensive, is designed to highlight important forms you need to file and when. It includes tax dates not only for individuals but for corporations as well. Key dates for employers are also highlighted. Taxpayers whose years end on dates other than December 31 must adjust these dates to their situation. Due dates that fall on a Saturday, Sunday, or legal holiday are automatically extended to the next business day.

INDIVIDUALS

January 15, 1997
- Form 1040-ES (declaration of estimated tax) for fourth quarter of prior year

April 15, 1997
- Form 1040 (individual income tax return, including the employment taxes for household employees) for prior year or Form 4868 (request for automatic four-month extension)
- Form 709 or 709A (gift tax return) for prior year or extension request (Form 4868 or letter)
- Form 1040-ES for first quarter of current year

June 16, 1997
- Form 1040-ES for second quarter

August 15, 1997
- Form 1040 for prior year, if previously extended by Form 4868 (if additional time is needed, a further two-month extension may be obtained by filing Form 2688)
- Form 709 or 709A, if previously extended by Form 4868 or letter (alternatively, request additional time to file by filing Form 2688 or by letter)

September 15, 1997
- Form 1040-ES for third quarter

October 15, 1997

- Form 1040 for prior year, if request for automatic four-month extension and additional two-month extension were previously filed

CORPORATIONS

March 17, 1997

- Form 1120 (corporate income tax return) (Form 1120S for an S corporation) for prior year or Form 7004 (request for automatic six-month extension)

April 15, 1997

- Deposit estimated tax for first quarter of current year

May 15, 1997

- Form 8752 (Required Payment or Refund Under Section 7519) for an S corporation using a year other than a calendar year

June 16, 1997

- Deposit estimated tax for second quarter of current year

September 15, 1997

- Form 1120 (Form 1120S for an S corporation) if previously extended by Form 7004
- Deposit estimated tax for third quarter of current year

December 15, 1997

- Deposit estimated tax for fourth quarter of current year

EMPLOYERS

(Includes businesses and individuals. Consult your tax advisor for the various dates that employment taxes must be deposited.)

January 31, 1997

- Form 941 (employer's quarterly federal tax return) for fourth quarter of prior year

- Form 940 (employer's federal unemployment tax return) for prior year
- Distribute withholding statements and information returns, including Forms W-2 (Wage and Tax Statement), W-2P (Statement for Recipients of Annuities, Pensions, Retired Pay, or IRA Payments), and 1099-R (Total Distributions from Profit-Sharing Retirement Plans, Individual Retirement Arrangements, Insurance Contracts, etc.) to employees

February 28, 1997

- File Form W-3 (Transmittal of Income and Tax Statements) with Forms W-2 and/or W-2P and for prior year with IRS and Social Security Administration
- File Form 1096 (Annual Summary and Transmittal of U.S. Information Returns) with Form 1099-R for prior year with IRS

April 30, 1997

- Form 941 for first quarter of current year

July 31, 1997

- Form 941 for second quarter

October 31, 1997

- Form 941 for third quarter

Index

Survivor annuities, company retirement
plans, retirement planning, 189–90

T
Tangible property, depreciation, business
planning strategies, 227–28
Taxable year, S corporation, 260
Tax credit(s), 149–52
alternative minimum tax, 149
business tax credit, 152
C corporations, business income
determination, 248–50
dependent care expenses, 150
earned income credit, 150
elderly and disabled, 150–51
estate taxes, estate and gift planning,
199–200
excise tax paid on gasoline and fuels,
152
foreign income tax, taxes paid,
deductions, 41
foreign tax credit, 151
foreign tax credit, citizens living
abroad, filing requirements, 144
investment tax credit, 152
investment tax credit recapture, S
corporation, 260
Taxes paid:
business income determination, 243
individual deductions, 41–42
individual year-end planning, 168
Tax-exempt interest:
income determination, 25–26
mutual funds, 125–26
Tax-exempt securities, deductions, 44
Tax-free gifts, described, 204–6
Tax preference items, alternative
minimum tax, 146–47
Tax preparation fees, deductions, 52
Tax rate, 267–70
capital gains and losses, 115
C corporations, business income
determination, 246
estate taxes, estate and gift planning,
199
filing requirements, 145
Tax refunds, deductions, 42
Tax shelters, investment planning,
186–87
Termination of status, S corporation,
260–61
Theft. *See* Casualty and theft losses
Tickets:
athletic tickets, charitable
contributions, 100
travel and entertainment expenses,
62–63
Time extensions, filing requirements,
137
Timing:

of income and deductions, business
year-end planning, 262–63
of payment, year-end planning
(individuals), 170–72
Totten trust, estate and gift planning, 208
Transactions, between companies, state
tax considerations, business year-
end planning, 266
Travel and entertainment expenses,
54–68
accounting log, 66
automobile expenses, 59
business meals, 63
charitable contributions, 100–101
club dues, 64
conventions and investment seminars,
55
cruise ships, conventions on, 57
deductions, sole proprietorship,
business income determination,
244
disallowed expenses, 68
domestic travel, 56
employee travel and transportation
(unreimbursed), 55–56
entertainment, 62
entertainment facilities, 63–64
expense account allowance, 65–66
50% limitation, 54–56
fixed-amount reimbursement
arrangements, 67–68
foreign business travel, 57–58
foreign conventions, 58
luxury skyboxes, 63
luxury water transportation, 56–57
meetings, 58
overview of, 54
record-keeping, 64–65
special rules, 58–59
standard reimbursement
arrangements, 66–67
tickets, 62–63
Truck expenses, deductions, sole
proprietorship, business income
determination, 242
Trustee's administrative fee, deductions,
51
Trusts, estate and gift planning, 209–11
2%-of-adjusted-gross-income limit,
deductions, 48–49

U
Underpayment penalty:
C corporations, business income
determination, 247
estimated payments, 154–55
Unemployment benefits:
income determination, 23
supplemental, deductions, 53